The Object-Oriented Development Process

Developing and Managing a Robust Process for Object-Oriented Development

ISBN 0-13-030621-5

90000

9 780130 306210

The Object-Oriented Development Process

Developing and Managing a Robust Process for Object-Oriented Development

Tom Rowlett

Prentice Hall PTR
Upper Saddle River, NJ 07458
www.phptr.com

Library of Congress Cataloging-in-Publication Data

Rowlett, Tom.
     The object-oriented development process : developing and
    managing a robust process for object-oriented development /
    Tom Rowlett.
      p. cm.
    Includes bibliographical references and index.
    ISBN 0-13-030621-5
      1. Object-oriented programming (Computer science) 2. Computer
    software—Development. I. Title.
QA76.64 .R679 2001
005.11'7—dc21

                                    00-064997

Editorial/production supervision: *BooksCraft, Inc., Indianapolis, IN*
Acquisitions editor: *Mike Meehan*
Editorial assistant: *Linda Ramagnano*
Marketing manager: *Debbie vanDijk*
Buyer: *Maura Zaldivar*
Cover design director: *Jerry Votta*
Cover designer: *Talar Agasyan*
Project coordinator: *Anne Trowbridge*

© 2001 by Prentice Hall PTR
Prentice-Hall, Inc.
Upper Saddle River, NJ 07458

Prentice Hall books are widely used by corporations and government agencies for
training, marketing, and resale.

The publisher offers discounts on this book when ordered in bulk quantities.
For more information, contact:
Corporate Sales Department
Phone: 800-382-3419   Fax: 201-236-7141
E-mail: corpsales@prenhall.com

Or write:
Prentice Hall PTR
Corporate Sales Department
One Lake Street
Upper Saddle River, NJ 07458

All product names mentioned herein are the trademarks of their respective owners.

All rights reserved. No part of this book may be reproduced, in any form
or by any means, without permission in writing from the publisher.

Printed in the United States of America

10 9 8 7 6 5 4 3 2 1

ISBN: 0-13-030621-5

Prentice-Hall International (UK) Limited, *London*
Prentice-Hall of Australia Pty. Limited, *Sydney*
Prentice-Hall Canada Inc., *Toronto*
Prentice-Hall Hispanoamericana, S.A., *Mexico*
Prentice-Hall of India Private Limited, *New Delhi*
Prentice-Hall of Japan, Inc., *Tokyo*
Pearson Education Asia Pte. Ltd.
Editora Prentice-Hall do Brasil, Ltda., *Rio de Janeiro*

This book is dedicated to my wife, Paula, who has patiently and lovingly stood beside me while I traveled all over the world to gain the experience and knowledge that helped me develop and refine this material; and to MM and PM for just being our friends.

Contents

I The Object-Oriented Development Process

II An Example Creating OODP Deliverables

III Reference

Preface

This book presents the details of a complete software development process using the methods and tools of object technology. It is based on my work as a consultant, mentor, and instructor over the last 17 years. The process architecture is based on ideas originally presented in [Radice88], and I have refined it over the years to integrate elements of [Jacobson92] with my own experiences in software engineering.

Readers should have a working knowledge of object-oriented concepts and terminology. For readers unfamiliar with the terminology of object technology, I suggest [Firesmith95] and [Taylor90] as good references.

WHAT THIS BOOK IS ABOUT

I intend this book to be a tool that enhances object-oriented software development by providing a step-by-step flow for application by project teams wishing to blend software engineering principles with object-oriented methods. With that in mind, the book is organized around process work products (deliverables) that act as vehicles for refining detail from original requirements to delivered code. All defined work products are accompanied by a set of criteria, in a check-list format, that the development team can use to objectively evaluate whether the deliverable is correct for the given product requirements.

WHO SHOULD READ THIS BOOK

The details of object-oriented software development I present are intended to help software analysts, designers, programmers, and testers develop software with rigor rather than speculation. The book is also intended to help project managers and leaders create a formal process for managing the development of the software itself.

HOW THE BOOK IS ORGANIZED

Part I describes the object-oriented development process (OODP). Chapter 1 defines a generic process architecture and chapter 2 provides the rationale behind OODP. Chapters 3–12 provide the details of each step in the OODP, starting with requirements and continuing through implementation and test. Among these are chapters on class design, persistence, test planning, and user interface development. This part concludes with a discussion of the major issues that a project manager would face as he or she attempted to integrate the technologies of object orientation into the organization's software development process.

Part II takes a medium-sized example and develops a complete solution with all of the deliverables of OODP. It develops the solution in four increments and reviews the steps of each activity as the deliverables are created.

Acknowledgments

*M*any of these concepts and ideas were developed as a result of the experience I gained during my tenure with IBM's Software Engineering Institute and later with its Object Technology University. Several of my colleagues from those organizations contributed a considerable amount of their time to review one or more of the many drafts of this book. I especially want to thank Don McKenna, Steve Spector, Roger Miller, Marilyn Bates, and Bernie Rackmales. In addition I want to thank Les Hellenack and Paula Rowlett for their time and effort in reviewing and proofreading the volumes of paper that I produced while developing this book. And finally I wish to thank the many other associates and friends who over the years have listened and contributed to my raw ideas and helped refine them into the practices that make up the object-oriented development process. And finally a special thanks to "SDHI" for encouraging me to start writing.

I made every effort to be complete and accurate with the information presented. I hope you find this book to be as useful as I intended it. I welcome your comments, questions, and criticisms. Please feel free to contact me via email at ***tom@obps.com***.

The Object-Oriented Development Process

This part of the book describes the architecture and details of the object-oriented development process. Chapters 1 and 2 describe the process architecture and incremental model. Chapters 3 through 12 elaborate on the details of each activity within the process. Chapter 13 discusses several project management issues related to object-oriented development.

The Process Model

*O*bject-oriented software development is still evolving, but every year more and more organizations choose to apply it to industrial-strength applications. Although the process architecture discussed in this chapter is effective for any set of software development methods, its instantiation with the use case discussed in Chapter 2 is built around the artifacts normally associated with object-oriented development. This chapter examines the need for a process during development and the essential elements of any process. A nonsoftware example is used to look at the components of a process.

1.1 WHY A PROCESS?

Today's software development environment is rich with methodology. The dictionary defines methodology as "a study of methods," but in software it appears that a methodology is any collection of tips and techniques that helps create a deliverable. This compendium of practices may be useful to developers involved in object-oriented development, but there is still a larger element of this activity that needs to be addressed. Assembling software involves more than merely performing a series of disjoint tasks. What is needed to bring these tasks together is a process, which shall be defined here as a series of interrelated and dependent activities that combine to complete larger and more complex tasks.

Methodologies merely describe independent activities, whereas processes link activities to achieve a predefined goal. The remainder of this chapter describes a process model that can be applied to object-oriented development. It addresses those elements that some methodologies may have chosen to ignore and applies a rigor that is essential in the development of robust, maintainable, high-quality software.

1.2 PROCESS ARCHITECTURE

A good process is based on good process architecture. The process architecture described here is composed of a series of activities that have some level of dependence on each other. This dependency is based on either deliverables passed from one activity to the next or a temporal relationship that requires the first activity to be completed before the second can begin.

An example of the former is where the input for the test activity is the compiled code that was the output of the implementation activity. A deliverable dependency is created when specific information created in a prior step is required by a subsequent dependent step.

The latter kind of dependency, described as temporal, occurs when there is no deliverable passed from one activity to the next, but the predecessor activity still must complete first. Consider the following nonsoftware example. People who wish to take a plane from New York to Rome cannot commence that activity until they have completed the activity that gets them to the New York airport from which their flight to Rome departs.

An example of a temporal dependency in software would be that extensive stress and performance testing cannot begin until functional testing is complete.

1.2.1 Process components

To understand the software process, we must first understand its primary component, the process activity. Each activity in a process has three major elements: its *input* (or requirement), its *output* (or deliverable), and the *method* (this is the definition of how the input is to be refined into the deliverable). The method component has five subcomponents. (See Figure 1-1.)

- ☞ The first element is the definition of the task that **transforms** the input to output. For example, consider a travel itinerary that lists the order and stopover durations of the cities to be visited.
- ☞ The second element is the state that the input is **assumed** to be in. For example, the foregoing travel itinerary assumes that you are at the

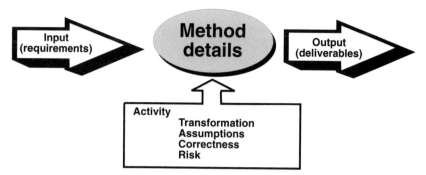

Fig. 1-1 A process activity architecture.

origination city. The process may define a separate activity to ensure that the input meets the pre-condition.

☞ The third element provides the details of the ***deliverable*** to be created. This is often combined with the fourth subcomponent of the method, which is the criterion used to measure whether the activity was performed ***correctly***. Together these two describe the post-condition of the method's output. Because there is considerable overlap on these subcomponents, they are usually combined into a simple checklist. The checklist can be used to ensure that the activity was performed correctly.

☞ The final element, which is discussed later in the chapter, is the ***risk*** element. It is the logic and common sense that can be used to override the other process rules. For example, the directions state that the traveler is to be in Cincinnati for two days beginning on May 7. However, a statement of risk may add that if it is determined that the business to be conducted is not proving fruitful, then an earlier departure would be acceptable. This is the rule that can override the others. The intent of risk in the process is to allow for adaptation to the real world. In software this usually means making the decision to proceed to a subsequent activity in the process before all the items in the activity checklist have been completed. Most risks will be project specific.

1.2.2 Deliverable dependency

Because activities are linked, the output of one becomes the input to the next, creating a dependency. Hence, the entrance requirement of the input of an activity should drive the correctness criteria of the activity that created the artifact. In general, correctness criteria of a deliverable should be a superset of all input requirements that use that deliverable.

Since all processes have deliverable dependencies, strict adherence to the rules would require that an activity provide all required deliverables before beginning an activity that needed those artifacts. Here is where risk provides some guidance on breaking this rule. Travelers have the option to make decisions on their own and to take some risk, if they believe that the overall process (trip) would benefit. The same is true during the software process if the developer chooses to start implementation before the design is complete. Rather than leave the decisions to the team in the throes of schedule pressure, consider adding a risk statement to the process that explains when deviations from the rules are acceptable.

1.3 AN EXAMPLE

Assume a family wishes to define a process for taking a vacation. The activities are vacation planning, vacation scheduling, packing for vacation, traveling to the vacation destination, and vacationing. Assume that vacation scheduling and packing are dependent on vacation planning; traveling is dependent on scheduling and packing; and vacationing is dependent on traveling. Figure 1-2 shows these dependencies graphically.

The process begins with the family performing some basic planning. This activity identifies a potential list of vacation sites and some criteria for climate and tour opportunities. The planning activity is followed by discussions on what clothing is appropriate and how much apparel should be packed. The last element involves transportation and lodging, which is based on budget as well as group preference.

Further assume that the goal of this process is to give the majority of the family a good time. The next five tables show the details of each of these activities.

Notice that the Vacation Planning activity in Table 1-1 includes steps and details for creating the deliverable: "locations rated on a scale of 1 to 5." The transformation is described in terms of the inputs. This is critical for process description. If it had said, "Dad then selects the location based on where his next business trip is," one would question why all the other inputs were

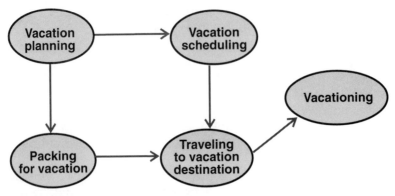

Fig. 1-2 Dependency diagram for vacation process activities.

Table 1-1 Vacation planning activity detail.

Activity	Vacation Planning
Requirement	Participants, desired time frame, geographical region, climate, activities, and maximum cost.
Deliverables	Target city or location and time frame. Cost allotments for travel, lodging, meals, and entertainment. Range of travel dates.
Transformation	Each participant's objectives in terms of climate, geography, and activities are prioritized against resorts in selected cities based on max cost. The participants rate all resorts and locations, using a five-point scale, on climate, region, and activities. The sum of the values is used to determine the target location.
Assumptions	Participants have had an opportunity to list their preferences for the selection criteria.
Correctness	At least a majority of the participants accept the chosen location. If not, it is deleted and the process is restarted.
Risk	If participants are biased to their preferred choice, consensus may need to be modified to plurality after all voting is complete. Cost and/or time frame may need to be fixed and removed from voting process.

provided and why "next business trip info" was not listed as one of the inputs to the activity.

Correctness of the deliverable is also tied to the requirements: "At least a majority of the participants accept the chosen location. If not, it is deleted and the process is restarted." It is assumed that participants (family members) represent the team, so they will accept the correctness question: "Do we agree on the solution with respect to the input provided?"

In the Vacation Scheduling activity in Table 1-2, notice that "location and time frame" refers to the output of the Vacation Planning activity. Travel cost allotment is a process input provided by the vacationing family as opposed to the output of a previous activity. This activity assumes that the location and the time frame are fixed, which implies that these were finalized during the Vacation Planning activity. To be completely correct, Vacation Planning should have the additional correctness question: "All participants accept and agree on the time frame selected." There was already a correctness question that stipulated that a majority of the family agreed on the vacation location.

1.3.1 Risk

Look at risk in the Packing for Vacation activity in Table 1-3. The method states that all family members have their own suitcases, and the assumption is that everyone's clothes will fit into his or her cases. From experience the family knows that this assumption is probably not realistic so a risk clause is added that allows for individuals to share travel cases when necessary.

Another risk is that all suitcases may not arrive at the same time as the traveler. The risk guidelines in the Traveling to Vacation Destination activity (Table 1-4) plan for this, and allow the process to continue. Without risk, the

Table 1-2 Vacation scheduling activity detail.

Activity	Vacation Scheduling
Requirement	Location and date range from planning, travel cost allotment.
Deliverable	Travel plans, including means of travel and reservations if appropriate.
Transformation	The selected location(s) is inspected for available accommodations on the dates and duration provided. Each accommodation is weighed based on cost and any other pluses. Travel alternatives (car, plane, bus, etc.) are examined, and the lowest cost alternative given the duration and dates is selected. Any savings beyond the travel allocation are distributed among meals and entertainment.
Assumptions	Location and time frame are now fixed.
Correctness	Total travel and lodging costs do not exceed allotments.
Risk	Lowest cost travel may waste too much time or involve unnecessary inconvenience and may be discarded with consensus.

Table 1-3 Vacation packing activity detail.

Activity	Packing for Vacation
Requirement	Location and dates from planning. Travel schedule from scheduling.
Deliverable	Correct amount, style, and climate-appropriate clothing for the duration for each family member.
Transformation	Each family member is allotted one or more suitcases and asked to provide a list of the items that he or she can safely place in that case.
Assumptions	Travel location and dates provide sufficient data to allow members to decide on appropriate clothing.
Correctness	Each case may be filled to no more than 90% of capacity. More senior family members agree on appropriateness of all packed items.
Risk	Not enough suitcases are available for each family member to have their own. Multiple family members may need to share the same case.

Table 1-4 Vacation traveling activity detail.

Activity	Traveling to Vacation Destination
Requirement	Transportation method from scheduling. Packed suitcases from packing.
Deliverable	N/A
Transformation	If appropriate, purchase travel vouchers. Make any prerequisite arrangements—taxi, limo, etc. Using travel medium, transport family and suitcases to vacation location.
Assumptions	Scheduling and packing completion criteria have been met.
Correctness	Entire family has arrived at planned location with all suitcases. Lodging accommodations are ready.
Risk	All travel cases may not have arrived at the same time as the family. In some cases vacationing may start without them, provided planned arrival is acceptable to all family members.

family would be forced to suspend their vacation until ALL of the suitcases arrived.

A team will most likely choose to not alter most of the elements of the process from project to project, but it is almost a certainty that some risk items will be restated.

1.3.2 Post mortem

The right way to end any project is with a post mortem as in the Vacationing activity in Table 1-5. The goal of a post mortem should always be to evaluate the process, not the project, not the team, or even the product. Time should be spent looking for what could be done differently next time. Perhaps some of

Table 1-5 Vacationing activity detail.

Activity	Vacationing
Requirement	N/A
Deliverable	Relaxation and fun.
Transformation	Have fun upon arrival. Make notes at end of vacation about changes that should be made on future vacations.
Assumptions	Travel completion criteria have been met.
Correctness	Vacation post mortem has been completed.
Risk	N/A

the risk items in this process are a result of a post mortem from a prior vacation that went bad.

Although it is not necessary to agree with details of this vacationing process, the process is nonetheless correct with respect to process structure and its elements. It is natural to modify an organization's standard process to accommodate the current project. The modifications include adding and removing process activities as well as modifying the details of one or more activities.

1.4 PROCESS MODELS

In addition to the process architecture just described, there are several process models that can serve as a pattern for any process. This chapter discusses four: waterfall, iterative, incremental, and spiral. These have traditionally been associated with object-oriented development, but in some cases were mistakenly believed to have been developed explicitly for object technology.

1.4.1 Waterfall

The waterfall model (Figure 1-3) is the basis for most process models. When applied with the rigor discussed earlier, it is an extremely effective and manageable process. Its weakness lies in its inability to revert to a prior activity when requirements change. Instead the current deliverable is modified, in the current activity, to accommodate the change. This results in changes to the design or code that have only been reviewed in the context of that portion of the deliverable that are adjacent to the change. Often a coding change may result in a re-inspection of only a few lines within the module that contained the change. This makes for fragmented rather than holistic logic. Changes implemented in this way usually produce code so closely coupled to the code

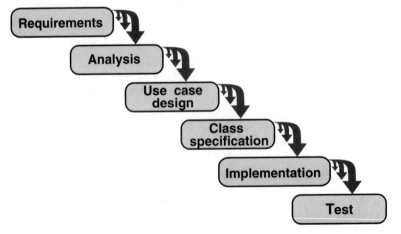

Fig. 1-3 The waterfall process model.

adjoining it, that when changes to the module's design occur, the associated code must be placed within *if* and *case* blocks, to isolate them from the flow of the rest of the module. The waterfall process's popularity is that it allows the process to get to the implementation activity quickly. However, its major drawback is that this is at the expense of change integration. The alternative would be to stop development for every change and to restart the process with the adjusted set of requirements. That is an alternative that would not be widely accepted in the current software development culture.

1.4.2 Iterative

One way to forestall changes is to identify all requirements and potential changes as early in the process as possible. Ideally this would be done before starting analysis. The iterative model depicted in Figure 1-4 is offered as one way to accomplish this. Notice that it differs from the waterfall model in that it not only allows returning to a prior activity but also encourages it. With this approach, requirements can be revisited as often as necessary, but if analysis is done with that knowledge, progress is slow until all requirements have been identified. Additionally, the requirements-analysis iteration can last indefinitely. Also if this model is continued into design, implementation, and test, the process becomes totally unmanageable and begins to look more like hacking than software engineering. This is not to say that iteration is detrimental to good software development. Quite the contrary, one purpose of analysis is to discover what was missed during requirements. Every design activity has the potential of raising questions that require reentering analysis; likewise, implementation can cause the developer to consider redesigning some pieces of the application. Yet in these instances it is expected that there will be only infrequent and brief revisiting of prior activities. The waterfall diagram in Figure 1-3 shows the allowable activity overlap graphically, but

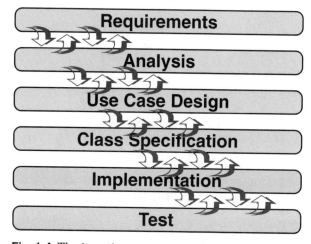

Fig. 1-4 The iterative process model.

the percentage of overlap should not be literally interpreted from the relative size and position of the boxes representing the activities. The goal should be that 90 percent of each activity will complete before entering the next phase and so reversing course occurs infrequently, not as a matter of policy that encourages premature exiting of each phase. Chapter 13 on project management discusses how to manage to this 90 percent target.

1.4.3 Incremental

A better alternative for dealing with incomplete requirements is to use an incremental approach. See Figure 1-5. In this model the entire waterfall process is applied to a portion of the known requirements. When testing has proven that increment correct, the waterfall process is repeated in its entirety on another portion of the requirements.

With incremental development, new requirements can normally be deferred to the next increment, and they, therefore, enter the process at the top and go through analysis and design before being made a part of the software implementation. The key to effective incremental development is being able to partition the development into several increments. You should expect to see only minor increase in the overall time required to complete all the increments as compared to the time to develop the product in a single pass. Use cases and objects, as we will see in the design chapters, are particularly suited to enabling this. The incremental process has several distinct advantages compared to other models.

☞ Each increment deals with a smaller work product, which should make the development more manageable, require a smaller team, and, therefore, yield higher productivity.

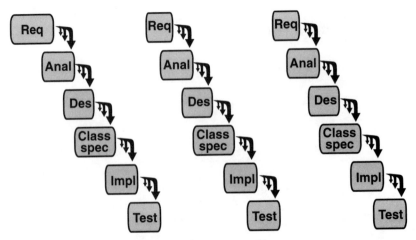

Fig. 1-5 The incremental process model.

☞ Each pass of the incremental process uses the waterfall process as its underlying model. Although the increments are smaller, they must still be managed as a robust process; but because each increment is a complete process, it will be far easier to manage than a process that uses the iterative model.

☞ The early increments can serve as prototypes to help the client understand better what to expect from the final product, and perhaps to provide more timely input if changes are required. This can help in those cases early in the development when the requirement is too big for the proposed schedule.

☞ With careful partitioning it may be possible to deliver an early increment with enough functionality to satisfy the client within the required schedule. This can buy the team another increment or two to finish the job with some of the pressure relaxed.

☞ When an organization deals with a new technology like object-oriented, the first increment can serve as a "practice run" to get the kinks out of the process. This approach will give the team a little extra time to improve its skills before diving into the more complex and detailed part of the product.

1.4.4 Spiral

The **spiral** model is vastly different from the others discussed. It is explained here only because the spiral, iterative, and rapid prototype models are often confused. Barry Bohem [Bohem88] developed the spiral model in the mid 1980s as a vehicle for risk management. Figure 1-6 shows the four phases of risk management as quadrants on the spiral.

Each revolution represents the completion of four risk management activities for one or more risks. Each risk is assessed and prioritized based on impact. In this model the most serious risk items are addressed before development begins. The final spiral develops the product and begins when it is determined that the cost of further risk evaluation and assessment is greater than the cost of managing the remaining risks as part of the software development process.

1.5 INCREMENTAL WITH USE CASES

The remainder of this book assumes an incremental process approach and the process architecture described in Chapter 1. The process will be built around use cases as the primary functional component.

The next chapter describes use cases, the object-oriented development process details, and the deliverables specific to it. Chapters 3, 4, and 5 describe using use cases in requirements gathering, analysis, and design,

Evaluation   **Identification**

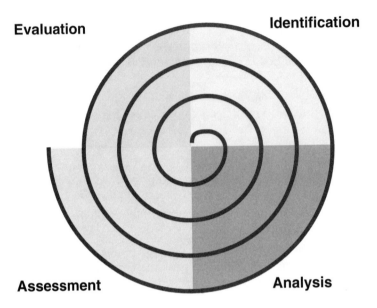

Assessment   **Analysis**

Fig. 1-6 The spiral process.

respectively. Chapter 6 discusses the issues of robust class design and documentation with special attention paid to developing inheritance hierarchies.
Chapter 7 briefly discusses the considerations related to persistence. This
chapter does not cover this topic exhaustively since most of these considerations depend on the particular environment and the database tools in use.
Chapter 8 looks at those considerations left for implementation. Chapters 9
and 10 cover testing. Chapter 11 talks about developing an independent user
interface. Chapter 12 deals with maintenance, and Chapter 13 discusses some
project management considerations for object technology.

This book is intended as both a tutorial and a reference guide on object-
oriented development. We recommend, the first time, you read the book all
the way through. Then use the individual chapters and the associated examples in the appendix as a reference to help you through each phase of software development.

The process described in this book has been applied successfully on several projects. Although each project adapted the process to its own organizational style, each project still followed the fundamental use case approach of
OODP.

Please contact me if you have any questions or comments, and enjoy the
remainder of the book.

CHAPTER 2

The Object-Oriented Development Process

*T*his chapter describes the use case and the object-oriented development process, using the architecture presented in Chapter 1. It describes the characteristics of a robust software development process and the detail of how the use case integrates into all of the process activities.

2.1 HIGH-LEVEL USE CASE DEFINITION

A use case is a transaction that begins with a user stimulus and ends with a response. In between the program logic accepts and validates the input and then determines the required actions, which may include updates to business data. This definition of a use case is not the same as that suggested by [Jacobson93]. This use case definition is intended to be more granular and rigorous. This granularity is essential to the correctness issues discussed in the details of OODP.

Consider the use case as the definition of all possible responses to an external event. Events are those needs that motivate a user of the system to stimulate it by pressing a key, manipulating a mouse, or performing any other activity that the interface will recognize as a stimulus. Events are described with phrases such as: "The customer wishes to transfer money," "The customer wants to rent a video," and "The manager needs to add a new item to the inventory." The wants and needs phrases are intended to show the motivation of the user of the system, a need that the application must fulfill.

When identifying use cases, it is important to differentiate them from business processes. A single business process may be composed of several use cases. For example, the business process shown in Figure 2-1 is actually composed of several potential use cases.

To do effective requirements gathering, it is important to recognize that this business process involves, not one, but four use cases. Chapter 3 on requirements definition elaborates on the rules that help make the distinction between use case and business processes. Many analysts, in a rush to find use cases, will identify the business processes instead. Organizations that struggle with identifying use cases often do so because they do not see beyond the business processes. One client team was trying to find the use case in an inventory management application. The business process analysts were arguing over whether the count of items in inventory should be updated when the order was received on the dock, delivered to the storage facility, or placed in the bin. The software analysts were frustrated because they could not get agreement on business rules. When they finally realized that the use case was "Update inventory" and not "Receive inventory and update quantity in hand," the use case and the business rules became simple to differentiate.

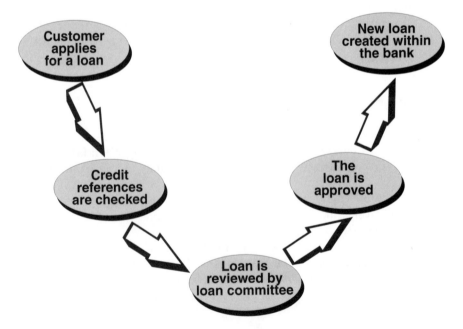

Fig. 2-1 A business process for a loan application.

2.2 THE RATIONALE BEHIND THE USE CASE MODEL

The business process model could have been used as a vehicle for require-ments gathering, but the use case as defined was chosen for OODP instead for the following reasons:

☞ Business processes are too complex and often involve steps that are not part of the application. For example, the banking application may be able to accept a loan request, obtain the credit report, and create the loan, but the process for approving the loan is a human activity.

☞ As use cases are combined into a single requirement, it multiplies their complexities. When they are treated separately, system complexity grows linearly.

☞ Business processes are more likely to change than the individual use cases, and often a business process change can be accommodated without ever adding or changing a use case.

☞ Each transaction can be validated as its own entity with its own specifi-cation, which makes it easier for the design and implementation to be validated. This concept of a use case, as an independent entity, is dis-cussed further in the use case design chapter.

2.3 HOW USE CASES LINK THE PROCESS

The following topics describe the role that use cases play in each OODP activ-ity and demonstrate how the use case model integrates into the process archi-tecture of Chapter 1.

2.3.1 Requirements

The application's functionality is recorded as use cases. For each use case, the requirements capture its inputs and outcomes.

2.3.2 Analysis

The use case is partitioned into scenarios, each with its own pre-condition, post-condition, and output. This is the detail that defines the business rules for the use case.

2.3.3 Design

Each use case is designed by creating a series of messages that determine the scenario in effect at the time the use case is instantiated. This is followed by additional messages to update the business object attributes with the values defined in the scenario's post-condition.

2.3.4 Implementation

The use case design messages are implemented as methods in the application objects. A special application class with a method for each use case is written to manage the control flow within an individual use case.

2.3.5 Test

One or more test cases are created for every scenario in a use case.

2.3.6 User interface

If the use case is triggered by a user interface event, it is the interface's responsibility to gather the inputs required for that use case and send a message with those inputs to the appropriate method in the application object.

2.4 CRITERIA FOR A ROBUST PROCESS

During the design of the object-oriented development process, the elements of several methodologies were reviewed. It became apparent that what was needed was not another methodology but a formal software process that would support object-oriented development. Methodologies tend to lack cohesion and structure. They often focus on only a few software activities or deliverables and ignore the process aspects. One of the results of this study was a set of criteria that could be used to evaluate any operational software process. These were not abstract properties like *effective*, *usable*, or *modern* but rather the following concrete and measurable attributes:

- ☞ Complete
- ☞ Consistent
- ☞ Verifiable
- ☞ Traceable
- ☞ Incrementable
- ☞ Testable

The definition of each of these attributes is discussed in the following topics. Subsequent chapters will refer to these attributes and measure the object-oriented development process against them.

2.4.1 Complete

A **complete** process is one that starts with basic minimal requirements as input and includes the details necessary to progress through all the required software development activities and to deliver a tested working product. This is an essential element often overlooked in many methodologies. The process is incomplete when, for example, it provides complete details on the analysis activity but omits the details for design and implementation. When using a process that is not complete, the project team may not know whether it is doing analysis or design, and more importantly, it may not know when it is done. The process architecture described in Chapter 1 can be an aid to ensure that the process has not omitted critical steps. The end of this chapter contains a short description of the activities and deliverables for the object-oriented development process.

2.4.2 Consistent

Hand in hand with a complete process is one that is **consistent.** That means that, except for the first activity, every input to a process activity must be a deliverable from a previous one. When methods, attributes, objects, and associations seem to appear out of thin air, there is no way to know when all of them have been found or how many may still be missing. A robust process should have only one ill-defined input, that is the user's requirements, and all other activity inputs should have been created by a prior step in the process. A corollary to this principle says that no deliverable should be created that is not either input to a subsequent process step or is considered one of the deliverables that was promised to the client as part of building the application. These include the machine-runnable code and documentation.

2.4.3 Verifiable

Verifiable processes are those whose activities contain deliverable correctness criteria. This is a checklist of objective questions that assert that the deliverable was correctly created from the input and that it will meet the entrance criteria of the input of subsequent activities. If the initial set of requirements is checked to see that they are what the customer requires, and the analysis deliverables are validated against those requirements, then we can reason that the analysis use cases are a correct refinement of the requirements. If design and implementation continue this practice for their inputs and outputs and the process is consistent, then the delivered code will also meet the user's requirements. Often a process relies on testing to validate that the product has met requirements. Testing is an important activity, but it is inefficient and sometimes ineffective in terms of correctness. Testing to validate correctness incorrectly assumes the following:

- ☞ All defects can be discovered during test.
- ☞ There is time to redesign and retest when defects are found.
- ☞ The test cases will test the requirements.

By ensuring correctness of each deliverable with respect to its input verification is streamlined, errors are detected sooner, and testing becomes confirmation that the team was successful in building the right piece of software.

2.4.4 Traceable

A **traceable** process has two components:

☞ Every deliverable can be associated with a requirement.

☞ For each product requirement, the deliverables that implement it can be identified.

The first rule prevents overbuilding the software; the second makes maintenance as efficient as possible. If a product will never be changed and no new requirements will surface during development, perhaps the traceable attribute could be ignored; however, since this is almost never the case, there needs to be a way that, when requirements do change, each and every deliverable in the product need not be scrutinized to see if it is affected by the change. A traceable process allows swift identification of a few pieces of the application that together completely encapsulate the change. This attribute not only includes delivered code but design, analysis, and test deliverables as well. Use cases are designed and implemented in a way that makes them independent of each other. That is, a use case has its own design and a discrete set of methods and objects that implement it, which means that only they need to be considered for rework when that use case changes. This approach will normally involve a very small and manageable piece of the product. Of course, some new methods, attributes, or objects may be required as well, but even they can be localized. Because of these characteristics, traceable is sometimes referred to as maintainable.

2.4.5 Incrementable

The **incrementable** characteristic implies that the requirements can be partitioned such that the effort required to build the application in pieces is virtually the same as if it were built as a single unit. This approach allows for tremendous flexibility in work distribution and includes all the advantages of incremental development discussed in Chapter 1. The important part of the incrementable property is that the cost of partitioning the problem into several smaller pieces approaches zero. It eliminates, as much as possible, rewriting or removing running code. Use cases make this approach possible because they are implemented as independent entities.

2.4.6 Testable

Finally, the process must be **testable**, which means that test cases can be developed from the requirements. This condition implies that requirements either do not change or are always maintained to reflect the software being built. It has been said about some development efforts, that when a delivered product's functionality matches its requirement it is known as "coincidence."

Testability requires that as the specification, design, or code changes, so must the associated requirement use case definition, and all the existing intermediate deliverables as well. The only thing worse than missing documentation is incorrect documentation.

Since all use cases will not be detailed during analysis, it must be possible to design some use cases directly from the requirements. If the design is also omitted, or later deleted, the code for this use case must be developed directly from the requirements. Whenever the decision is made to eliminate some of the process deliverables, the developer must develop the remainder of the solution from the lowest level documentation available. This implies that requirements can *never* be eliminated and must always accurately reflect the current application. This is the summation of the rules for a testable process. "The requirements use case definitions must always be complete and accurate."

2.5 OVERVIEW OF THE ACTIVITIES OF OODP

An abbreviated description of the activities in the object-oriented development process follows. It includes a short definition of the purpose of each activity, its inputs (requirements), and its outputs (deliverables). It does not contain all the process detail described in Chapter 1, but that information can be found in Appendix A where the process and its activities are fully explained. It is the intent here to highlight the flow among the activities of OODP while providing a brief definition of each one. The details of each activity are covered in Chapters 3 through 12.

Figure 2-2 shows the flow and deliverables of the activities that make up the object-oriented development process. The ovals represent the activities and the lines between the activities represent the deliverables of one activity that flow into the next. Additional details on these activities can be found in Appendix A.

One project may refer to an activity as "analysis," whereas another calls the same activity "requirements gathering." OODP's activity naming is not intended to be definitive, but it is important to understand the terms used within the process definition. The remainder of the book will assume the names and activities as defined here.

2.5.1 Requirements gathering

The purpose of requirements is to bound the problem space and provide the team with enough information to grasp its scope without getting mired in the details of analysis. There should be sufficient information about the product to develop a project resource plan, estimate, and schedule and to begin the activities of analysis, test planning, and user interface design.

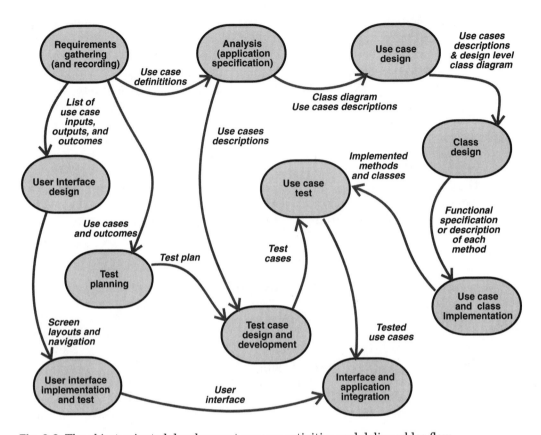

Fig. 2-2 The object-oriented development process activities and deliverables flow.

Input	Textual statement of need
Deliverables	Use case definitions
	Initial list of objects, attributes, and actors
	Incremental plan

2.5.2 Test planning

Once the scope and functionality of the product is captured the test team needs to demonstrate that they can test this application thoroughly. The test plan is provided so the client can review the tests and concur that the tested product will deliver all the required capabilities.

Input	Use case definitions (for the current increment)
Deliverables	Details on how each scenario will be tested

2.5.3 Analysis (and application specification)

If requirements define the product breadth then analysis defines its depth. Analysis captures, records, and validates the business rules for each scenario of every use case. That means supplementing the use case inputs and outcomes by adding a pre-condition and post-condition for each scenario. The last step is to get the client's concurrence that the use case descriptions completely and correctly define the application's response to every event.

Input	Use case definitions (for current increment)
	Initial list of object and attributes
Deliverables	Use case descriptions
	Data dictionary
	Class diagram
	Updated test plan

2.5.4 User interface design

Requirements record the application's functionality, but it is still necessary to show the user how that functionality will look and feel in a production environment. User interface design, while considered a nonsoftware related activity within OODP, is still necessary. The screen designs created and approved by the client are input to the user interface implementation activity.

Input	Use case definitions (from requirements)
	Client/user input on look and feel
Deliverables	Screen designs and flow

2.5.5 User interface implementation and test

This step in the process addresses the creation of the user interface after it has been designed. It involves implementing the user interface independent of any application and testing to ensure that it meets the criteria specified by the requirements use case definitions.

Input	(Screen designs)
	Use case definitions
	Scenario semantics (includes input types)
Deliverables	A set of user interfaces that send the correct messages to the application for each use case

2.5.6 Test case design and development

When analysis is complete and the scenario pre-conditions and post-conditions are defined, the test plan must be reviewed for correctness and completeness, and, when necessary, updated. While the development team is doing use case design and implementation the test team will be writing the test cases based on the updated test plan.

Input	Use case descriptions
	Updated test plan
Deliverables	Details of messages for each test case in this increment
	List of attributes required for test case validation, for the current increment

2.5.7 Use case design

Use cases are designed by creating a sequence of messages that first determine the correct scenario and then modify the attributes of the business objects to achieve the required state of the use case scenario as specified in the post-condition.

Input	Use case descriptions
Deliverables	Design of each use case recorded with a sequence diagram
	Design data model for the current increment

2.5.8 Class design

Use case design is followed by class design and method specification. The methods are those that the designers determined were required to support the design of the use case for this increment and those that the testers required to support test case validation.

Input	Use case designs
	Updated data model
Deliverables	Class specifications
	Updated design data model

2.5.9 Use case and class implementation

Each use case is implemented as a separate method in the application. Classes as defined in support of the design are created as well.

Input   Use case designs

                 Class specifications and design

                 Test case attribute references

Deliverables   Coded and compiled classes

2.5.10 Use case test

During test, every test case must run correctly, with no intervening failures. That means that if a failure occurs during a test run, then all the tests must be rerun once the defects are found and fixed. This requires a program capable of running all tests without intervention. As failures are discovered, the test and development teams work together to determine if the flaw is in the use case design, the implementation, or the test case itself.

Input   Test cases

                 Compiled classes

Deliverables   Test results

2.5.11 Interface and application integration

Since OODP tests the application without using the user interface and the user interface is developed without using the application, a final integration test is required when the user interface and application are joined. More traditional testing including performance, stress, integration, and system follows this.

Input   Tested use cases

                 Installed classes

                 User interface implementation

Deliverables   Integrated tested product

Do not expect to completely understand this process from the brief amount of information shown so far. This section was intended only to present the flow of OODP at a high level. The information required to implement and execute this process with confidence is contained in the details of the chapters that follow.

Requirements Definition

*T*his chapter describes the process of gathering requirements, how to record them as a use case definition, and the importance of requirements to other activities in the process. It discusses how incremental development applies to use cases and introduces a small case study to be used as an example for the rest of this book.

3.1 THE USE CASE

The use case is closely aligned with the concept of a transaction. It embodies the system's response to a user request. It is defined during requirements gathering as a set of inputs, outcomes, and an optional response. The concept of transactions, especially on large mainframe software has been around a long time. It is well understood and can easily be applied to the use case.

For readers familiar with the use case as defined in [Jacobson93] or the popular definition from the Unified Modeling Language, they will find that the use case of OODP is much more finely and rigorously defined. The rules presented here for a use case are necessary to effectively apply the process characteristics defined in Chapter 2.

3.2 RULES OF GRANULARITY

To understand what constitutes the correct amount of information in a use case, three rules need to be satisfied.

☞ The use case must define a complete transaction. The request must contain enough information that the application can process the request completely without returning to the user for additional information. This rule describes the minimum content of the use cases. Consider a request to withdraw some funds from an account where the only information provided is the account number. This demonstrates what is meant by incomplete. Too little information is available to complete the transaction. At the very least, the amount to be withdrawn must also be included. In all cases, the client will make the final decision about what the inputs to a use case must be.

☞ The use case must be a discrete unit of work. A use case that creates a loan and opens a savings account to guarantee that loan is a complex use case. It violates the single unit of work rule by performing two separate tasks. In the larger banking application, these two transactions will not always be done at the same time. Break this transaction into two use cases—one that opens a new savings account, and one that creates a loan—and perhaps even a third use case that guarantees the loan with funds from the savings account. The user interface chapter will discuss how primary use cases can be combined to appear as a single transaction from the user's perspective.

☞ Finally keep the use case simple. In other words, use case definitions should avoid multiple identical inputs, when these inputs logically belong to separate transactions. Suppose we wanted a use case that would allow a clerk to satisfy a loan by transferring funds from up to three separate accounts. The use case signature would then look something like

> **pay a loan (loan number, from-account number 1, amount 1, from-account number 2, amount 2, from-account 3, amount 3).**

This use case has three pairs of semantically identical inputs and the possibility that two of these inputs may be null. A better way to handle this transaction is to have one use case to initiate the loan payment, a second use case to specify each payment source, and a third to complete the loan payment process. While this may seem like more work and confusing at first, it greatly simplifies the design and implementation, while still giving the user the ability through the user interface to have the capability to enter all three account numbers and amounts at the same time.

The rules of use case granularity

♦ The use case must be **complete**. It should contain enough information that the application can process the request without
returning to the user for additional information.

♦ The use case should be a **discrete** unit of work. Business processes should be decomposed into individual use cases each with
its own inputs and outcomes.

♦ Keep use cases **simple**, by avoiding multiple identical inputs,
when these inputs logically belong to separate transactions.

3.3 USE CASE SIGNATURE

A great amount of detail is required to define a use case completely, and the
majority of this detail will be deferred until analysis, when the client supplies
the business rules. During requirements, the goal is to

☞ Bound the problem space.
☞ Record enough use case details to allow other dependent process activi-
ties to begin.
☞ Document the known requirements as quickly as possible.

To accomplish these goals, limit requirements use cases to four pieces of
information, which will be referred to as the use case signature.

☞ The inputs (and their order)
☞ The input types
☞ The use case outcomes
☞ Any returned information

All remaining detail will be developed during analysis and user interface
design.

3.3.1 Inputs

Suppose that there is a use case to transfer money from one financial account
to another. What are its inputs? One might assume that at a minimum there
are two account identifiers and the amount to be transferred. Since the client
has the responsibility to define all of the details of the requirements, including
use case inputs, they may require additional information, such as account
owner identification, pin number, or social security number. Assume the client

requires that the users enter their pin number as well. In this case the inputs for the use case definition would be

```
transfer (from-account number, to-account number, amount, pin number)
```

This may appear to violate the second or third rule of granularity since the two account numbers are essentially identical items; the transaction could be broken into a withdraw and a deposit. However, the use case does not violate these rules since there will always be two account numbers and logically a transfer can be viewed as a single event.

3.3.2 Input type

To correctly edit the information entered on the screen, the user interface implementer will need to know the type of every input. *Type* is the syntactic definition of what makes an input valid. For some attributes, the answer may seem trivial because everyone assumes that the application is working in the domain with which they are most familiar; however always check with the client first. Consider the transfer amount in the preceding use case; the logical assumption is that it involves U.S. currency and that the format is therefore a decimal number representing dollars and cents. However, what if these are brokerage accounts where the units might be $1/64^{th}$ and a two-digit decimal would not provide enough accuracy? Requirements gathering is the responsibility of the development team, but requirements definition is the responsibility of the client and that includes input type definitions. Based on the transfer example begun earlier, assume the use case input type definitions specified by the client are

```
transfer (from-account number, to-account number, amount, pin number)
    from-account number:   String(8)
    to-account number:     String(8)
    amount:                Decimal(12,2)
    pin number:            String(4)
```

3.3.3 Outcomes

The third element of the use case signature is its outcomes. Outcomes are the different possible logical results of the transaction. In the example of transferring funds from one account to another, a successful transfer is one outcome, but there is the possibility that the from-account balance is too small to accommodate the transfer. The user may have also entered an invalid account number or perhaps an expired pin. Once again, defer to the client to determine what logical outcomes are required. Rewriting the use case with outcomes gives the following use case definition. The convention in OODP is to show outcomes in braces, after the use case inputs.

```
transfer (from-account number, to-account number, amount, pin number)
{OK, invalid from-account number, invalid to-account number, wrong pin
    number, insufficient funds}
```

Sometimes outcomes will be referred to as scenarios in requirements. Chapter 4, Analysis, will show that there is a subtle difference between the two. Since that difference is difficult to detect during requirements, OODP uses outcomes for the use case definition in requirements and scenarios for the use case descriptions during analysis.

3.3.4 Returned data

The client may require that one or more of the outcomes return information to the user. For example, if the transfer from-account has insufficient funds, then the client may require that the available balance be returned. When the transfer is successful, it may be the practice that the new balances of both accounts are provided to the user. If both of these practices are part of the bank's policy, then the final use case definition is as shown here. The returned values are in parentheses following the associated outcome.

```
transfer (from-account number, to-account number, amount, pin number)
{OK (updated from-account balance updated to-account balance),
invalid from-account number,
invalid to-account number,
wrong pin number,
insufficient funds (from-account available balance)}
```

3.4 WHY THIS LEVEL OF USE CASE DETAIL DURING REQUIREMENTS?

To some it may seem that the amount of information recorded in requirements use cases is too little, whereas others may feel that there is more information here than is necessary for simple requirements recording. However, the four elements of the use case signature represent the minimum amount of information required to support the process activities for which they are the input. Consider how and where these requirements definitions will be used.

3.4.1 Use of requirements

Five activities are dependent on the requirements:

- ☞ Project estimating and planning
- ☞ User interface development
- ☞ Test
- ☞ Analysis
- ☞ Increment partitioning

Recall that an objective of the use case definitions in requirements was to provide enough detail for these five activities to be completed. The next few topics describe the role of the use case definition in each activity. They describe and explain why the information as specified is essential and minimal. Subsequent chapters will elaborate on these activities.

3.4.1.1 The estimate and the plan   A use case is not just one of the functions of an application; it also represents a logical unit of work for the analyst, designer, tester, and implementer. This makes the use case the ideal metric for planning because it represents a task that can be assigned to a developer. By identifying use cases during requirements, a plan can be developed based on the deliverables associated with each use case. To weight these tasks so that resource estimates can be added to the plan, use outcomes instead of use cases as the metric for computing effort. As the number of outcomes increases, so will the amount of effort required to complete the project.

3.4.1.2 User interface   OODP is structured so that the user interface and development teams can work independently. The user interface will most likely not be built incrementally and will be driven more by end user tasks than by individual use cases. In order for these teams to integrate successfully later in the process, there must be an agreed to interface defined. That interface is the use case signature, which defines how the user interface will communicate with the application. It is the only reason that the order and types of the use case inputs and returned information are required so early in the process.

3.4.1.3 Test   When testers test use cases, they do so by testing the individual scenarios of the use cases. During requirements, outcomes are a good approximation of a use case's scenarios. That means that the testers can use outcomes to begin use case test planning.

3.4.1.4 Analysis   The analyst's job is to elaborate the use case outcomes into scenarios and add their business rules. These rules will be expressed in terms of the inputs to the use cases and the attributes of the business objects. Both the analyst and the user interface designer may uncover missing inputs or scenarios during these activities. By agreeing on when and how the requirements will be defined, it will be easier to communicate changes to the teams later.

3.4.1.5 Incremental planning   The last activity dependent on requirements is the creation of the incremental plan. This requires a few assumptions about the use case that have not yet been identified; but by having the inputs and returned information available, a reasonable incremental plan can be developed. The outcomes and returned information help to identify use case dependencies, which are key elements in developing this plan.

3.4.2 The ideal amount of information for requirements

It should be clear that less information than described here would make it difficult, if not impossible, to continue with the other development activities. If more information were collected, the requirements gathering activity would take too long. Remember that the goal is to bound the problem space as quickly as possible so that an estimate and incremental plan can be created. If it takes more than a few weeks to accomplish this, there is a good chance that use case definition will be rushed or skipped. On the other hand, if the details are too sparse, then there will be insufficient information available to accomplish the dependent tasks, especially planning, and that may jeopardize the entire project.

3.5 THE RAW REQUIREMENTS (THE WAY THEY NORMALLY ARE PROVIDED)

Once it is understood how requirements will be recorded and used, it will be easier to interrogate the client to gather the essential information. Requirements start out in many forms: statements of needs, list of functions, descriptions of tasks that the user wants to perform, or information gathered as a result of interviewing the current or future system users. Interviews are a good technique to determine how the business operates today and to find out how the users want it to work tomorrow. The one item that all these forms have in common is that they can be recorded as text. Therefore, start the requirements gathering process by examining this text and using grammar to identify objects, attributes, actors, and function.

3.5.1 Vocabulary

The goal is to record these terms in the data dictionary and create a vocabulary for the problem domain. For requirements it is enough to identify each term and to make sure that both the client and the analyst agree on the meaning of each one. When the vocabulary is established, technical documentation should be limited to only these terms.

3.5.2 Nouns

Nouns will be the key element of the vocabulary of the client's problem domain. Categorize the nouns as object/attribute, actor, alias, or not applicable. At this point, whether a given noun is an object or an attribute is not important.

Identifying and labeling nouns this way will keep the analyst from overlooking important terms in the written requirements. A classification of "not applicable" needs to be validated by the client to ensure that it is an element that is truly outside the problem space.

Aliases need to be recorded with their primary term, and a determination must be made as to which is the most preferred word or phrase.

An actor is a direct or indirect user of the system and will serve as a source to identify and elaborate use cases, based on the tasks they perform.

3.5.3 Adjectives

Some attributes appear in requirements as adjectives that represent their values. For example, overdrawn or closed is really a value of the account status attribute. During requirements it is not important how a closed account will be represented but only that there needs to be an attribute that defines that state.

3.5.4 Verb phrases

Verbs are also useful, but it is important to examine them in the context of the words that surround them. Consider the verb "pay." By itself, it sheds little to no light on requirements, but "pay off a loan" and "pay yearly safe deposit box fee" are use cases that should be discussed with the client. On the other hand, "pay a visit to the bank" is not significant in terms of use case identification. In general, verbs should be combined with other adjacent nouns to create the *essential* phrase. This union is considered the candidate use case.

3.5.5 Actors, roles, and use cases

A bank may have actors like a loan officer, teller, or customer, and possibly others not obvious from the text of the requirements. In the day-to-day banking operation, the customers may never directly interact with the banking system but they are still responsible for several events that the system must respond to and that need to be considered as sources of use cases. Once identified, actors can be assigned roles based on the tasks that they perform. For example, bank officers may step into a role that has them opening new accounts, taking loan applications, or even making simple withdrawals and deposits on behalf of their customers. These roles are the source of use cases.

The role/use case relationship is used rather than the actor/use case relationship because more than one actor may perform the identical task in a similar role. A teller might query for the balance of an account because of a customer's request. The loan officer may also need to check the balance of an account because of a loan application. If there were a web interface available, even customers would have the capability to query their account balance. In these instances, the system response, and therefore the use case, would be the same. One use case can support many users, all of them operating in the same role. The only difference is the interface presented to each of these actors.

3.5.5.1 Nonhuman actors   Actors are not all human beings. Systems that require information from the application are considered actors since they trigger events that require a response by the application. Business processes can

also be considered actors since they may initiate use cases. For example, the business cycle calendar defines temporal events that trigger periodic reports. In all cases where the actor is a business process or a nonhuman actor, find the individual most responsible for these activities (the programmer, the business analyst) and have him or her assume the role of surrogate actor to help identify the details of the use cases.

3.5.6 Paper and pencil user interface prototypes

One way to facilitate requirements gathering with actors is to provide them with an *informal* view of a user interface (see Figure 3-1). This allows the analyst to walk through the related use cases with the user to discuss the following:

☞ Where inputs will be entered
☞ How the event is triggered
☞ Where the outcomes are displayed

This process may help discover missing inputs to an existing use case, or even to entire use cases.

> *The analyst would point to the input field "Customer identification" and explain that the teller will enter the customer number there. Then pointing to the next two fields, the analyst would show where the withdrawal amount and account numbers would be supplied. Finally, the analyst would point to the withdraw button and explain that it causes the withdrawal application to be performed. The conversation might continue something like: "If the application determines that the account number does not exist or that the account balance is too low to allow the withdrawal, a message will appear here (point to the output message) and the withdrawal process will abort."*

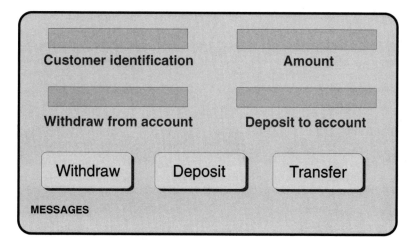

Fig. 3-1 Sample paper-and-pencil user interface prototype.

The clients might agree that this correctly describes the use case, or they might ask a question like "where do you enter the pin number?" or "how does the program determine how much money is available in the account to make a withdrawal?" This dialog can help to determine if an additional input (such as pin number) is required, or if there are complex business rules for determining if an account has insufficient funds for a withdrawal transaction.

Use cases and inputs are easy to visualize in this way. Outcomes are not as obvious, so they must be verbalized as each event is reviewed with the user. Do not let the clients believe that they are designing the user interface and do not waste time on user interface issues. User interface professionals will do these tasks later. The purpose of the walkthrough sessions with the clients is to search for use cases, inputs, and outcomes. One way to convey this message is to hand draw the user interfaces so that it is clear that this is an informal view and not a design.

The walkthrough of the use cases should follow some logical order such as "add a customer," followed by "open an account," then "make a deposit" and "make a withdrawal." This flow will help identify missing use cases that support the business process.

3.6 SEARCHING FOR USE CASES FROM KNOWN INFORMATION

Existing objects, attributes, use cases, and outcomes can be an aid to finding new use cases. The next few topics elaborate on this process.

3.6.1 Use cases from objects and attributes

Every attribute must have a use case that initially sets its value. Look at every attribute and ask if there is a use case that creates or initializes this attribute. Also ask if there is a use case that uses its value and whether there needs to be a use case that changes its value. A similar rule applies to objects. There must be a use case that creates the object and another that deletes it.

3.6.2 The inverse rule

Almost every use case will have an inverse. A banking system that allows deposits will most likely need a withdraw as well. A use case to add new customers implies that there should be a way to remove them when they no longer do business with the bank. Examine each use case discovered so far and ask if there is an inverse that should be included.

3.7 FINDING SCENARIOS

Every use case has a successful outcome, and almost all have one or more failure outcomes. Failures come in three forms.

☞ The input data is invalid, not syntactically but semantically. For example, the account number specified on the deposit does not exist, or the customer is not a client of this bank. Most inputs to use case will lead a failure of this type.

☞ When creating new objects, the object or the identifier associated with the object may already exist, such as trying to add a customer with an identifier that has already been assigned.

☞ The last category of scenarios is logical errors defined by the business. The customer already has the maximum number of accounts, or the customer is trying to withdraw an amount that would make the balance lower than the minimum required by the bank. Although the rules that define these exceptions will not be detailed until analysis, try to define the known outcomes during requirements.

3.8 WHEN TO STOP LOOKING FOR MORE USE CASES

The goal is that requirements will identify 90 percent of the use cases and about 95 percent of the scenarios for the application. It is reasonable to assume that as long as new use cases are being discovered, there are others that have not been found. In this case, the search for additional use cases should continue. However, when the techniques described stop yielding new use cases, and it appears that the cost of finding more may be more than the cost of dealing with them as changes, a reasonable assumption is that enough of them have been found. If post-project review shows that the 90/95 percent goal was not reached, review the thoroughness of the requirements process and try to determine how these activities could have uncovered more. Then stress those activities on the next project. This aspect of process improvement is discussed further in Chapter 13 on project management.

3.9 THE CASE STUDY

The case study that follows provides the opportunity to walk through an example that applies these rules and the details of the activities of OODP. Assume that the project begins with an informal requirement for a video store (see Figure 3-2). This is a subset of a larger problem presented in its entirety in Part 2.

The video store is chosen as an example because it is a well-understood domain, which makes it easier for the reader to take on the perspective of either the client or the analyst/designer. It is large enough to demonstrate all the features of OODP and small enough to be able to provide a complete solution.

3.9.1 Identify nouns, adjectives, and verb phrases

Given the requirement, the interesting parts of speech would be nouns, adjectives, and verbs. Figure 3-3 shows the identification of the nouns.

> Create a video rental tracking system that allows any member with a
> credit card on file to rent any available video for a maximum of three
> days. Members can rent at most four videos at a time. When the member
> brings a video to the counter, the clerk scans or types the video identifier
> and the member's identification. The video is then rented. If the video is
> returned late, the member must pay a 2 dollar per day late fee.
> Members with outstanding late fees or overdue videos cannot rent movies.

Fig. 3-2 Video store statement of requirements.

> Create a video rental tracking system that allows any member with a
> credit card on file to rent any available video for a maximum of three
> days. Members can rent at most four videos at a time. When the member
> brings a video to the counter, the clerk scans or types the video identifier
> and the member's identification. The video is then rented. If the video is
> returned late, the member must pay a dollar per day late fee.
> Members with outstanding late fees or overdue videos cannot rent movies.

Fig. 3-3 Video store statement of requirements, with nouns identified.

Scanning the requirements for the other parts of speech and performing a similar analysis for attributes and verb phrases would yield the following vocabulary:

Nouns—system, member, credit card, video, days, counter, clerk, (video) identifier, (member) number, (2) dollar, day, (late) fee

Adjectives—three (days), four (videos), late, outstanding (fees), rented, returned, overdue

Verb phrases—rent a video, scans the identifier, video is returned, pay a 2 dollar per day late fee

3.9.2 Objects and attributes

Elements that can be represented as primitive types like number, string, character, or boolean are atomic and should be considered attributes. Complex terms that contain multiple elements are most likely objects. Given those

Member   Video
    identifier   identifier
    fees outstanding   status {rented, late, returned}
    late videos
    rented videos

Fig. 3-4 Initial selection of application business objects.

guidelines and the previously listed nouns and adjectives, it is reasonable to presume the objects and attributes in Figure 3-4.

3.9.3 Identify use cases

Using the rules for identifying use cases from verb phrases, actors, attributes, objects, and inverses, the following use cases are suggested. Note that "scans the identifier" has been omitted since it was determined to be part of the user interface and therefore outside the scope of the application.

Verb phrases

    rent a video
    return a video
    pay a late fee

Actors

member

    pay late fee (amount, member id)

clerk

    rent video (identifier, member id)
    return video (identifier)

Attribute or value / set or update

    set video status to rented (rent)
    set video status to late (????)
    set video status to returned (return)
    set member fees outstanding (return)
    set member videos rented (rent)
    set member video late (????)

    (???? indicates that no use cases currently exist that set this state. This condition would indicate that a discussion with the client is necessary to determine if additional use cases are needed.)

Object create and destroy

> add member
>
> delete member
>
> add video
>
> remove video

Inverses

> Given the use case *pay late fee* the inverse would be:
>
> Charge late fee (return)

Although this fact was stated before, it is worth repeating. The final decision as to what use cases are or are not to be included in the application is the responsibility of the client. Based on this analysis, the list of use cases that would be presented to the client as the base requirement follows (inputs are shown in parentheses, outcomes have not yet been determined):

☞ Rent a video (id, customer)

☞ Return a rented video (id)

☞ Add a new video to the inventory (id, title)

☞ Create a new member (id, credit card)

☞ Delete an existing video (id)

☞ Delete an existing member (id)

☞ Make a video late

☞ Pay overdue fees

3.9.4 Finding outcomes

Use the client's knowledge of the domain to find the outcomes based on business policy. Use the guidelines for outcomes based on inputs to discover other potential outcomes.

3.9.4.1 Logically invalid input For the use cases rent, return, delete video, and delete member, the id of the video or the member may not exist in the system. A rented video may already be rented and a returned video may have a status indicating that it was never rented.

3.9.4.2 Duplication when creating new objects For add new video or create a new member, the id may already exist in the system.

3.9.4.3 Business rules These outcomes are the hardest to find since they often require the client to provide them. Some will be suggested by the requirements. Scan the requirements for words like *if, when, until,* and *must.* Then have the client elaborate to define the outcomes. Discovering others may require walking through the user interface prototypes. Here are the business rule outcomes from the video store:

☞ A member with outstanding fines or videos may not rent videos.

☞ Members have a maximum number of videos that can be rented.

☞ Videos are considered late after three days.

3.9.5 Final proposed set of use cases

The inputs and outcomes of the use cases identified using the rules discussed follow. The inputs follow the use case in parentheses (), and the outcomes are shown in italics within brackets {}.

☞ Rent a video (video id, member id)
   {OK, video not found, member not found, member has max videos rented, member owes fines (amount)}

☞ Return a rented video (video id)
   {OK, video not found, video not rented, video is overdue (fines owed)}

☞ Add a new video to the inventory (video id, title)
   {OK, video id already exists}

☞ Delete a video (video id)
   {OK, video not found, video is rented (due back)}

☞ Create a new member (member id, credit card no.)
   {OK, duplicate member id, invalid credit card}

☞ Delete an existing member (member id)
   {OK, member not found, member owes fines, member has outstanding rentals}

☞ Pay fines owed by member (member id, amount)
   {OK, member not found, member owes no fines, member overpaid by (amount), member still owes fines (amount) }

All the use cases, inputs, and outcomes were found deductively. This list must be presented to the client for verification. The techniques presented here to identify requirements are suggestions and aids based on our experience, but do not be fooled into thinking that they represent a magic formula that will find every use case. The rules of thumb can only stimulate the client and the developer to help remember some important facts that would have been overlooked in an informal requirements recording activity.

3.9.6 Typing the inputs

The use case inputs must be typed for the user interface team. They will need the type definitions to do basic input editing before sending the data to the application. This is discussed further in Chapter 11 on user interface.

The following list is an example of what that deliverable might look like:

```
video id         String(8) + NumericString(3)
member id        String(6..10)
title            String(1..30)
credit card no   String(16)
amount           String(0..9) + . + String(0..2)
```

3.10 CORRECTNESS

Remember that the client will decide which use cases are to be parts of the product and what outcomes the program should check for. End the requirements gathering activity with a semiformal walkthrough of the use cases, where the clients and developers review and agree to the use cases and their signatures. The questions to be asked and agreed to are:

☞ Have all use cases within the scope of the application been considered?

☞ Are the use case inputs and their types correct?

☞ Have all the outcomes and the outputs for each use case been identified?

3.11 PARTITIONING THE PROBLEM BY USE CASE

If the discussion and review yield no new use cases, assume the goal of finding 90 percent of the use cases was achieved and move on to the last activity within requirements, that of partitioning the use cases into increments. Use cases are ideal for partitioning because they map directly to functional requirements. The rule for partitioning is that all use cases in an increment may only be dependent on other use cases in the current increment or a previous increment.

Use case A is dependent on use case B, if B is necessary to create a pre-condition state for any scenario in use case A.

Note that the definition of dependence involves scenario pre-conditions that have not yet been defined. For that reason, it may be necessary during analysis to alter the content of the current increment when the scenario post-conditions are understood.

It is possible to define an increment where all dependent use cases are not available but enough exist to establish pre-conditions for a subset of the use case scenarios. This approach may seem useful, but it requires considerably more work during later increments. For example, if the first increment contained only the use cases "add video," "add member," and "rent video," it would not be possible to test the scenario where a rental was rejected because the member owed fines. Creation of that state requires the return use case. When the increment containing "return video" is finally completed, "rent video" will need to be re-tested, and existing tested code may need to be changed. The use of this style of partitioning is discouraged.

3.11.1 A larger video store example

The number of use cases identified for the requirements seen so for is too small to define interesting increments, so consider the use cases from a larger video store. These are the use cases based on the example from Part 2. The outcomes are shown in braces and any output associated with an outcome follows the outcome in parentheses (). Figure 3-5 shows the intra use case dependencies graphically. The arrows point from the independent use case to the dependent use case.

Add category (category)

{OK, category exists}

Add vendor (vendor name, address, royalty, type)

{OK (vendor id), vendor exists}

Remove vendor (vendor id)

{OK, vendor not found}

Add video (title, category, rating, vendor id, rental fee, late fee, days)

{OK, title exists, category not found, vendor not found}

Remove video (title)

{OK, copies exist, title not found}

Define branch (branch number)

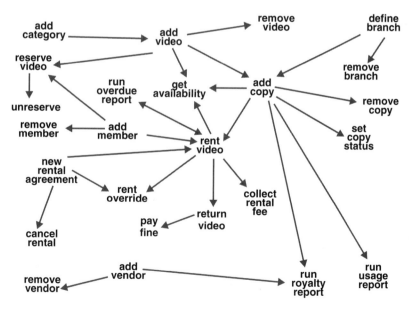

Fig. 3-5 Video store application use case dependency diagram.

{OK, branch exists}

Remove branch (branch number)

{OK, branch not found}

Add copy (title, copy number, branch number)

{OK, title not found, copy exists, branch not found}

Remove copy (title, copy number)

{OK, last copy, title not found, copy not found}

Add member (member name, phone, member flag)

{OK (member id), member and phone exist}

Remove member (member id, phone)

{OK, member and phone not found}

New rental agreement ()

{OK, rental active}

Rent video (title, copy number, member id)

{OK, title reserved, member ineligible, copy not available, title not found, copy not found, member not found}

Rent override (title, copy number, member id)

{OK, title not found, copy not found, member not found}

Collect rental fee (amount)

{OK, insufficient amount, change due(amt)}

Cancel rental agreement

{OK, no rental active}

Reserve video (title, member id)

{OK, title available, title not found, member not found, member ineligible}

Remove member from wait list (title, member id)

{OK, video not found, member not on list}

Run overdue report()

{OK}

Return video (title, copy number)

{OK, overdue (days), next reserved (cust), title not found, overdue (days) and next reserved (cust), copy not found, wrong branch}

Pay fine (member id, amount)

{OK, member not found, change due (amt), still owes (amt)}

Get availability (title, branch number)

{on shelf, due back (date), at branch (branch)}

Set copy status (title, copy number, branch number, status)

{OK, title not found, copy not found, branch not found}

Run royalty report()

{OK}

Run usage report()

{OK}

3.11.2 Partitioning strategies

There are many ways to partition a set of use cases correctly. Project leaders will choose one or more based on the goal of each increment. This topic starts with a discussion of a few of the many potential partitioning strategies and ends with an example of incremental partitioning and the associated strategies.

Easiest first: This approach is useful when trying to ease the development team into working with use cases or objects. The easier use cases allow for time to evaluate the methods and tools. If the methods are ineffective and need to be abandoned, very little effort is lost.

Target use cases for operational support: This strategy attempts to get a comprehensive set of use cases operational as soon as possible (typically within the first or second increment). It allows the system to be used to perform tasks such as loading the database. An example would be to include the use cases to add videos, categories, and vendors so that, while the team is working on developing increments two and three, the stores are able to begin the tedious task of adding all those videos. Remember that with incremental development, a tested increment delivers the complete and final functionality for those use cases. The only way that this effort would be wasted is if the basic requirements are changed.

Provide most functionality as soon as possible: Here the goal is to demonstrate as much of the system's capability as soon as possible. This is particularly useful when trying to show capability and feasibility very early. Even though the final product will not be completed for another two or three increments, in many cases an operational system can be delivered several months early. Meanwhile, the remaining use cases with a much lower probability of use are developed. Consider delaying use cases to delete a member, video, vendor, category, or copy. Also some of the lesser used reports like those that track high turnover videos could easily be delayed for two or three months. The result is that the product is delivered sooner and a lot of pressure is removed from the development team.

Support end user training: This plan creates use cases to provide most application operations but not enough to run in production mode. An example would be to add use cases to add videos and customers and to rent and possibly return videos. Functions like cancel, reserve, override, check availability, pay fine, and the like could be deferred, but the delivered system would have enough functionality to allow the clerks to use the system in training mode. This approach often requires two or more increments, but the result is a level of functionality that allows the client to have their users work with the system while there is still time to make changes. The drawback to this approach is that a fairly complete user interface is also required. These strategies help to emphasize the benefits of an incremental development process.

3.11.3 Example increments and strategies

Normally it is enough to plan one increment at a time. Requirements will change, new requirements will surface, and even the strategy for the next increment may change by the time it is ready to begin. However, there is no danger in planning future increments, if that is desired, as long as everyone realizes that the plan needs to be revisited at the start of each increment.

The example that follows shows an incremental plan and the associated strategies for each increment of the 23 uses cases identified in the larger video store example from Part 2. It shows a 4/5 incremental plan. That means that the plan has committed to the delivery of increments 1 through 4 based on the required schedule. Increment 5 has been declared optional and will be delivered in this release of the product only if the development team feels that there is sufficient time.

3.11.3.1 Increment 1

Use cases:

> Add category
>
> Define branch
>
> Add vendor
>
> Add video
>
> Add copy

Strategy: This is the first object-oriented project for the team; therefore, the first increment has been kept small and simple. This will allow it to be used as a practice increment and not endanger any critical code if the team falters. In addition, if they are successful, the client may be able to put the increment to use by beginning the process of creating the database of videos.

3.11.3.2 Increment 2

Use cases:

> Add member
>
> New rental agreement

Rent video

Run overdue report

Return video

Collect rental fee

Reserve video

Strategy: The second increment plans to deliver most of the core function to operate the store and to demonstrate a fairly complete system. The user can evaluate functionality, assuming a minimal user interface prototype is available. There is plenty of time to react to required changes.

3.11.3.3 Increment 3

Use cases:

Rent override

Get availability

Pay fines

Run royalty report

Run usage report

Cancel rental

Strategy: This increment provides all but a few of the required use cases to consider the system operational. It is expected that there will be an operational user interface available during this increment, even though it may not be fully tested and approved by the client. Increment 4 is still available to make minor adjustments.

3.11.3.4 Increment 4

Use cases:

Remove copy

Remove video

Remove member

Remove vendor

Set copy status

Rent override

Remove member from wait list (unreserve video)

Strategy: The use cases in this increment are noncritical. If the project flounders and runs excessively late, increment 3 could be used as the operational system for a short period of time until increment 4 is complete.

3.11.3.5 Increment 5

Use cases:

> Search for video information
>
> Find movies with actor
>
> Find movies by director
>
> Show video clip

Strategy: It was determined that the kiosk station for use by the member was an entirely different subsystem that required a much larger database. To meet schedule constraints and contract deadlines, it was agreed that increment 5 would be considered optional and renegotiated as a separate contract after completion of increment 3.

3.11.4 Guidelines for incremental planning

Use case effort does not distribute evenly across increments.   If the use cases were apportioned, so that every increment had the same number of scenarios, increment 1 would take longer than any other increment and the final increment would require the least amount of effort. This is because the implementation of increment n will create classes and methods that will be reused in increments n+1. In addition, as the team completes the analysis and design of the use cases for the current increment, the understanding of both problem and solution space that results from these activities makes the design and analysis of subsequent increments go more quickly. The recommendation is to make the first increment the smallest in terms of functionality and gradually to build up to larger increments. The exception is the last increment, which should be smaller and easier so that any required redesign can be accommodated.

Plan on surprises in the first increment.   By definition, projects begin analysis without a full understanding of the problem. As the use case descriptions are developed for the first increment, the analysis team is likely to discover that they are more complex than expected, or that it has omitted a dependent use case or two. Much of the project housekeeping usually gets done in increment 1; so if increment one takes longer than planned, it does not necessarily follow that every other increment will overrun its schedule as well. Wait until the end of increment 2 to make that assessment. It should also be expected that there would be a few less surprises in increment 2.

Plan at a detailed level only for the current increment.   Plan to replan at the start of each new increment, especially for organizations that are new to object technology, or to use cases. The lessons learned in increment 1 will, and should, change the way you approach the rest of the project. This will be true to some extent in every increment. For this reason, it is probably ineffective and inefficient to include the same amount of detail in the plan for follow-on increments as for the current one. Also, by deferring that detail, you are forcing the team to revisit the plan at the start of each new increment.

Defer any changes until the next increment when analysis is complete. Don't even tell the team about them. Changes include new scenarios or changes to existing scenarios. Even though it may seem more practical to go ahead and incorporate a change to a use case while it is being developed, the benefit of the analysis activity cannot be overstated. Changes in the business rules of one use case can affect other use cases; when change is integrated during design and implementation, the reviews that should resolve these conflicts are almost always skipped. One of the big advantages of the incremental process is that it has the ability to process all changes from the top of the process. Do not circumvent that feature.

Try to incorporate all of a use case's scenarios in the same increment. It is possible to implement a use case where only some of the scenarios are operational. For example, it may be decided that the extra work required to make a video overdue will be postponed, and not be included in the increment that contains rent. This will prevent testing the outcome where a member is prohibited from renting more videos until they have returned and paid the fines on their overdue videos. This plan may be reasonable, but it has the following drawbacks.

- ☞ There will often be some stub code required to make this work that will later need to be removed, or, worse, it may be that if the function is used, runtime errors may result.
- ☞ It will be necessary to retest the entire use case when the missing scenarios are added in. If this extra effort later in the process is weighed against the value of simplifying the current increment, it will be easy to see why this approach is discouraged.
- ☞ This approach makes it difficult to see the full function of the use case from the user's perspective.

Finish increments in four months or less. If the plan has a very large number, or too many very small increments, it will diminish the productivity value of the model. An increment should typically take about 8 to 16 weeks for analysis, design, code, and functional test. It is acceptable for one or two of the early increments to be much smaller. Sometimes their duration will be as short as two to four weeks. But as the team gains experience, productivity will suffer with many small increments. A good rule for teams new to object technology (OT) and incremental development is to make your estimate for how long the project should take and assume that it will take about as long as it did under the old method of program development; then break up the schedule so that each increment takes about two to three months. For example, suppose that the estimate for the project is 14 months to complete. Divide the requirements so that there are five increments. (14 divided by 2.5

is approximately 5.) Furthermore, assume that there are 100 use cases (the 100 is just a round number for demonstration). The plan could have 10, 15, 25, 30, and 20 respectively in each of the five increments. Schedule and resource planning are covered further in the project management chapter.

3.12 DISTRIBUTING AND MAINTAINING THE REQUIREMENTS

When the requirements are finalized, give the list of use cases for the first increment to designer/analysts so they may begin the process of implementing it. The same list goes to the test team to begin creating the test plan. The user interface team gets the entire list of requirements since they will not be working incrementally.

The requirements are the project definition, and it is essential that everyone work from the same list. Place the document under change control. If one team member discovers a missing use case or scenario or if another team member finds an omission or errors in the use case signature, everyone on the team needs to be informed. When it is agreed that this is a required change, update the requirements document and, if applicable, the incremental plan. Then, redistribute them to the teams with the changes highlighted.

3.13 USE CASE NAMING CONVENTIONS

There is just one more item to cover before leaving requirements. To this point, the names and parameters of use cases have been written using Standard English adjective, noun, or verb phrases. To maintain identical names for these items throughout the process, it would be better to adopt a style that is more suited to design and implementation. The Java, Smalltalk, and C++ naming style creates single identifiers for use cases, methods, objects, and attributes, omitting blanks and capitalizing any intermediate words. They also have the convention of beginning only classes with a capital letter, and objects, methods, attributes, and other variables with lowercase letters. Therefore, *Rent a Video* becomes *rentVideo*, and *movie title* becomes *movieTitle*, and the *video* class becomes *Video*. The Unified Modeling Language (UML), which is discussed in the next chapter, has become the de facto standard for notation of object-oriented analysis and design artifacts. It has adopted this naming convention. As a result, the same name can be used to reference a variable, attribute, use case, or parameter in analysis, in design, and when writing code. Therefore, consistent terminology can span the entire process. This gives the reader of the artifacts a tremendous advantage with respect to understanding and eliminates the translation normally required between these phases. It is recommended that you write your requirements in the same manner. That means, for example, that the rent and return use cases should have been written as follows:

rentVideo (videoId, memberId)

{OK, member ineligible, videoId not available, videoId not found, member not found}

return (videoId)

{OK, overdue (days), videoId not found, videoId not rented }

The remaining chapters will adopt this naming style.

Analysis

This chapter describes the details of the use case specification and how it should be recorded. It elaborates on the relationship between the use case and the class diagram and discusses the role of the Unified Modeling Language (UML) in analysis. It also reviews several other analysis models associated with object technology that are helpful in identifying use cases. It begins with a discussion on the difference between analysis and design.

4.1 ANALYSIS VS. DESIGN

It is important to understand the difference between analysis and design. A frequently asked question is "when does analysis end, and design begin?" Some will say, "analysis is the *what* and design is the *how*," but others prefer "analysis is the statement of the problem and design is the description of the solution." Another interpretation of the question could be "how does one determine if the task being performed is part of analysis or part of design?" That question has a more objective answer.

Analysis is the activity within the process where the client is in charge and makes *all* the decisions. They decide what function is to be included and how its behavior will be defined. The client defines all the business rules, and the analyst may not change them without approval. Developers naturally interject cautions based on cost or technical concerns, but they may not make business policy. For example, if a banking application has a withdraw use case, it is not up to the developer to decide that the function of the withdraw use case will be to increase the account balance rather than reduce it.

Conversely, during design, it is the developer who is responsible for making *all* the decisions. To allow the client to decide that "tables will be arrays rather than trees" would have a serious impact on the designer's ability to optimize the application. This clarification of roles within the process can simplify the decision as to what details of deliverables should be added where. When examining a deliverable, if there are choices and tradeoffs to be made, they are usually part of design. On the other hand, if the questions relate to critical information needed to define the problem, then it belongs in requirements or analysis.

4.2 PURPOSE OF ANALYSIS

Since analysis is the definition of the problem, any activities that can help clarify the problem should become part of the analysis activities. Analysis requires staying focused on the problem. During requirements the objective was to bound the scope of the problem space quickly so that the team could move on to the tasks of sizing, estimating, and planning. In analysis the focus is on understanding the business rules that specify the application. With that in mind, consider stating the goals of analysis as

☞ To better understand the problem domain
☞ To capture the business rules and policies
☞ To identify missing requirements as quickly as possible
☞ To reach agreement between the client and development team on the problem specification.

If activities do not support one of these four goals, determine whether it is an activity that the client needs to participate in, then defer those, which they do not, until design. The next few paragraphs briefly describe the techniques that will be applied to reach these goals.

4.2.1 Understand the problem domain

Start with the vocabulary developed from the nouns and other textual references collected from the textual documents in requirements. Use these terms to develop the core of the data dictionary. For each entry in the data dictionary, record a definition that is applicable to the problem domain. Even though the analyst will usually write these definitions, the client will need to review them for accuracy.

4.2.2 Identify the business rules and policies

For every use case, record the business rules that define the outcomes. For each outcome, record the information that application must remember. The application remembers information by storing values in the business object attributes. For example, the way a bank remembers that a deposit was made is by increasing the account balance by the deposit amount. The amount that the balance is increased by is considered part of the business rules.

4.2.3 Identify any missing requirements

Several models allow the team to view the problem from different perspectives. Each has the goal of capturing or validating a business rule, a use case, a scenario, or operational data. The models employed are the decision table, the state diagram, the class diagram, and the sequence diagram. These models are reviewed with the client during a walk-through that allows the development team to suggest potential gaps in the specification and hopefully trigger missing requirements in the client's mind.

4.2.4 Agree on the problem specification

The goal of the walk-though is to have everyone agree on the problem to be solved. Use structured reviews with the developers to assert consistency between the models. Use formal semantic reviews with the client teams to assert its correctness.

4.3 DETAILS OF THE ANALYSIS ACTIVITY

The discovery and recording steps that the analyst progresses through to achieve the goals of analysis follow:

- ☞ For each use case, record the business rules for each outcome.
- ☞ For every noun in a use case, create a data dictionary entry with an associated client agreed-to definition.
- ☞ For nouns that represent business data, create class diagram components for them.
- ☞ Use any analysis models to reinforce everyone's understanding of the problem and assist in creating a complete specification.
- ☞ Conduct a walk-through with the client to review the use case details and obtain agreement on the application specification.

These activities are presented sequentially and independently; however, during a real project they would overlap. As new use cases discover additional vocabulary, the terms will be defined and recorded in the data dictionary and at the same time added to the appropriate place on the class diagram. As complex objects are discovered, it may be helpful to use state diagrams to better understand their role in the application even though the complete class definition will evolve over several increments.

4.3.1 Recording the business rules for the scenarios

Requirements referred to use case outcomes. In analysis these are refined into scenarios. Before proceeding, it is appropriate to define the difference between an outcome and a scenario.

4.3.1.1 Scenarios vs. outcomes   Requirements identified one or more logical outcomes for each use case. This abstraction was a means to determine project breadth without enumerating all the details. However, internally the business may have variations on the way it achieves an outcome. For example, the successful (OK) outcome of the withdraw use case that provided the cash requested may be made up of several scenarios. The bank may enact a transaction charge if the account balance is below a certain amount, or the status of the account may change from preferred to nonpreferred because the new balance is below some threshold. Another bank may have a policy to charge a fee when the number of transactions per month exceeds some fixed number. Each of these transactions represents a unique logical path through the use case and is therefore a separate scenario. Since requirements do not refer to state there was no way to distinguish between scenarios at that time. In requirements it was possible only to identify a successful withdraw, but when the details of the business rules were uncovered in analysis, this outcome encompassed more than one rule, and, therefore, involved multiple scenarios. During analysis, detail each logical rule separately. From this point on, in the process, use case scenarios will be used instead of outcomes.

4.3.1.2 Scenario pre-conditions   Each scenario is defined using a combination of the use case inputs and the pre-transaction values of one or more attributes in the business objects. For example, the withdraw amount (input) must be less than or equal to the account balance (business object attribute). As such, every scenario has a unique pre-condition, defined by the client and based on the rules that their business operates under. Consider the definition of insufficient funds. One bank may require that a withdraw leave a balance greater than some minimum, whereas another may require some of the account assets to be frozen and unavailable if they are used to guarantee a loan.

4.3.1.3 Scenario post-conditions   For each scenario there is also a post-condition. This is the detail of how the attributes of the business objects are to be altered. The post-condition also identifies the information returned to the user.

The withdraw use case must reduce the account balance by the withdraw amount and charge a transaction fee based on the type of account and the original available balance (see rule 23.a). After a successful withdrawal the new account balance is returned.

Each post-condition is paired with its pre-condition to define the business rules. When all the scenarios for a use case are combined, they create the analysis use case description.

The correctness questions for scenarios within a use case are:

☞ The pre-conditions must completely cover the input space; that is, there can be no state of the system that is not covered by some pre-condition.

☞ The pre-conditions must be disjoint. That means there can be no system state that satisfies more than one pre-condition.

☞ The post-conditions must be unique, so no two scenarios can have the same post-condition. Violating this rule may merely mean that the two scenarios need to be combined, but often it is an indication that a portion of the post-condition of one of the scenarios was omitted.

☞ The business rules must not be ambiguous. This fourth rule is not as easy to enforce as the others since the word *ambiguous* may itself be ambiguous.

Consider the following use case description for withdrawing funds, as part of the banking application:

Use Case: Withdraw (account number, amount)

Outcomes: OK, insufficient funds (NSF), invalid account number

Business Rules: If the account number supplied is *invalid* or there is *insufficient money* in the account, then reject the transaction. Otherwise, *update* the account balance and return the new balance to the customer.

The previous example meets the conditions of the first three correctness questions for both pre-condition and post-condition, but it fails to meet the condition of question four, since the business rules are not well defined. Specifically the following questions cannot be answered based on the existing use case description:

☞ What makes an account number *invalid*?

☞ What does *insufficient money* mean?

☞ How is the account balance *updated*?

The rules as stated are detailed, but the details are ambiguous. The problem is that, to the client, they have very precise meanings, but these meanings were not captured in a way that the developers can precisely interpret them. For example, invalid account number might mean that no account with that number was found, or it might include the case that the associated account was closed or frozen. Insufficient funds could be interpreted as the account balance being less than the withdraw amount, or it could be based on a minimum balance required by the bank. Even the update account balance does not specify whether to add or subtract an amount from the account balance. Furthermore, what amount should be used to adjust the account balance: the withdraw amount or an amount that includes a service charge.

Here are the guidelines for recording business rules that can help eliminate the ambiguity seen in the last example.

☞ Use only terms from the data dictionary. The use case should be written using a combination of business object, attributes, and input parameters defined for the use case. By limiting the use case definition to the vocabulary of the domain, there is a better chance of the client identifying any errors.

☞ Use identical words when the meaning is identical. Good prose uses synonyms to avoid making the sentences appear repetitive and boring. A good use case specification should do just the opposite. Use the same words over and over to ensure that the meaning is clear.

☞ Avoid adjectives. Although adding colorful adjectives enhances readability, if these adjectives are not integral to the problem domain, then the sentence while beautiful may be less clear. Remember that the goal here is precision, not reading enjoyment. This rule excludes terms like *insufficient balance*, enhancing the likelihood that the analyst will be forced into recording the precise formula for insufficient balance instead.

☞ Use formulae instead of ambiguous verb phrases. The terms of the formulae should be the use case inputs, the attributes of the business objects, and the business object attribute values. Phrases like "reduce account balance" would be replaced with the textual formula: "new balance is the old balance minus the withdraw amount plus a 2 dollar service charge." Even more precision could be achieved with the arithmetic formula: "account balance = account balance − (withdraw amount + $2.00)."

4.3.1.4 A nonambiguous use case   Here is the withdraw use case rewritten to remove the ambiguity.

Withdraw (account number, amount)

{OK, insufficient funds, invalid account number}

If the account number is invalid (**does not exist or the account is closed**), or there is insufficient money in the account (**the account balance is not at least 100 dollars greater than the withdraw amount**), then reject the transaction.

Otherwise update the account balance (**decrease the account balance by the withdraw amount plus $2.00**), and return the new balance to the customer.

The new business rules for withdraw are specific about the phrases "insufficient balance" and "update account balance" because a formula was used instead of ill-defined adjectives and verb phrases. It should be clear that terminology in use cases must be limited to a vocabulary that is well understood by the client and the development team.

Whatever the client's policy, the use case must capture it in the scenario's business rules. The danger is that these rules are easy to overlook, when the analysts are working on what they consider a familiar problem domain. The client usually knows precisely what the business rules are but the developers only assume that they know them. This miscommunication results because developers have some knowledge or experience with the domain. The result is that the business rules do not get captured and recorded, or at least verbalized, and the resultant misunderstandings may not surface until much later in the development cycle.

4.3.2 A precise model for recording complete use cases

One way to ensure that the use case description is complete is to use an underlying robust model based on good software engineering practice to record it. There are two candidate models common to software specification: the mathematical function model and the state machine model.

4.3.2.1 Function model   A mathematical function always produces the same output given an identical input. Remember $y = f(x)$. The formula will always yield identical values for y given the same value for x. The function model is based on the mathematical function, and is ideal for recording those elements of a use case where algorithms exist that are based solely on the input parameters and are independent of any state data. Using the function model guarantees that whenever the users enter a mortgage amount, an interest rate, and a payment period, they will get the same payment amount every time.

4.3.2.2 State machine model   The second model is the state machine model. It is more suited to the use case since its functionality is based on a combination of use case inputs and the state (values) of the business objects. For example, using an automated teller machine, a customer withdraws $100 from her savings account, and the ATM provides her with the requested cash. The next day when she attempts the same transaction, she is informed that there are insufficient funds in her account. Here are two identical transactions with completely different outcomes. That is because the business rules of the withdraw use case are defined in terms of how much they want to withdraw *and* what is the available balance in the account. Figure 4-1 shows the state machine model. It has an input arrow for the current system state as well as the external input. Furthermore, notice that the model has an arrow representing both the output and the update to the state data.

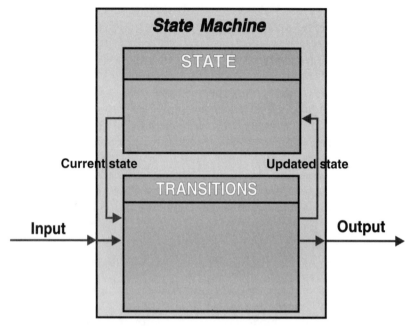

Fig. 4-1 State machine model.

The use case is best modeled by incorporating the features of the state machine. Most transactions include as input to their behavior, the information remembered within the business object. Figure 4-2 shows the components of the use case overlaid on the state machine model.

The use case model maps the inputs of the state machine to the inputs of the use case and the output of the use case to the outcomes of the use case. The values of the attributes of the business objects, before the transaction, make up the current state and with the input values, define the scenario pre-condition. The scenario post-condition identifies state changes and any output information. Although this model is very precise, enforcement of this level of detail is the responsibility of the team, and no less rigorous form will suffice as a specification. If the client does not specify the exact pre-condition that defines each scenario, and exactly what changes must be made to all attributes for the scenario, then the requirements are incomplete and, there-fore, so is the specification. As an extreme example, imagine a situation where the developers were so naive about the banking domain that they did not know that a deposit should increase the user's bank balance. If this informa-tion was omitted, how would the application designers be able to create a cor-rect solution. Every day developers work on problems for which they are just as unaware and no one would question that in these cases they would expect a level of detail and precision that matches the rules stated here.

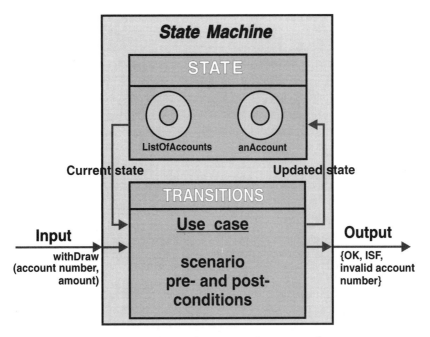

Fig. 4-2 State machine model with associated use case elements.

4.4 ANOTHER USE CASE MODEL

In the days of structured analysis, a popular tool for specifying business policies was the decision table. It is an ideal tool for recording both the pre-conditions and the post-conditions of use case scenarios. Table 4-1 shows a decision table for renting a video. The top half of the table is used to describe the conditions on the input and state; the bottom section details the state changes and any outputs.

In a decision table each column represents a scenario. The **T** (true) or **F** (false) in the top half identifies the values of each condition for a given scenario. A blank indicates that, for this scenario, the condition does not apply or does not matter. In the example in Table 4-1, if the video cannot be found, it is irrelevant whether or not the video is available or if the customer id is legitimate. The check marks in the lower half of the table indicate the actions associated with this scenario. Do not feel limited by the size of the boxes in a decision table. It is acceptable to simply place a reference to a more detailed description of the action or condition which may be a complex algorithm, a long checklist of items, or even another decision table. The condition "Member is eligible to rent" and the action "Rent video" show examples of this convention.

When the use case is recorded as a decision table, the three correctness questions for use cases and their scenarios, described earlier, can more easily be verified. Those questions are repeated here.

Table 4-1 The rentVideo use case recorded as a decision table.

RentVideo(videoId, memberId)	Scenarios				
	1	2	3	4	5
Conditions					
videoId exist	F	T	T	T	T
videoId is available (not rented)		F	T	T	T
memberId is on file			F	T	T
Member is eligible to rent*				F	T
Actions					
Reject rental and provide a message	X	X	X	X	
Rent video†					X

*Member must have fewer than three videos currently rented, none of which can be overdue. He or she must also have a fine balance of zero.

†The rental process includes marking the copy as rented, creating a record of the rental that contains the customer, the copy, and the due date, and increasing the rental count by one for this customer.

1. The pre-conditions must be complete. Every combination of conditions must be covered in one of the scenarios. One way to create an exhaustive set of conditions is to create a column for every possible combination of T and F. This technique guarantees coverage but makes for a large table. If there are n conditions in the pre-condition half of the table, then there are potentially 2^n columns. That means that the rent example in Table 4-1 would require a 16-column table ($2^4 = 16$), like the one shown in Table 4-2.

The alternative is to show that the five columns defined represent all 16 possible conditions. To validate this assumption, refer to Table 4-1 and look at the third scenario, which actually represents two of the possible 16 columns, since there would be one column when the last condition was false and one where it was true. Using the same logic, scenario two represents four columns (TT, TF, FT, FF), and the first scenario represents eight more. That means that the decision table columns covered eight, four, two, one, and one conditions, respectively, for a total of 16.

Table 4-2 Example of exhaustive identification of combination of conditions.

Scenarios	1	2	3	4	5	6	7	8	9	10	11	12	12	14	15	16
Condition one	T	T	T	T	T	T	T	T	F	F	F	F	F	F	F	F
Condition two	T	T	T	T	F	F	F	F	T	T	T	T	F	F	F	F
Condition three	T	T	F	F	T	T	F	F	T	T	F	F	T	T	F	F
Condition four	T	F	T	F	T	F	T	F	T	F	T	F	T	F	T	F

There a few guidelines to recording don't cares (blanks) for this simple math to work. They are discussed in the next correctness question.

2. The pre-conditions must be disjoint. No system state can be satisfied by more than one pre-condition. In the decision table, that means that there can be no set of values where pre-conditions in more than one column apply. If the technique of exhaustively defining every column and then adding the actions is used, then this correctness question like the previous one is guaranteed. It is only when blanks (don't care/does not apply) appear in the pre-condition section of the table that this rule can be violated. Consider the partial decision table in Table 4-3 with three conditions.

Notice that scenarios 2 and 3 overlap. The condition "Member owes fines" can be true or false in scenario 2, and "Member has videos still rented" can be true or false in scenario 3. That means that the condition where a customer to be deleted has both fines due and videos still rented is covered by both scenarios. This violates rule 2.

A technique to help avoid this problem is to address as few new conditions as possible (preferably one) at one time in a column. Then in the next column to the right, immediately negate the previous condition.

By picking the strongest conditions first, this guideline is easier to follow. Assume that the condition "Member exists in the system" is false (F) as the condition in the first column. It is the strongest condition because if the member does not exist, the other questions are not applicable and can be left blank. In the remaining columns, immediately record true (T) as the value of that condition. Now assume that "Member has videos still rented" is the next strongest condition to address. When that condition is true, it does not matter if the member has fines due as well since the deletion will be rejected anyway. The decision table now looks as shown in Table 4-4.

The condition "Member has videos still rented" was set to false (F) in the remaining columns. The final condition "Member owes fines," can be either true or false, so the pre-condition section of the decision table is complete as shown in Table 4-5.

An additional scenario had to be added to separate the overlapping scenarios. Since the virtual number of columns in the decision table in Table 4-3 totaled eight, this error was not detected by the first correctness question.

Table 4-3 Decision table with overlapping scenarios.

	Scenarios		
removeMember	**1**	**2**	**3**
Member exists in the system	F	T	T
Member has videos still rented		T	
Member owes fines			T

Table 4-4 Partial decision table for removeMember use case.

removeMember	Scenarios		
	1	2	3
Member exists in the system	F	T	T
Member has videos still rented		T	F
Member owes fines			

Table 4-5 Complete conditions for removeMember decision table.

removeMember	Scenarios			
	1	2	3	4
Member exists in the system	F	T	T	T
Member has videos still rented		T	F	F
Member owes fines			T	F

Notice that when a customer has both videos overdue and outstanding fines, the decision table as recorded specifies reporting only videos overdue. Technically, a separate scenario could be required to report that both conditions are true. The client may be willing to combine these scenarios, or they may require an explicit message to the user making the number of scenarios five. Most applications will have several situations where the business rules fall into this multiple-error-conditions category. Even though the impact of deferring the decision is minor, address it with the client early in the process.

3. The post-conditions must be unique.   When it has been established that pre-conditions are complete (correctness question 1) and disjoint (correctness question 2) a visual check is made to see that no two scenarios have the same actions. A violation here is a minor offense that is more of an inconvenience than a flaw in the specification. In the decision table for paying overdue fines in Table 4-6, notice that the actions for scenarios 3 and 5 are identical. This decision table is correct, as long as the business rules are interpreted to mean that change due is allowed to be zero.

Identical actions specified for multiple scenarios are a flag that this rule should be reviewed. It may suggest one of the following:

☞ The identical scenarios should be combined.

☞ The business rules are incomplete. Either a condition or action for one of the identical columns is missing.

☞ The client expects a different response when they pay the exact amount of their fines vs. an overpayment.

Table 4-6 Complete decision table for use case payOverdueFines.

payOverdueFines(memberId, amount)	1	2	3	4	5
Conditions					
Member exists in system	F	T	T	T	N
Member does not owe any fines		T	F	F	F
Amount paid is greater than the amount owed			T		
Amount paid is less than the amount owed				T	
Amount paid is equal to the amount owed					T
Actions					
Reject transaction	X				
Tell customer that they own nothing		X			
Set fines to zero			X		X
Reduce fines by amount paid				X	
Inform customer they still owe fines				X	
Return any change due			X		X

4. The business rules must not be ambiguous. Use the same guidelines as before to eliminate ambiguity.

Most use cases for an application will be undocumented in analysis. Usually only about 30 to 40 percent of the use cases will be detailed. This is because, as understanding of the problem improves, the writing of use cases adds no additional insight into the problem. About 80 percent or less of the critical use cases will require a decision table.

4.5 CREATING THE DATA DICTIONARY

For every meaningful noun, there must be a data dictionary entry with a client agreed-to definition. As mentioned earlier, these activities happen in parallel, but use case validation should check there are no terms used in the use case that have not been defined in the data dictionary. During requirements and analysis the data dictionary is more like a glossary than a dictionary. The dictionary will evolve during the development process.

4.5.1 Attributes

As the design is developed, information about type is added to the attributes, and data structure definition is added for objects. During implementation, details about physical representation of the data may need to be included. When attribute values are included, they should include their meaning.

4.5.2 Objects

For objects, record information about its role in the application or the business as a whole. Consider the video object as an example:

> **Video:** *Information about a title that is available for rent at one or more of the branches.*

The significant detail recorded here is that a video object exists in the system, for only those titles that are available to rent in one of the branches.

4.5.3 Aliases and words with different meanings

Words that are aliases for other words should point to the original word. Words with duplicate meanings should be flagged in the data dictionary as not to be used, and new words should be added to differentiate between the multiple definitions. These new terms replace all references to the original in the use cases. Make the new words clearly different from the original; the goal is to discourage even the client from using the ambiguous phrase. For example, consider that the word *tape* has several meanings depending on the specific user. The purchasing manager uses *tape* to refer to a movie title while the clerk's meaning of *tape* includes the copy number as well. The inventory department uses *tape* to mean the physical cassette that is assigned an inventory number and a shelf location. The data dictionary entries for the word *tape* and its replacement terms might be the following:

> **tape** *(duplicate meanings)—do not use. See title, videoIdentifier, or cassette.*

> **title**—*Information about a movie carried in the store. Information stored here is considered to be identical for all copies of the same title.*

> **videoIdentifier**—*attribute of Video. Uniquely identifies each copy of a title carried in the store.*

> **cassette** *(Physical)—the encoded plastic cartridge that the customer takes with them when they rent a movie.*

4.5.4 Verb phrases

Occasionally verb phrases will need to be included in the dictionary. This occurs when a phrase refers to key business processes that are not implemented as use cases, but the activity triggers a use case or operates as a result of the output of a use case. Phrases such as these may need to be referred to in the use case for clarification and, therefore, require a data dictionary entry. For example, when new videos are received, it is the company policy that they should be entered into the database within 24 hours. The add video use case might refer to flagging a video if it were not received within the previous 24 hours.

4.5.5 Algorithms and formulae

When critical algorithms are part of the requirement and have a common term that is used to refer to them, include the formula as the definition of the term in the data dictionary. For example, a formula for "calculate rocket trajectory" or "compute loan payment" will need to be precisely described by the client, and the definition may not be deferred until design. They are therefore part of the specification, so include them in the data dictionary. This allows them to be used as basic action verbs in use case descriptions.

4.6 CREATING THE CLASS DIAGRAM

The second major deliverable of analysis is the class diagram. It is a model that depicts the known classes, their attributes, and the relationships between them. (See Figure 4-3.) Begin with the use case nouns that represent business data; use them to create the class diagram. During requirements, it was not necessary to categorize attributes and objects separately. When the nouns are transferred to the class diagram, it will be necessary to make a decision as to which category they belong. Every noun that is part of a use case description must be considered as a business object, an attribute of a business object, or a potential value of an attribute. An exception is a noun that represents an actor. If a noun does not fall into one of those four categories, question its usage. However, since most use cases will be unwritten, it is possible that a piece of data will get overlooked. Therefore, it is very important during the analysis review to at least verbalize every use case and every scenario. Developing the class diagram from the use case descriptions guarantees that it will contain no extraneous information.

4.6.1 Duplicate attributes

When the class diagram is constructed in this way, the model may have the same information in more than one place. Make a determination as to which class should own the attribute; then delete the duplicate attribute in the other class and draw an association line between the two classes. This line can be annotated with a descriptive phrase to explain why the association exists. These class-to-class associations are exactly the same as what a data modeler would call an entity-to-entity relationship. The associated classes' potential number of objects that participate in this association can be recorded at the point where the association line intersects with the object's class. Figure 4-3 shows the class diagram for the video store application based on the use cases identified so far.

4.6.2 Associations

The association from rental to video indicates that either there is information in the video object that the rental needs or vice versa. The decision as to

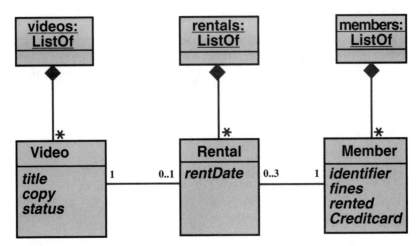

Fig. 4-3 Class diagram for video store.

whether the video will point to the rental, the rental will point to the video, or perhaps both is deferred until design, and the association is merely an abstraction for use during analysis. The 0..3 next to Rental class is referred to as the association's multiplicity. Multiplicity indicates the number of objects of each class that may participate in this association. 0..3 means that a customer may have as few as zero, and at most 3, rental objects associated with it. The 1 next to the Member class means a rental must be associated with exactly one customer. The convention is that if these numbers are unknown, leave them blank until they are determined.

4.6.3 The data model vs. the class diagram

Class diagrams are based on the widely accepted data model. Although object modeling includes the extra relationships of specialization and aggregation, the data model will work effectively as class diagram. Recall that what distinguished analysis and design was who made the decisions. It is easy to see that decisions about aggregation and inheritance are best made during design, so if the class diagram is used as an analysis tool, it is better to omit these special object/class relationships until design.

4.6.4 Optimizing the grouping of attributes in objects

Wouldn't it be wonderful if all the business object attributes could be thrown into a big pile, and a tool would magically rearrange them into small piles that would be the business objects? This tool would keep attributes that were logically related to each other in the same piles and, when appropriate, assign one of the attributes to be the object identifier.

The good news is that such a tool does exist. It is called normalization. Data modelers have used it for years to optimize the organization of databases. It naturally groups attributes that are dependent on a common primary attribute, which represents the key of the group. That grouping is exactly what you would get if you applied the rule that an object should contain only those attributes that are directly related to each other. When all the attributes have been added, make a pass at normalizing the data and removing as much redundancy as possible.

There is sometimes reluctance among object-oriented analysts to use this natural method of grouping. Their concern is that it is based on data modeling and not on objects. That concern is unfounded. Data modeling is a long time proven technique for minimizing data storage and information ambiguity. Even though it may be that a given application could operate in a faster manner with un-normalized data, it is also true that most perform better when the tables are normalized. The recommendation is that the initial analysis class diagram be developed as a normalized data model, and then as application design and performance considerations that require a different structure surface, add aggregation and inheritance and, when absolutely necessary, de-normalize.

4.6.5 Class diagram role

The importance of capturing all the business policies in the use case cannot be overstated. As important as a class diagram may seem, it is a model that is redundant and must be accompanied by the use case descriptions. Programs must have a functional specification; the use case provides that and the class diagram does not.

4.7 UNIFIED MODELING LANGUAGE NOTATION

The class diagrams in this book are drawn using UML as the notation language. UML is well documented [Fowler97] in the literature and its object modeling notation is similar to object modeling technique (OMT) [Rumbaugh91]. Further discussion on UML will be deferred until design.

4.8 OTHER WAYS TO IDENTIFY USE CASES

There are three other models that are sometimes used as part of analysis. These models or variations may be useful in augmenting the use case identification techniques described for requirements gathering. They are presented here because they require some of the details of analysis that were not available during requirements.

4.8.1 CRC analysis

CRC stands for Class Responsibility Collaboration. CRC cards were introduced by [Beck89] and elaborated by [WirfsBrock90]. They are used to document object collaborations and behavior with respect to functional requirements. The first step for the analysis team is to write the name of each class on the top of a large (4×6) index card. The lower portion of the card is divided so that the left side contains the responsibilities of the class and the right side contains all its collaborating classes (see Figure 4-4). As responsibilities are extracted from requirements, the team discusses which class was best suited to own them. The plan is that each responsibility will become a method in the respective class, and the collaborators will define the class's associations. This responsibility driven approach to analysis assumes that, during analysis, all functional requirements can be assigned to a class, representative of a business object. Figure 4-5 shows partial CRC card for the Rental, Copy, and Video classes.

Given the requirement "rent a video," the team will decide to which class the "rent video" responsibility will be assigned. Although it is possible to choose a class to assign the responsibility during analysis, it is a choice better made during design. Since it is not the client who should decide this assignment, and it adds little or no additional understanding of the problem, this is not an analysis activity.

Although CRCs are useful, they are too informal to scale up, and they assume that the business classes will be responsible for implementing the

Class Name	
Responsibility	Collaborator
	Collaborator
Responsibility	Collaborator
Responsibility	Collaborator
	Collaborator

Fig. 4-4 CRC card elements.

Rental		Copy		Video	
Maintains details of each rented copy	Copy Member	Keeps track of copies for a branch Remembers the status of	Branch	Maintains details of every title carried by the branches	Vendor Copy Wait list

Fig. 4-5 Video store application CRC cards.

requirements—something that is not desirable. CRC analysis requires getting far too deep into design. Because there is no way to reverse the process to determine which class is collaborating with a given responsibility or which responsibility a given collaboration supports, process traceability is not supported.

4.8.1.1 Using responsibilities to identify use cases
Even though CRC cards have limited value because of their informal nature and their inability to scale up, they do recognize that requirements are often provided as a series of phrases that are something like "the new program shall:" followed by a functional capability. These references to system responsibilities do need to be captured, and requirements validation needs to guarantee that they have been included. When reviewing the use cases within the team, make a check to see that every responsibility, identified from the raw requirements, has been captured. These *musts* and *shalls* show up as verb phrases that need to be associated with some use case. If no use case contains their behavior, then a requirement may have been missed.

4.8.2 Sequence diagrams

Another model for requirements analysis is the sequence diagram. It is used to describe a single scenario and mixes physical and logical business activities similar to the physical models recorded in structured analysis. Sequence diagrams can show details of the walk-through similar to the one conducted during requirements with the user interface mockups. They allow everyone to see how individual scenarios fit into a larger business process and can help identify the components that will become part of the application, and those that will not. Consider the scenario of a customer searching for and finding a video and then successfully renting it. The diagram in Figure 4-6 shows the physical process graphically based on the flow of information. The customer walks into the store, searches the shelves for a movie, and takes that video to the counter. There the clerk validates the customer's membership, removes the video ticket, records the due date and the customer on it, and stores the ticket in the rental file.

Although the individual actions can be seen in Figure 4-6, the order in which they occur cannot. The sequence diagram (shown in Figure 4-7) allows adding order to the flow of information. The drawback to a sequence diagram is that it can only show one scenario so it is an impractical replacement for a decision table.

An advantage of sequence diagrams is that they can be expanded to encompass several use cases. This allows the analyst to capture an entire business process that involves a maximum number of use cases and scenarios.

Consider the following activities. The video store manager adds a new member and a new video title, the member rents the video and is late in returning it. Now the member tries to rent another video (which is rejected) and subsequently pays the fines owed. Finally, both the video and the customer

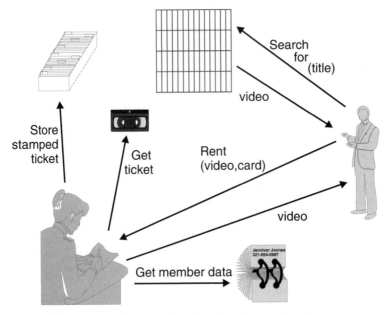

Fig. 4-6 Customer selects and rents a tape from video store.

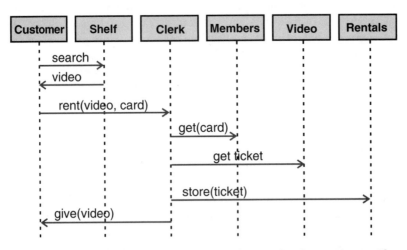

Fig. 4-7 Sequence diagram showing actor interaction for renting a video.

are deleted. This process includes six use cases and seven scenarios from the business process. A graphic like the one shown in Figure 4-6 would be an ineffective tool for understanding this complex flow, but the model as drawn in Figure 4-8 would work well. It not only accommodates a much more elaborate flow but also includes the details of the order in which these activities occur, which aids in the understanding of the client's environment. Even though this

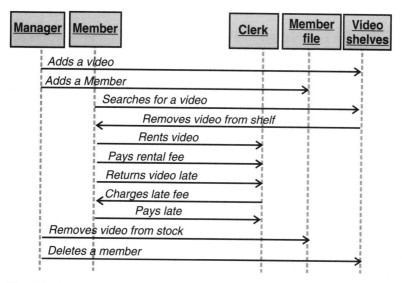

Fig. 4-8 Sequence diagram with multiple use cases with a business process.

sequence diagram (Figure 4-8) shows all the interactions between business objects and actors, it is scenario based, so use cases are still required to capture the business rules.

Even when using sequence diagrams to describe the flow of just a single use case, care needs to be taken that too much emphasis is not placed on the process. It is important that the model is not assumed to represent the application's use cases. (See the rules for use cases in this chapter.)

Look at the sequence diagram shown in Figure 4-9; it shows the interaction when the customer withdraws cash from the bank's ATM. Someone familiar with the business processes but not familiar with a rigorous definition of use cases might view this physical model as the problem specification and record the use case description as follows:

> *The customer walks up to the ATM and inserts his bankcard. The ATM asks the customer to enter his pin; then it asks the customer what transaction he wishes to perform. The customer selects withdraw, and the ATM asks for the amount and account number. The customer supplies the information, and the ATM asks the customer what denominations he prefers. The ATM provides the cash to the customer.*

The problem is that this description completely ignores the business rules of the scenario and focuses instead on the process of interacting with the ATM interface. This style of use case and the associated sequence diagrams are all too often used as the problem description without regard for the details of the business rules. Textual use cases are an acceptable way to capture business rules, but the decision table forces the analyst and client into looking at

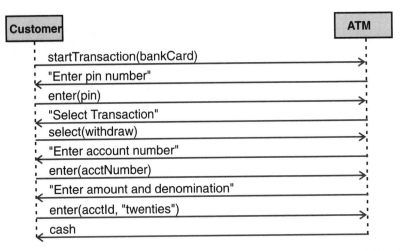

Fig. 4-9 Sequence diagram depicting scenario of customer successfully withdrawing funds using an ATM.

the logical questions. Table 4-7 shows the complete use case description as a decision table for the withdrawal transaction.

The recommendation is to use these physical models as part of the requirements-gathering activity, to help identify use cases, and then to rewrite them as decision tables during analysis. The sequence diagram can be discarded after requirements (since they will not represent the system being built), or the client and analyst may wish to retain these models for an understanding of how individual use cases fit into the business process.

Table 4-7 Decision table showing business rules for account withdrawal.

Customer makes a withdrawal (account number, pin number, amount)	1	2	3	4	5
Conditions					
Account number exists in system	F	T	T	T	T
Account is open		F	T	F	F
Pin number is valid			F	T	T
Amount is less than (account balance less $100)				F	T
Actions					
Reject transaction	X	X	X	X	
Inform customer that they have insufficient funds				X	
Reduce account balance by (amount + $1.00)					X
Inform customer of new account balance					X

4.8.3 State diagrams

The final analytical model helpful in identifying use cases is the state diagram. It can be extremely useful in uncovering missing or incomplete requirements, but it does not apply in all cases. The basic role of this artifact is to identify the potential states of an object and to record any transitions between the states, using the Finite State Machine (FSM) as the model. The FSM shows all possible states and the legal transitions between them.

Assume the following states for a video: *does not exist, available, rented, overdue,* and *deleted.* The model highlights the initial and final state with a solid circle and a circle within a circle (in this case these are: *does not exist* and *deleted,* respectively). It also shows the legal transitions between states, and not all states are directly accessible from every other state. The rules for creating a correct state diagram follow:

☞ Every state must be reachable from the initial state using some sequence of transactions. (Reachable means along some path using the transitions.)

☞ The final state must be reachable from every other state using some sequence of transitions.

☞ Every state must be definable in terms of values of business object attributes.

☞ Every transition must have at least one scenario of a use case that is its trigger.

☞ The object may not exist in more than one state at any time between use cases.

☞ The same use case scenario may not transition from the same old state to different new states.

The diagram in Figure 4-10 shows the complete state diagram for the video object.

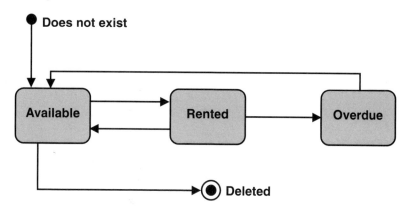

Fig. 4-10 State diagram for a video.

4.8.3.1 Interpreting the model   The model indicates that a video may transition from *does not exist* to *available* and then to *rented*. From there it may go back to *available* or to *overdue*, from *overdue* to *available*, and only from *available* can it transition to *deleted*. According to the diagram no other state changes are legal.

4.8.3.2 Using the model to help identify use cases   Even though this use of the state model is popular in many object-oriented analysis methods, if it cannot be linked to the process of defining requirements, its value is diminished. Understanding the values of attributes that define a state is more of a design activity if it is not tied to functional requirements. Rule 4 for the state diagram states that for a correct state diagram every state change must be a result of some use case. Therefore, there must exist at least one use case that can cause the state model to move along a transition from one valid state to another. If not, then either a use case was overlooked, or an impossible state has been defined. Table 4-8 itemizes these transitions, and it can be seen that all but one has a corresponding use case. That exception is the transition from rented to overdue. No use case causes a tape to enter the *overdue* state.

If no scenario has behavior that is dependent on this state, then it may represent a nonexistent state and can be deleted. However, if a business rule exists in the pre-condition of any use case that refers to an overdue video, then the state is valid and either a use case is missing or there is a post-condition of some other use case that needs to include making the video overdue.

The returnVideo use case has unique actions based on overdue videos, but it determines if a video is overdue at the time of rent. This action would indicate that overdue is a nonexistent state of copy, and just a special case of rented. One could argue that there is a temporal event that occurs at midnight that makes the video overdue, but that event has no corresponding use case in the video store application.

The rentVideo use case refers to members having overdue videos, and the actions for this scenario are different than for members who have no overdue videos. In this case, it may be necessary to view the state diagram for the

Table 4-8 Video object state transitions and associated use cases.

From State	To State	Use Case
Does not exist	Available	addVideo
Available	Deleted	removeVideo
Available	Rented	rentVideo
Rented	Available	returnVideo
Rented	Overdue	?????
Overdue	Available	returnVideo

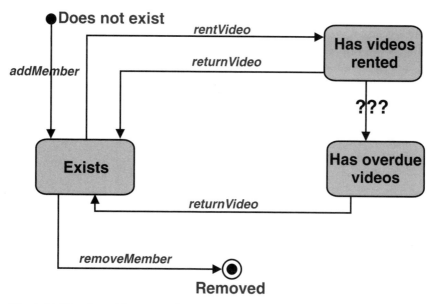

Fig. 4-11 Member object state diagram.

member object (Figure 4-11), to see how it achieves the "has overdue videos" state. For this state diagram the existing use cases to support the transitions have been shown on the transitions arrows.

Again it would be possible to have the rentVideo use case search for any videos rented to this member that were overdue. For performance reasons the analysts could suggest to the client that a new use case be added to put the member into this state when his or her rented videos become overdue. This would require something like a batch job run every night to check for tapes that should have been returned that day that marks the renter as overdue. This is, of course, the client's decision, but the analysts are free to make a recommendation.

As with sequence diagrams, do not let the state diagram become the deliverable; this may lead to a proliferation of state diagrams, of which only a few were actually needed. These models can be useful for understanding the problem and for stimulating the analysis process; but like the class diagram and sequence diagram, they are redundant models, and their information needs to find its way into one or more use cases. Both the sequence diagram and state diagram have an alternative use during design, but in this activity, the developers define its content.

4.9 ANALYSIS REVIEW

Step 5 in the analysis process is to conduct reviews with the analysis team to validate the model for consistency and to walk through the use case descriptions with the client to review the use case details and acquire agreement on the product specification.

4.9.1 Analysis model consistency

Only the client can assert the correctness of a use case. However, before the walk-through with the client, the development team should review the analysis models for consistency and try to discover errors or oversights that can be brought to the attention of the reviewers. In addition to the correctness questions for scenarios and use cases, discussed later, there are six consistency rules that can be applied against the analysis models.

- ☞ Does every noun that is part of a use case description appear in the data dictionary and on the object model?
- ☞ Is the use of aliases in use case descriptions appropriate?
- ☞ Are all ambiguous use case terms replaced with their nonambiguous alternatives?
- ☞ Does every class diagram object appear in some use case?
- ☞ For every attribute in the class diagram, is there both a use case that creates the attribute and one that uses it?
- ☞ For enumerated attributes, does every value appear in a use case where the associated attribute is set to that value, and another where that value is used?

The state diagram is not included as part of the model consistency check because, unlike the class diagram, which will be the basis for database design, the state diagram has little value after analysis. If the client wishes to keep the diagram, the rules for the state diagram will suffice for correctness questions.

The next few paragraphs consider each of the consistency questions in greater detail.

Does every noun in a use case appear in the class diagram and the data dictionary? This is a simple check that guarantees that every term used to explain a business rule for this application is defined in terms that the client understands. Omissions must be fixed by either adding a class diagram entry or renaming the reference in the use case. Normally a violation of this rule is an oversight, but it can indicate a previously overlooked class or attribute. Be sure to make this check for unwritten use cases as well.

Ensure that no terms in the data dictionary defined as ambiguous are used in the use case descriptions. When ambiguous terms are used in use cases, there is always the chance that individual users will interpret their meaning, and therefore the use case, differently. The data dictionary rule was to create new and unique words that represent each of the terms that are used among the different actor groups so as to avoid the problem described earlier.

This check guarantees that the new terms are used instead of the old ambiguous one.

Are aliases from the data dictionary used only when appropriate? Aliases for primary business terms should be used only when the use case is associated with an actor whose task descriptions use the alias almost exclusively. The important question when describing the rules of the use case to the primary user (actor) is "Is the term used the one that they would most often use and will they understand its meaning?"

Is every class diagram object referenced in some use case? When an object is not used in any use case, it indicates that either a major use case has been overlooked or that all the use cases that reference the object were trivial enough that a description was not required. Verbalizing the unwritten use cases and mentioning the class is enough to satisfy this rule. If no use case can be found that references the object, consider deleting it.

Is every attribute initialized and referenced in a use case? If an attribute has no use case that initializes it, it is possible that it does not need to be part of the application. Likewise, if its value is set but never referenced, question why it exists in the first place. It is possible that when the objects are part of a database that is shared by another application, applications may use the information stored by the use case, or one of the use cases will use the information stored by the other application. These conditions satisfy this rule. For a stand-alone application, failing this check indicates a possible missing use case or one that has not been formally recorded for review. Verbalizing the unwritten use case business rules may show that this condition is satisfied.

Does each enumerated attribute have every one of its values set and referenced in some use case? This rule is a variation on the preceding one, except that it focuses on the specific values that an attribute might hold. However, the rule is the same. If, for example, no use case sets a video's status to missing, then that use case has not been defined, it is not detailed, or that particular status of the video is not required.

4.9.2 Static vs. dynamic models

The majority of the business rules will have been documented in the use case descriptions, and any rules documented on the class diagram should have been transcribed in the use case as well. However, this does not imply that the class diagram should be omitted. It is an important model that provides value to the analysis process. First, it is the basis of the data base design, and, secondly, it will become useful in reviewing use cases with the client. Together the use case and the class diagram give two orthogonal views of the problem space. The use case is a dynamic model that enumerates all behavior, which is not possible with the class diagram because it is a static model and can only represent potential states. On the other hand, the use case focuses on a vertical view of the problem and is less valuable for describing the big picture. Here is an example to demonstrate the differences between static and dynamic models, the roles that they play, and the importance of the dynamic model.

> Imagine arriving at an airport and wanting to get to a particular place, like the Holiday Inn. There are two separate abstractions available: the first (a road map) is the static model, perhaps provided by a rental car agency or a travel company. It shows all the nearby places and the roadways that connect them. This model provides details on all the routes (choices) available but no detail on how to go to a particular place. However, it has the *potential* to solve almost any local travel problem. The second tool available is a set of detailed directions (this is the dynamic model). It guides its user from one place (probably the airport in this example) to another (Holiday Inn). Its details show what to look for, how far to drive, when to turn, whether to go left, right, north, or south, and what street you should be using. Now suppose that while following the instructions to Holiday Inn, you remember that your reservations are at the Marriott. Now what are your alternatives? Continue following the written direction to the Holiday Inn (no longer a desirable option) or return to the airport, by executing the directions in reverse. If, however, the road map (or static model) is available, it can be used to determine: current location, desired location, and alternative routes to get there. Now a new dynamic model to the new location can be written or at least developed informally in the mind, and the new plan executed.

In this story, it is important to note that no progress toward any destination was possible without the dynamic model. This fact, when overlooked, has frustrated object-oriented developers for years. It is important to recognize that the application is defined by its dynamic view, and the analysis effort needs to shift its focus to that area. Class diagrams may be useless unless they are accompanied by the use case descriptions.

4.9.3 Static model

The mind works better when pictures accompany details. The class diagram makes a nice *picture* of the system. It is something that the client can look at as the analysis team walks through the scenarios. It is also a useful tool to use as a reference when questions arise or changes are suggested that are not part of the current use case descriptions. It can help in the discussion of what the correct dynamic model should be, but the dynamic model is still the key element in the specification of the problem. The static model can help find the alternatives when the problem changes, but a new dynamic model (as in the new directions to the Marriott) must be created.

4.9.4 Correctness

Since there is no formal way to determine the correctness of use cases during analysis, the team must rely on the subjective perspective of the client and the analysis review to confirm that it correctly represents the requirements. This review is critical to the rest of the development effort. The problem with such an informal process is that it cannot guarantee correctness. Try to put as much information in front of the client as possible but remain abstract enough that the details are not overwhelming. The decision table is an excellent vehicle for presenting the business rules to the client in a precise form that they can understand.

Changes will arise in the review meeting, and that is a good thing. New requirements are inevitable, and the best place to discover them is up front in the process where they can be evaluated, prioritized, and included or excluded. When requirements are discovered late in the process, there is often no choice but to include them. This often happens at a time when it may be too late to remove use cases to offset the new ones. Changes that arise in the review, should not cause new use cases to be rewritten on the spot. That would be impractical and would probably cause problems later, but it may be appropriate to have some discussion immediately to make sure the change is understood. The class diagram will facilitate this discussion. Dealing with changes and new requirements is discussed in detail in Chapter 12.

Once the use cases have been reviewed and approved by the client, and the development team is comfortable that the goal of finding 95 percent of the use cases has been achieved, consider the analysis activity compete and move into the use case design phase.

Before ending the discussion on analysis, it is worth noting that all the techniques mentioned so far are applicable in the development of software that is not object-oriented. All these techniques should apply to any type of software development, even legacy systems where most projects are pure maintenance.

CHAPTER 5

Use Case Design

*T*his chapter looks at a pattern for designing use cases and discusses the roles of the user interface objects, the control objects, and the business objects. It demonstrates recording the design using a sequence diagram and provides a set of correctness questions to validate the design against the analysis use case description.

5.1 MAPPING THE ANALYSIS USE CASE TO DESIGN

The essential elements of a use case are its inputs, outcomes, and business rules that define the scenario. The design should cover every scenario in the use case. The first step is to interrogate the business objects and determine which scenario applies. The second step is to send the business objects the appropriate messages to update their attributes as specified by the scenario post-condition.

5.1.1 The sequence diagram

As the designers decide on the messages that need to be sent, they are recorded using the sequence diagram. Figure 5-1 shows a sequence diagram for the design of a customer paying fines for overdue tapes. The rectangles on the top, and the lines that descend from them, represent the objects.

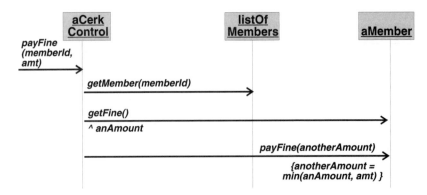

Fig. 5-1 A sample sequence diagram for payFine use case.

5.1.2 Objects

The rectangles at the top of the diagram contain the names of the objects that will participate in the design of this use case. If the object has a name, write it in the box with an underscore. (Underscore is the way UML differentiates an object from a class.) If the object is unnamed, write the class name in the box preceded by a colon and underscore it. When a message is to be sent to a class, write the class name in the box and omit both the colon and the underscore.

5.1.3 Messages

Horizontal arrows represent messages from one object to another. The name of the method being called and the parameters being passed are written on the line. UML uses a separate line for information that is returned from a method. The notation in this book records the returned information below the line with the original message. The returned information is preceded by a caret ($^\wedge$) to highlight it.

The topmost message on the left apparently emanating from no object is the method that invokes the use case. This message can come from many sources, but the most common sender of this message will be the user interface. It is not necessary to show the interface object since it is not part of the application, and the application design should be independent of any interface.

5.2 THE MVC DESIGN PATTERN

Jacobson in his book *Object-Oriented Software Engineering* [Jacobson92] describes a design pattern for use cases that involves three components: the user interface object, the control object, and the business objects. This has come to be called MVC from the name given to the user interface pattern made popular by Smalltalk 80. MVC in this pattern stands for model (the business objects), view (the interface objects), and control (the application objects).

5.2.1 The interface (view) objects

The **interface objects** have the responsibility to communicate with the user, obtain the information specified as input to the use case, and validate that the supplied information is correct with respect to the required input type. For example, the use case signature may have specified that an input parameter must be an integer, two place decimal, string of some fixed or maximum length, date, etc. The process of collecting these inputs may involve several interactions with the user that require more than one user interface window. After the collected data are edited for type, a message with the validated information is sent to the second component of MVC, the **control object**.

5.2.2 The application (control) objects

The control object is the application. Its methods implement the business rules for the use cases. There will be a method in the control object for each use case. This method is a refinement of the analysis use case and will be verified against the associated decision table. When the control object has received the message from the interface object, it sends a series of messages to the **business objects** (the third component) to first determine the correct scenario and then to make the required updates to the business objects. The decision table was developed by choosing the strongest conditions first and placing them in the leftmost columns. The design should take the same approach when creating the sequence diagram. Record first the messages that check the pre-conditions of the first column of the decision table followed by messages to check the remaining pre-conditions. On the sequence diagram, time is assumed to move downward. The topmost message will be the first sent. When the action for a scenario is to reject or return an error status, show a message from the control object back to the interface object. The sequence diagrams in this book use a dashed arrow to show an error condition return.

When the post-condition from the analysis use case specifies that changes to the state are required, insert those in the top down flow as well.

As with any class, it is good practice to partition tasks among several methods. This keeps the function of the individual methods small and simple, helps eliminate redundant code, and allows for some reuse. This type of decomposition may require a single use case to have more than one method in the control or interface objects.

5.2.3 The business objects (model)

The business objects, unlike the control and interface objects, are not application specific but can be shared across many applications. The business objects exist to store information that the company requires to operate its business. Many business objects will have only getter and setter methods.

5.2.4 Advantages of this pattern

This pattern has several advantages. The control object's methods isolate the use case, and the business objects remain application independent. The control objects are interface independent and can respond to requests from any source. For example, a transfer request to the control object could initiate from an ATM, the bank teller's terminal, a dial-up interface that communicates with the user via voice or the telephone keypad, or the use case test cases. All these interface objects would send the same message to the control object. This encapsulation of the application component allows testing of the use cases without having the user interface implemented. If either the interface design or the application business rules change, the other is not affected, and in most cases neither are the business objects.

When the control object embodies the entire application, the business objects have little or no responsibility of their own, so their behavior is limited to mainly getter and setter methods. This approach of placing all responsibility in the control object has it sending almost all the messages required to implement the function of the use case, and the sequence diagrams look like the one shown in Figure 5-2. Because the message arrows all flow from a single vertical line representing the control object, Jacobson refers to this design patter as "fork."

Contrast this to a design where the application's responsibilities are distributed across all the business objects. Figure 5-3 shows a design of the rent-Video use case based on this pattern. Jacobson describes this approach as a "stair" because the messages have the look of staircase risers when drawn as a sequence diagram.

In the early years of OT, it was believed that the stair approach was best suited to objects and encapsulation. When building class libraries or frameworks, even small ones, it is probably the most effective technique. But today enormous applications are being developed using objects, and these programs

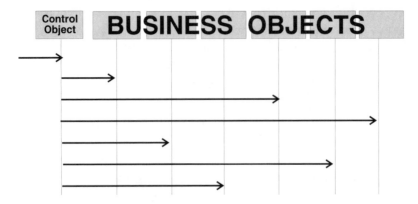

Fig. 5-2 Sequence diagram skeleton showing the fork pattern.

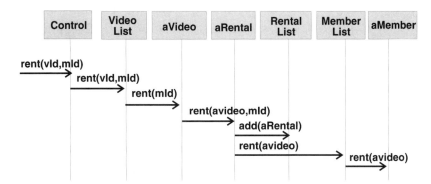

Fig. 5-3 A use case designed with the stair pattern.

undergo design changes month after month. In this environment the advantages of the fork pattern shown in Figure 5-2 far outweigh those of stair. These advantages occur in three major areas:

☞ Maintenance

☞ Error recovery

☞ Reuse

5.2.4.1 Maintenance Development and maintenance are simplified because all the code for a use case is located in a single method in the control object. This means that, when a use case changes, only one method will need to be investigated and modified to accommodate that change. Similarly, when designing and implementing new use cases, the developer will be working on fewer classes simultaneously, which simplifies the process and reduces the probability of errors. When business class methods are limited to performing primitive operations, like getters and setters, fewer method function conflicts arise. That means that there is a lower probability that multiple programmers will need to work on the same method. Compare that with the situation where multiple use cases require a method that performs an *almost* identical function. The *almost* will drive the developers crazy. Also, the opportunity to either write or use the wrong method increases with the complexity of the methods available from which to choose. In the fork version of MVC, all complex function is encapsulated within the methods of the control object. This keeps the business objects compliant with the object-oriented principle that says a method should avoid complex behavior and do only one thing.

5.2.4.2 Error recovery Consider the design in Figure 5-3. What if the rent method in member encountered an unrecoverable error? Each method along the message path would have to check for and handle that error, and any others. This approach would require extra code and execution time in every one of those methods, plus an in-depth understanding of the behavior of all the collaborating methods. This makes each of the individual methods unnecessarily more complex. The fork approach allows error handling and recovery to be encapsulated entirely within the control object.

5.2.4.3 Reuse   Finally the fork pattern facilitates reuse of the business objects. Since there are no methods in the business objects written for a specific application, they are more suited to work with all applications. Remember that the key to reuse is generalization and simplification. When responsibilities are buried deep in business object methods, these methods may become too powerful and too complex to have any reuse value. So, although these methods are powerful, their complexity may keep them from ever being appropriate for a second application; therefore, they may never be reused. Getters and setters, and other single function primitive methods like incrementCount(), getBalance(), or isAvailable() on the other hand, are so primitive that their reuse is guaranteed.

5.2.5 But which is more object-oriented?

Even though the fork pattern is more efficient and more maintainable, it is often disregarded because the stair approach appears to be more object oriented. This can be emphasized with a short fable.

> Once upon a time, a programmer was walking through the woods, and it was a beautiful day. The sun was shining, and not a cloud was in sight. Then seemingly without warning clouds gathered, the sky darkened, and the rain began to fall in a deluge. As the programmer frantically searched for cover, he spotted a large oak tree that promised adequate protection from the rain. However, he quickly dismissed this idea as soon the thunder and lightning began. As he continued his search, he spotted a cottage perched on top of a small hill. Amazingly, as if fate had intervened, the cottage had a covered porch. Surely, the programmer thought to himself, the owner would not mind if I used the porch for cover until the rain stopped. So he rushed up onto the porch. As he did, he noticed that the cabin door was ajar and that a note was pinned to the door. The note said:
>
> **IF YOU ARE A PROGRAMMER CAUGHT IN ONE OF OUR SUMMER DOWNPOURS PLEASE FEEL FREE TO COME INSIDE, START A FIRE, HAVE A CUP OF TEA, AND RELAX UNTIL THE RAIN STOPS!**
>
> What luck, thought the programmer, and he decided to accept the invitation. He stepped into the cabin and looked around to review the available resources. (See Figure 5-4.) Now since he was a good programmer (and a procedural programmer at that), he decided that to do what the note suggested he would need a plan. After many iterations and revisions of the plan, he decided that he would use the bucket to draw some water from the well, fill the teapot with the water, and place it on the stove. Using the ax he would chop some wood and start a fire in the stove, which would boil the

Fig. 5-4 The participants in the "making a cup of tea" design.

water and allow him to enjoy his cup of tea. Exhausted from the planning and all the running around necessary to make the tea, he flopped in a chair to drink his tea and wait for the rain to stop.

Now as luck would have it, the very next day another programmer was walking in the forest and the exact scenario unfolded once again: the sun, the clouds, the rain, the thunder, the lightning, the porch, the door, the note. You are familiar with that part of the fable, but here the tale takes a turn. This time the programmer was an object-oriented programmer. When she entered the small cabin room, she decided to take a different tack to making her tea. She simply sent a message to the teapot asking it to perform the method "make a cup of tea." The teapot sent a message to the stove to "start a fire," which in turn collaborated with the tree's "get kindling" method. This method of the tree sent the necessary message to the ax, to fulfill its mortal contract. It is worth a pause at this time to point out that this is as close to a real destructor method as you will ever see. With its last breath the tree returned the kindling to the stove, which was now able to start the fire. While all of this was going on, the teapot had started a second thread that sent a "get water" message to the bucket, which, in turn, sent the "fill me" message to the pump. The pump filled the bucket, which returned the water to the teapot. The teapot was now able to boil its water and make the tea.

So what is the moral of this little *object story*? The moral is that people believe that "programming is always easier and faster when you use an *object-*

oriented approach." After all, the object-oriented programmer only had to send one message to a teapot and presto! no more of that time consuming planning and design. The teapot collaborated with its friends to do all the work on the programmer's behalf. The problem is that, in the early days of object technology, people listened to that story and thought to themselves, "WOW." Executives commissioned teams to start being as resourceful as the young woman in the story, and IT managers started searching for the "magical teapot" that would instantly make their programmers more productive. However, many of them overlooked the fact that all this was possible only if you have one very smart teapot (and one very stupid tree). How did the teapot and all the objects in the story acquire those skills? A programmer had to create a class for each of them and then design, implement, and test all of the methods involved. It required just as much work as the procedural approach. It was just organized differently. So the question becomes which is better. Should programmers build powerful teapots or customized control methods to do most of the work? The fact is that it is easier and safer to put all the code for a use case in one place. This does not mean returning to modules that contain several hundred lines of code. Even complex control methods will rarely exceed 40 or 50 lines of code. Some might point out that teaching the stove to build a fire is a capability that could be not only used by the teapot, but reused by the popcorn popper, the fry pan making eggs, and anyone that just wanted to warm up the room, and the fork approach would require that this same code be rewritten several times. Although this is a reasonable argument, using a control object to manage all the use case logic does not preclude that reuse. That portion of the use case that is required by several control methods can be made into a private method in the control class and shared by any use cases needing a hot stove.

On the other hand, when rich function is included in a business object, it may never be reused. When looking for a reusable function, programmers rarely consider complex methods whose function can be understood only by looking deep into all its collaborators. The developers will be more likely to review the private methods of the control class for reusable code than they will be to search through all an organization's business objects to find the appropriate method. The chapter on class design discusses the characteristics of good reusable classes, and a leftover function in complex methods of business objects does not qualify. Project teams will decide on their own what design patterns are best for their projects, but they should not rule out patterns like fork just because they do not feel object-oriented.

5.3 VARIATIONS ON MVC

5.3.1 Combined interface and control

Some object-oriented designs combine the function of interface and control into a single object. The disadvantage of this approach is that it requires that tested working application code be opened up whenever the design of the interface is changed. User interfaces are more susceptible to changes than the application, and it is detrimental to the application's integrity to allow non-functional modifications to slow down the development of the application. With this packaging the application and interface code get entwined and when what should have been a minor adjustment to the interface arises, it may cause a redesign of the use case. This approach also makes validation of the design more difficult because the reviewers must filter those elements that do not directly implement the business rules out of the use case design.

5.3.2 The control object drives the interface

Another variation is when the application is designed to drive the interface rather than the other way around. This approach requires that the application become involved with presentation as well as computation. It integrates the design of the interface with the use case in such a way that, when the client wishes to change the look and feel of the interface, the entire application may need to be altered. Even the interface itself becomes fragmented so that major presentation redesign is more difficult. When the use case is configured correctly, there should be no need to integrate the interface and application. Consider a withdrawal transaction at an ATM designed so that amount, pin, and account number all are elements of the transaction screen. Later the bank client decides, for security reasons, that they want the customer to enter the withdrawal amount twice. One solution would be to have the application open a pop-up window and ask for the amount to be re-entered. This design has tightly coupled the user interface and application. Any subsequent redesign of the pop-up window may affect deep application code. The pop-up window may be an effective way to implement the client's preference, but it should be done inside the user interface and not as part of the application. The model that has the application communicating directly with the user, while seemingly harmless, can cause development delays whenever simple editing changes that could have been encapsulated within the user interface occur.

5.4 AN EXAMPLE OF RECORDING A USE CASE DESIGN

When recording the use case design, start with the scenarios that eliminate the strongest conditions first. These are usually error conditions that return immediately to the user interface. Table 5-1 shows a decision table for the rentVideo use case. It follows the left to right flow of strongest scenario precondition to weakest.

To begin the design, start with a find(videoId) message to listOfVideos to locate the video with the title to be rented. If a video with that id is not found, this message returns a null. In that case, exit the control method with an indication of the failure. If a video object with the videoId is found, have the

Table 5-1 Decision table for rentVideo use case.

rentVideo (memberId, videoId)	Scenarios				
	1	2	3	4	5
Conditions					
VideoId exists	N	Y	Y	Y	Y
Video is available		N	Y	Y	Y
Member exists			N	Y	Y
Member is eligible				N	Y
Actions (post-conditions)					
Reject rental	X	X	X	X	
Mark video as rented					X
Assign the video a due date					X
Assign memberId to rented video					X
Increase member's rented video count by one					X

find(videoId) message return the video object. The next message would be to the video to retrieve its availability status. Figure 5-5 shows the sequence diagram for the design thus far.

Next aClerkControl will need to examine the video's status to see if the video is available for rent. (Since this simple logic does not involve messages between objects, it will not be included on the sequence diagram.) If the video's status is not "available," then the control method exits, and the interface is informed. If the video is "available," the design moves on to scenario 3 and sends the find(memberId) message to the listOfMembers to find the member object with the memberId of the renter. Once again this method returns the associated member object if it is found and returns null to indicate that the correct member object was not found. If a member object is returned, the control object's rent method will send the member a message to check its eligibility, and either reject the rental (scenario 4) or accept it (scenario 5). Figure 5-6 shows the sequence diagram based on the design to this point.

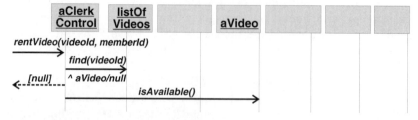

Fig. 5-5 Partial design of rentVideo use case.

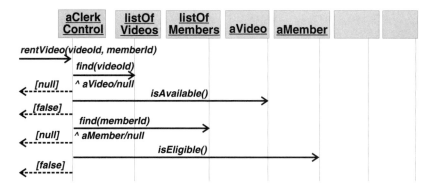

Fig. 5-6 Additional detail for the design of the rentVideo use case.

The decision table in Table 5-1 defines the following four actions to complete the successful rentVideo use case:

- ☞ Mark the video as rented.
- ☞ Assign the video a due date.
- ☞ Assign rented videoId to the member.
- ☞ Increase member's rent count by one.

By creating a new rental object with the memberId, videoId, and due-Date, actions 2 and 3 have been satisfied. However, this newly created object must be saved in the rentalList for future access. The last two messages from aClerkControl set the video's status (action 1) and increase the member's rent count (action 4), which completes the correct design of the rent use case as specified in the decision table. Figure 5-7 is the completed sequence diagram based on this design.

Notice that when the find() message is sent to any of the collection classes, the messages that they send to their collaborators are not shown. listOfVideos will need to send some type of a getVideoId() message to each video object it contains to determine whether that video object is the one it is searching for. The same is true for listOfMembers. These extra messages and associated logic have been encapsulated and hidden. This keeps the design simpler without any loss of accuracy or important detail.

5.5 OTHER DESIGN CONSIDERATIONS

During design the designer gets to make choices about what messages are sent and in what order they are sent. Arrows represent events in UML, which considers a response to a message as a separate event. UML uses one arrow to send a message and another for the response. UML also uses the message arrowhead to distinguish between asynchronous messaging, where the

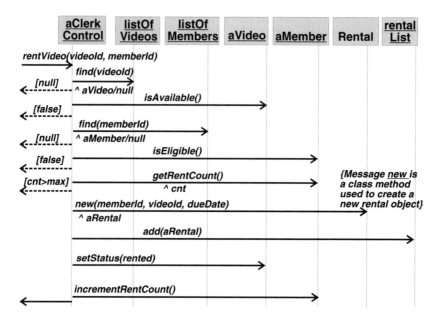

Fig. 5-7 Complete design for rentVideo use case.

invoked methods operate as separate threads, and those that suspend the calling method until the invoked method is complete. The sequence diagrams in this book all use messages with an open arrowhead.

5.5.1 Variations on notation

Also in this text, any returned information is shown below the message line and preceded by a caret (^) rather than as a separate event. If the response is considered obvious and is not referred to in the diagram, the response under the message arrow is omitted. For example, consider the message isAvailable(). Since a true or false response can be deduced from the message itself, the ^boolean response beneath the line is not shown. When the control object returns to the interface, an arrow is used instead of the caret notation. Since the control method has a separate return for each scenario, this allows the same sequence diagram to combine all the scenarios for a use case as part of the same graph. When the return from the control object is considered an error, the arrow is dashed rather than solid.

5.5.2 Objects vs. classes

UML and most object-oriented languages adopt the convention of naming classes with general nouns that begin with an uppercase letter. Names of objects begin with a lowercase letter and are often the class name prefixed by an article. An object of the Account class would be anAccount or theBankAccount. If several instances of the same class were required, the second name would appear as anotherAccount, or anAccount2. Methods that do not require access to an object's attributes can be invoked by sending a message directly to the class. These are referred to as class or static methods, and it may be useful to prefix these methods with a dollar sign ($).

5.5.3 Comments and other miscellaneous details

Use {braces} to add information that is not implicit from reading the message's text. The types of information that would be recorded in braces are algorithms, important actions that occur within the method, details on loops or conditions in the method logic, and special conditions that must become part of the method implementation like response time requirements.

5.5.4 Conditions

Any message sent conditionally can have the condition enclosed in brackets [ ] preceding the message text. When stating the condition, use the names defined in the current method. Defined names are names of attributes in the class to which the method belongs, parameter names supplied on the current method invocation, and names of values returned from a previous message sent from within this method. When the condition on a return from control is directly related to the last returned value from the last message sent, use the actual values returned.

5.5.5 Loops

UML indicates a loop within the logic of a sequence diagram by enclosing all messages that are within the loop's body in a box. The exit condition is recorded as a comment on the bottom of the box. Most often the box itself is enough, and the exit condition can be inferred from the semantics of the design. Figure 5-8 shows examples of these last few conventions.

The design begins with a loop that retrieves each rental object and examines its associated videoId. The loop terminates when there are no more rentals, or the rental with a video identifier (theId) matches the one being returned (videoId) from the getVideoId() method {While more rentals and videoId do not equal theId}. If the last retrieved video identifier (theId) does not match the one being returned [videoId ~= theId], the use case control method exits; otherwise, the associated video object is retrieved from the listOfVideos and its status is set to "available." After the member and due date are obtained from the rental, the rental due date is checked against today's date, and if the video is overdue [dueDate < today] a fine is charged to the associated member. The calculation of fine amount is indicated as a comment {amt is overdue days * late fee} just before the member is charged.

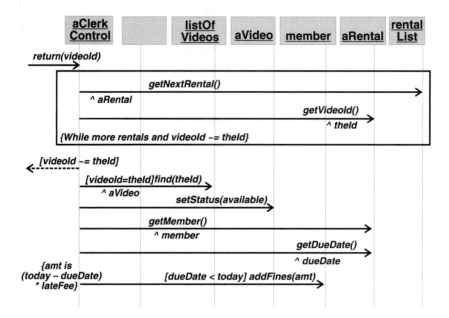

Fig. 5-8 Sequence diagram showing optional notations.

The bullets in Table 5-2 describe the ways that the sequence diagrams in this book differ from pure UML notation.

The sequence diagram should be viewed as a thinking and review tool, not a vehicle to necessarily record every detail of a use case's design. Jacobson [Jacobson93] suggested that a sequence diagram be accompanied by pseudo code. It would then be easy to see the logic as well as the message flow. The problem becomes one of real estate. If everything is recorded on the sequence

Table 5-2 Variations in notation for sequence diagrams.

- Interface objects are omitted.

- Returned information is not indicated with a separate event arrow; instead, it is written below the line and preceded by a ^.

- Returned data are included only when they are not obvious or are required for reference in another message.

- Conditions on messages and loop notation are included only if they are necessary for understanding the design.

- When the use case exists with an error condition, the return to the interface is shown as a dashed line.

- Braces {} are used for comments on functionality not recordable as part of the sequence diagram.

- Class methods are preceded by a $.

diagram, it may become cluttered and unreadable. The sequence diagram should contain only enough information to convey the design and allow it to be reviewed for correctness.

5.5.6 Capturing data design decisions

Use case design includes deciding to which class an attribute should belong. Many of these decisions about data organization will be based on deciding which use cases are most in need of the best performance and then reorganizing the data to make those use cases the most efficient. As these performance decisions are made, it will be necessary to make changes to the class definition. All nonlocal variable references in the sequence diagram must appear in the design class diagram refinement.

5.6 DESIGN CORRECTNESS QUESTIONS

It was impossible to determine formally the correctness of the use case descriptions developed in analysis because correctness in that case was based on the subjective evaluation of the client. However, given a use case decision table, it can be shown that the design is a correct refinement. There are six correctness questions required to make this assertion.

1. Does the signature of the control method for this use case match the signature that was defined in the requirements?
Since test and user interface development have all begun their work based on the signature of the original requirement, it is imperative that the control method's design matches the use case signature defined during requirements. This is an easy check to overlook. The recommendation is to copy the use case definition from the requirements document and make it a comment at the top of the control method's design.

2. Is every recipient of a message and every parameter on the message either:

    a. Part of the state of the object that is sending it,
    b. Passed in as a parameter to the method sending the new message,
    c. Returned from a previous message sent within the current method?

This is the law of Demeter [Lieberherr88,89]. Violations are an indication of tight coupling, or the design is wrong. The three conditions confirm that the sequence diagram is not making a reference to an object to which it has not yet established addressability. In most cases, the compiler will catch any violations; but with the three rules shown below they can be detected during design.

☞ In the design use the same names for attributes that were recorded on the class diagram.

☞ When referencing parameters within a method, use the same name that was used on the message signature for this method.

☞ When an object is returned as the response from a message, give that object a name preceded by a caret (^ returnedObject). Use that name whenever you reference the object again.

These rules will make it easier to see when the design is using the same variable in multiple places within a method. Then whenever a message is sent to a variable representing an object or a variable is used as a parameter within a message, it will be clear whether that variable was not initialized earlier (higher on the sequence diagram) within the current method. The most common mistakes are:

☞ Referring to an object like aVideo without first retrieving it from the VideoList using a method like find(videoId)

☞ Referring to another object's attribute as though it were public instead of using the attribute's getter method to obtain it

☞ Creating or acquiring an object in one method and then using that same object in a subsequent method without storing the reference as an attribute of the object's class

3. Does the signature and semantics of every message support the design of the method that sent the message?

As the control object is designed, it will require the services of other objects. Methods that perform some of these functions may already exist while others will need to be specified. If a new method is required, write a specification for it. (Method specifications are described in detail in the next chapter.) In the case of any undocumented complex method, consider summarizing its behavior as a comment on the design diagram. This will help in determining the logical correctness of the design. When specifying a method, refrain from basing any other use case design on it until the class owner has approved the method. That means that this correctness question may have to be delayed. Notice that most of these issues go away if the designer chooses the fork pattern and limits the business objects to getter and setter methods.

4. Compare the use case's decision table, recorded during analysis, with its design in the corresponding method of the control object. Then ask for each scenario:

a. Is the pre-condition determined correctly?

b. Are the correct updates made to establish the post-condition?

c. Are only the specified state changes included?

The previous correctness question asked if the behavior of methods that were invoked supported the current method design. This question asks if the design of the control method precisely implements its use case specification. Note that this question could apply to any method and its specification if it collaborates with other objects. The recommendation is to structure the design of the control method such that stronger pre-conditions are checked first. This makes it easier to see that the correct pre-condition is established for the more complex scenarios especially those involving state changes. If comments are included to describe the behavior of complex collaborator methods, this question is easier to assert. Part c of this question is harder to prove since it requires looking for a function that is not supposed to be there. Using the decision table design mapping technique, and the other suggestions for developing designs that were described earlier in this chapter, can help make this type of mistake more obvious.

5. Is every attribute that is assumed to be part of an object's state recorded on the class diagram?

During analysis, objects that needed reference to each other were noted on the class diagram with an association line between them. During design, decisions were made about which way these references should point. For example, Figure 5-9 shows the analysis and design views of the Rental and the Member classes.

In analysis, Member and Rental have an association named isRentedBy between them. Assume that the designer decided that the most efficient way to track a rental is to store the memberId of the member that rents a video in the rental object. That decision created a new attribute memberId in the Rental class that was not there in analysis. The design view shows the updated class diagram reflecting this change. It is important to show data structure changes as part of use case design.

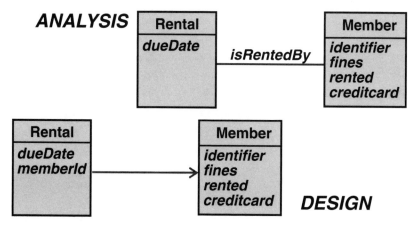

Fig. 5-9 Transformation of analysis association in design.

6. Is every newly created persistent object initialized and saved in a collection?

One of the most common mistakes that new object-oriented programmers make is assuming that just because an object is created it will always be addressable later. When an object will be needed by other use case designs, or later in the current one, it needs to be stored with a handle that allows for its retrieval. Temporary objects can simply be given a name. Permanent ones must be turned over to a collection or manager object to ensure their persistence. In these cases, the handle will be some unique identifier (or key) of the object. It is the responsibility of the collection objects to add new objects, delete them when no longer needed, and return a reference to them when presented with their identifier. Most object-oriented languages provide predefined classes that can perform these generic services. This is a subtle correctness question easily overlooked since the business rules do not usually spell out that the new object should be put in a safe place. Therefore, the rule is included here as a special consideration. The second part of this question is a reminder to ensure that newly created objects are initialized. This should have been spelled out in the use case specification but, if omitted, may not be detected by compilers.

The correctness questions for verifying the design of a use case sequence diagram against its analysis specification are summarized in Table 5-3.

Table 5-3 Design correctness questions.

---

1. Does the signature of the control method for this use case match the signature that was defined in the requirements?

2. Is every recipient of a message and every parameter on the message either:

    a. Part of the state of the object that is sending the message,

    b. Passed in as a parameter to the method sending the message,

    c. Returned from a previous message sent within the current method?

3. Do the signature and semantics of every message support the design of the methods that use it?

4. For every scenario in the use case:

    a. Does the control method correctly apply the business rules to check its pre-condition?

    b. Does the control method make the correct updates to establish the post-condition?

    c. Are any state changes made that are not required by the scenario?

5. Is every attribute assumed to be part of an object's state recorded on the class diagram?

6. Is every newly created persistent object initialized and saved in a collection?

5.7 AN EXAMPLE OF DESIGN VERIFICATION

Using as an example the rentVideo use case, this topic considers its correctness by reviewing each of the design correctness questions to verify the sequence diagram against its decision table. Table 5-4 and Figure 5-10 show the decision table and the sequence diagram design for renting a video.

1. Does the signature of the control method for this use case match the signature that was defined in the requirements?

Yes There are two parameters: the video identifier and member identifier, in that order, and both are of type String. Note that this question is correct even if the names used for these parameters differ between the decision table and the sequence diagram. It is strongly recommended that the names be kept the same.

2. Is every recipient of a message and every parameter on the message either:

    a. Part of the state of the object that is sending it,
    b. Passed in on the message that invoked the method sending the message,
    c. Returned from a previous message sent within the current method?

Yes listOfVideos and listOfMembers are part of the state of the ClerkControl.

    The memberId and videoId used in the find messages were passed in as parameters to the control method.

Table 5-4 Decision table for rentVideo use case.

rentVideo(videoId, memberId)	Scenarios					
	1	2	3	4	5	6
Conditions						
Video title exists	N	Y	Y	Y	Y	Y
Video is available		N	Y	Y	Y	Y
Customer is a member			N	Y	Y	Y
Member is eligible				N	Y	Y
Member has maximum videos currently rented					Y	N
Actions (post-conditions)						
A1—Reject rental	X	X	X	X	X	
A2—Mark video as rented						X
A3—Assign a video due date						X
A4—Assigned rented video to member						X
A5—Increase member's rented video count						X

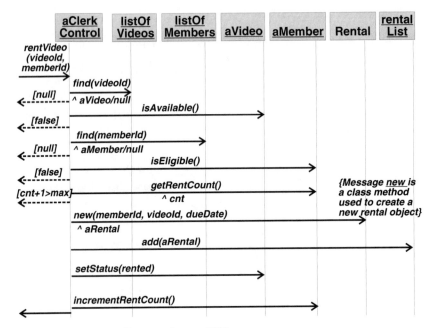

Fig. 5-10 Sequence diagram for rentVideo use case.

The isAvailable() message is sent to aVideo which was returned from the previous find.

The aMember object that is sent the isEligible() message was returned from the find sent to listOfMembers.

The use of the class Rental to create a new rental object does not violate these rules, since classes are considered to be global and are available to all methods in all objects.

The aRental object added to the rentalList was returned from the new() message sent to the Rental class, and the rentalList is part of aClerkControl's state.

3. Do the signature and semantics of every method support the design of the methods that use it?

listOfVideos.find(videoId)

Yes Returns the video object with the identifier videoId or returns null if no object is found.

listOfMembers.find(memberId)

Yes Returns the member object with the identifier memberId or returns null if no object is found.

aVideo.isAvailable()

Yes Returns true if video is not rented.

aMember.isEligible()

Yes Returns false if member owes fines or has overdue videos.

aMember.getRentCount()

Yes Returns number of videos currently rented by the member.

Rental.new (memberId, videoId, dueDate)

Yes Creates and returns a rental object with memberId, videoId, and due-Date.

rentalList.add (aRental)

Yes Adds the rental object to rentalList collection.

aVideo.setStatus (status)

Yes Sets the video status to the supplied value.

aMember.incrementRentCount()

Yes Adds 1 to the number of videos rented by this member.

Note that even though the specification comments following each method do support correctness, these methods, when designed, still need to be validated against these specifications.

4. For every scenario in the use case:

    a. Does the control method correctly apply the business rules to check its pre-condition?

        Scenario #1 Video not found

        Yes Action A1 and return.

        Scenario #2 Member not found

        Yes Action A1 and return.

        Scenario #3 Video not available

        Yes Action A1 and return.

        Scenario #4 Member owes fines or has an overdue video

        Yes Action A1 and return.

        Scenario #5 Member has max videos rented

        Yes Action A1 and return.

Scenario #6 OK

Yes Actions A2, A3, A4, A5, and return.

b. Does the control method correctly make the updates to establish the post-condition?

Scenario #6

Yes Action A1—Rental created with memberId, videoId, and dueDate (message #6—new)

Action 2—Video status set to rented (message 8—setStatus())

Action 3—Member rent count increased by one (message 9—incrementRentCount())

c. Ensure that no state changes are made that are not required by the scenario?

Yes All messages are in support of stated actions.

5. Is every attribute, assumed to be part of an object's state, recorded on the class diagram. (See design class diagram in Figure 5-11.)

Yes New attributes added (this use case).

aClerkControl:ClerkControl -

listOfVideos

listOfMembers

rentalList

Rental -

memberId

videoId

6. Is every persistent object that is created initialized and saved in a collection?

Scenario #6—The rental object created in Action #6 is stored in rentalList.

Yes Message 7—add().

5.7.1 Rules and pitfalls

The most common pitfalls of object-oriented design correctness verification are

☞ Forgetting to acquire addressability to an object before sending it a message

☞ Not saving a newly created object

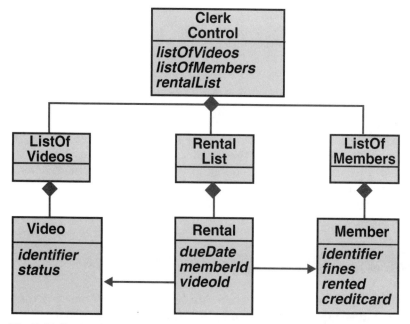

Fig. 5-11 Design level class diagram for the video tracking application.

☞ Forgetting to label objects, attributes, returned objects, and parameters consistently

☞ Making design decisions about object-to-object references and not recording them on the class diagram

5.8 DESIGN FROM REQUIREMENTS

It should be expected that approximately one-third of the total use cases defined during requirements will be detailed during analysis. Likewise, only about one-half to two-thirds of those use case descriptions will have their design formally recorded with a sequence diagram. Decision tables are created in analysis only when the business rules are complex enough to require extra scrutinizing of the deliverable during the review process. The purpose of creating a sequence diagram is much the same. Some designs are elaborate enough that their review without some visual representation would be difficult and informal validation would most likely miss some errors. Most sequence diagrams for a use case will be developed from the decision table. However, cases may exist where the business rules are easily understood without a decision table but the design is complex enough to require a formal sequence diagram. In this case, it will be necessary to develop the design directly from the requirement's use case. You might want to consider creating a decision table for the use case before you attempt the associated sequence diagram. Later, when the design is approved, if the decision table is believed to be of no further value, it can be eliminated.

5.9 LANGUAGE LIBRARY OBJECTS

Sequence diagrams show business and control objects but not necessarily all library objects. Library objects are those normally considered to be part of the language. For example, both Smalltalk and Java have predefined classes for Date and String, so it is reasonable at design time to consider these as language primitives. An exception to this rule is a collection object, which is integral to correctness. All collection objects that participate in the design should be included on the sequence diagram.

5.10 CREATING CONTROL AND INTERFACE OBJECTS

The control object has been shown to be a critical element of the use case design, but so far there has been no discussion of how it is instantiated or how multiple actors can interact with the application.

Multiple actors are accommodated by creating a control and interface object for each actor active in a defined role. When actors log on to the system, their application interface must be created. For them to perform the tasks associated with their job, they must also be provided with a control object with the methods supporting the use cases associated with their tasks. Figure 5-12 shows the logon and logoff events as a sequence diagram.

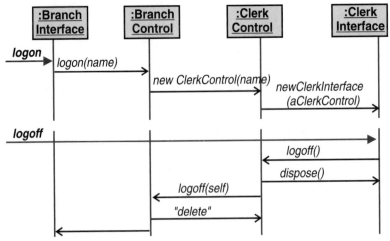

Fig. 5-12 Sequence diagram showing management of control and interface objects.

Both the control and interface classes instantiate an object for every active actor in the system and can be viewed as having a single method for each use case associated with a role for that actor. When actors share roles, they may share control methods even when they have unique interface methods.

Assume that the initial screen for the video store application is a welcome screen displayed by the branch interface. The BranchControl class currently contains only one method, logon (id,pw), (logoff() is in ClerkControl). Interface and control objects normally have a one-to-one relationship. Either the interface is created when an actor logs on and the interface object instantiates the corresponding control object or the control is created first and control creates the interface. The design in Figure 5-12 shows the former approach. When the clerk logs on to the Video application, the branchInterface object creates a new instance of the ClerkControl class, which in turn creates and displays the clerkInterface. When the actor logs off, the clerkInterface will return to branch control, which will remove both the clerk control and the clerk interface. The user interface has returned to the branchInterface and is ready for the next employee to log on.

5.10.1 Roles and actors

This model allows for defining the tasks associated with an actor by including in the control object only those use cases for which the clerk is authorized. When multiple actors are permitted some unique task but share others, the shared functions can be factored into a superclass like BranchControl or, if necessary, into a new abstract control class that holds the common methods.

5.10.2 Sharing global data

This refactoring [Johnson88] applies to attributes of the control classes as well as the methods. Collection classes will normally appear higher in the hierarchy, whereas actor-specific information will appear lower. The control classes can be organized into an inheritance hierarchy, as shown in Figure 5-13.

The design of the use cases is now complete, but several design-related activities need to be addressed. Specifically the new classes, methods, and attributes that were referenced within the sequence diagrams need to be documented. These topics and others related to class design will be covered in the next chapter.

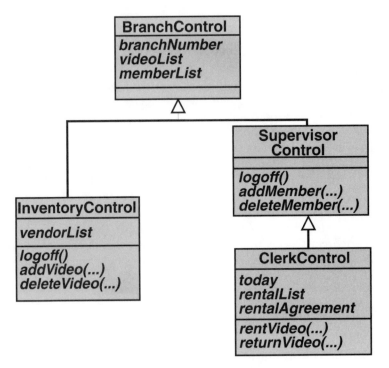

Fig. 5-13 Control class hierarchy.

CHAPTER 6

Class Design

This chapter defines the contents of the class specification and details the information that must be documented for the methods and attributes of each class. It discusses data design issues related to redundant attributes and attributes that reference other objects. It describes two project roles, that of the class owner and that of the use case owner, and shows how to design reusable inheritance hierarchies.

6.1 PURPOSE OF CLASS SPECIFICATION

The object-oriented programmer creates classes. Objects do not get created until runtime. The application designer needs to ensure that each class will provide the functionality and data structure necessary to support the design of the use cases in the current increment.

OODP considers class design and use case application design as separate activities. The reasons for the separation are listed here.

☞ Class design is not required on every project. Some projects work with existing classes and require no new class specifications.

☞ Class design is a skill different from application design; it requires experience with encapsulation and inheritance hierarchies.

☞ Design of inheritance hierarchies is a skill apart from the basic skills of object technology. It is best applied as part of class design after the application classes are well understood.

☞ Reuse is more a function of class design than application design since it is closely linked to the class definition.

Class design is where the business data structure is defined. Class designers need to work closely with the data modelers and Database Administrators (DBAs). They have the unique perspective of seeing how their classes are used across several applications so they can better evaluate the reuse potential.

Some approaches to object-oriented design suggest that designing, or at least defining, class behavior and data organization in advance of functional design is the more object-oriented approach. This strategy implies that the application is built in support of the data. This may be valid if the data are the objective, as with a program to support a research project gathering large amounts of information and performing extensive analysis on the data and forecasting or extrapolating results. However, most business applications exist to perform a function. In this case, it is the data that support the functional requirements. Objects exist to remember transactions, so it makes more sense to create to the application and then adapt the objects, their attributes, and associated methods in a way that facilitates application design.

6.1.1 Steps in class specification

The basic steps required to complete and record the design and specification of the classes for an increment are:

☞ Create new classes required for the current increment.

☞ Add methods and attributes to new and existing classes, based on the design of the current increment.

☞ For each new attribute, define its visibility, type, and initial value.

☞ For each new method, define its signature, visibility, return type, and behavior.

☞ Create getters and setters based on attribute visibility.

☞ Determine the procedure for updating information that is stored in more than one object.

☞ Create abstract classes and build inheritance hierarchies where necessary.

☞ Update the class diagram to reflect data structure design decisions.

6.2 CLASS SPECIFICATIONS

The class design specification contains the following elements:

☞ Class name, definition, hierarchy, and usage

☞ Attributes and their types

☞ Attribute scope, visibility, and initial value

☞ Method signature, visibility, type, usage, and behavior

☞ Events

6.2.1 Class name and definition

The class definition is a simple narrative sentence giving the class a name and purpose. It describes why this class is part of this application. It is almost identical to the description of the class recorded in the data dictionary.

> **Rental:** *Keeps track of videos that are rented, who rented them, and when they are due back*

6.2.2 Class hierarchy

The **class hierarchy** defines its immediate superclass and, when applicable, the complete class hierarchy. This is necessary to identify all the methods and attributes of the objects of the class. If the designer requires that the class have more than one immediate superclass, that is, it uses the object-oriented feature of multiple inheritance, the designer needs to be certain that the implementation language will support multiple inheritance hierarchies.

6.2.3 Class usage

Class **usage** is *concrete, abstract, or pure-abstract*, with concrete being the default. Abstract classes have no objects and are permitted to have both abstract and concrete methods. Pure-abstract classes have no concrete methods and no attributes; therefore, they do not participate in the implementation of business rules. When considering multiple inheritance hierarchy designs, pure-abstract classes are the preferred choice for secondary superclasses.

6.2.4 Attributes

The **attributes** of the class are named and given either a user-defined or a language-defined type. The language-defined type usually includes the primitives such as integer, float, and boolean.

6.2.4.1 Scope When **scope** is omitted, it defaults to *instance*. In this case, every object of the class will have its own copy of the attribute. That means that every object is capable of having a different value for the attribute. The second option for attribute scope is *static*. *Static* means that regardless of the number of objects of the class, only one copy of the variable will exist, and it will be shared by all the objects of the class. *Static* attributes are still treated as though they are part of each individual object's state. *Static* attributes are sometimes referred to as class variables. Finally, scope may be specified as *constant*. *Constant* attributes are *static* attributes that are not permitted to be altered and have meaning outside of the current class. In an encapsulated environment, *constant* attributes are effectively global data.

6.2.4.2 Initial value   When an **initial value** is critical to correctness, it should be specified at design; otherwise, it can be deferred to implementation. *Constant* attributes should always be given an initial value.

6.2.4.3 Visibility   Attribute **visibility** is either public or private. During design, if an attribute's visibility is public, the attribute has a getter, and perhaps a setter, method. Private variables have neither.

6.2.5 Method specification

The **method specification** defines its signature, semantics, usage, and visibility.

6.2.5.1 Signature   A method **signature** is the order and type of parameters for the method. If the method returns an object, the signature includes the type of the returned object. When a method has a pre-condition, it is part of the signature of the method. Chapter 8 (Implementation) discusses the use of method pre-conditions. The signature of a method is to its behavior as a requirements use case definition is to its analysis use case description. UML refers to a signature as an operation, and it uses the term *method* to refer to the implementation. UML defines polymorphism as two classes with the same operation but with different methods.

6.2.5.2 Semantics (behavior)   Method behavior must detail *every* state change, including those of attributes in other objects (sometimes referred to as side effects). It should state the details of the changes in terms of the method's parameters and the object's attributes.

Semantics is a key element of the class definition. Potential users of this class need to understand how its methods behave. The behavior described here should convey enough information to accomplish two things. First, the implementer of the class must understand exactly what is expected of this method for the application that uses it to behave correctly. Second, users of objects of this class can understand how its objects and their collaborators will be affected when this method is invoked. A method that is not easily understood by its potential users is of no value and may never be used, or worse, may be used incorrectly.

6.2.5.3 Usage   Method usage is optional, but can be *abstract* or *static*. Abstract methods will have no implementation, but the intended semantics should still be specified. A class that has one or more *abstract* methods is an abstract class. *Static* methods are those that can be invoked without an instance of the class (which in some languages includes the methods used to create instances of the class). *Static* methods are used to access static attributes and cannot reference nonstatic attributes. Most methods are neither *abstract* nor *static*. These methods must have an implementation, and may directly reference all the attributes of the object. A method can be both *static* and *abstract*, or neither.

6.2.5.4 Visibility Method visibility is either *public* or *private*. Public is a commitment on behalf of the implementer to guarantee that neither the signature nor the behavioral semantics of the method will ever change. Private indicates that both signature and semantics may change depending on the needs of the public methods of the class. Private methods should not be used by methods outside this class.

6.2.6 Events

With modern object-oriented languages like Java, the elements of an object have been redefined to include events. Objects contain information, and an object's methods are the means for other objects to access or manipulate that information. Events are the means for an object to communicate simultaneously with several objects for which they do not have a direct reference. Each event has a definition, related data, and registration and notification procedure.

6.2.6.1 Defining the event An event is logically defined based on the values of one or more attributes of this object, and perhaps other objects. The event occurs when these values are realized. Objects' attributes are changing constantly, but for the change to be considered an event, some other object must have a dependency on knowing when this change has occurred. For example, a simple state change may be that the price of a stock has changed by more that 5 percent within the last hour. If this information is required by the loan that this stock guarantees, or the portfolio with a stop loss order, or margin calls, then this 5 percent change could be defined as an event.

6.2.6.2 Registration After the event is defined, the class must provide a means for objects dependent on it to register their interest. This is accomplished by writing a method that dependent objects can invoke to request notification when the event occurs. A separate method would be required to specify that notification is no longer required.

6.2.6.3 Notification When an event occurs, the owning class notifies all currently registered objects by sending them a prearranged message. The message can be fixed and defined as part of the event, as in Java, or it can be specified as part of the registration, as in Smalltalk. When the notification message is defined as part of the event, it can include an object that contains specifics about the event. In the case of the stock fluctuation, it might include the current stock price, the object representing the stock, or both. The object firing the event is often passed as part of the event notification, in case the notified object needs to communicate with the object that "fired" the event to obtain additional information. Example 6-1 is an example of a partial class specification. It shows some of the elements just described.

Example 6-1 An example of a class specification.

```
Class Video subclass of Object
    Defines a title carried by one of the video store's branches
Attributes
    title          String[1..40]          public
    waitList       Vector of Customer     private
    copyList       Vector of Copy         public
    category       String[10]             public
    rating         {G,PG13,PG,R,NR}       public
Methods - public (excluding getters)
    getCopyCount () returns integer {returns the number of copies for this
        title currently carried by the store}
    reserve (Customer customer) returns void {Adds this customer to the end of
        the waitList}
Methods—private
    getFirstWaiting() returns Customer {removes and returns the customer
        object that has been on the waitList the longest}
Events
    The last copy of this video has been deleted.
        Registration -
            addZeroCopiesListener(Object)
            removeZeroCopiesListener(Object)
        Notification
            zeroCopies(String title)
```

6.3 LANGUAGE TYPES AND LEGAL VALUES

Some attributes' legal values are a subset of the standard language-defined types. For example, all languages define a type for integers, but many do not have a type for the ordinal numbers (integers greater than zero). Consider a case where the business object represents account balance as a floating-point number, but there is an additional constraint that balance must always be greater than or equal to 0.0. A simple comment can be used to record the constraint in the class specification, and perhaps on the class diagram. Example 6-2 shows using a constraint to define a subtype. Enumerated types such as a string defining the rating categories for video title (G, PG, PG13, etc.) are another example of a subtype constraint.

Example 6-2 Specifying attributes.

```
Attributes
    rentCount    0 >= Integer > 4      public
    finesDue     Decimal(5,2) >0.0     public
    status       {OK, INELIGIBLE}      private
```

6.4 UML CONSTRAINTS

There are also cases where the legal values of one attribute are dependent on the current values of one or more attributes in this object and other objects. Suppose that all checking accounts must be guaranteed with a personal loan. When a check amount exceeds the available balance, the loan principle is automatically increased to cover the overdraft. One way to capture this relationship is with an invariant.

6.4.1 Invariants

An invariant is one type of constraint. It states a relationship that must be preserved within the object's state.

6.4.1.1 The single object invariant Assume an invariant in a BankAccount class that specifies that the balance attribute must always have a value that is greater than or equal to zero. Preservation of this invariant is the responsibility of the withdraw method and any other method that changes the value of the balance attribute. The rules follow:

☞ The method may assume that the invariant is true at the beginning of the method.

☞ It is okay for the attribute of an object to be in an invalid state while the method is executing provided it is not possible for another thread to access that attribute in the same object while in the invalid state.

☞ The method must exit with the invariant true.

6.4.1.2 Recording business rules in constraints vs. use cases This constraint that balance must be greater than or equal to zero is a business rule, and business rules must still be captured in the recording of the use case description (decision table); therefore, this is a class design correctness question.

Figure 6-1 shows a more complex constraint and how it would be represented in a class diagram using UML. The expression in braces at the bottom of Figure 6-1 is the constraint. It states that the account attribute of the Account class (object) plus the principle attribute in the object that shares the association isCoveredBy with the Account class must be *greater than or equal*

{*Account.balance* **+** *Account.isCoveredBy.principle* ≥ *0.0*}

Fig. 6-1 Constraint involving attributes in multiple objects.

to zero. Simple text saying that *account overdrafts are automatically covered by a loan* could also have been included as a comment in the class specification, as part of the attribute definitions.

Given the invariant in Figure 6-1, assume that the design of the withdraw method first reduces the account balance by the withdraw amount and checks for a negative result. If the balance is negative, it increases the principle of the loan. In this design there is a point where the account balance and loan principle have values that violate this constraint, even though it is restored to true before the withdraw method completes. If the account withdraw transaction was handled by a separate manager method that used a getter and a setter method to obtain and modify account balance, the getter and setter would not conform to the invariant rules since the setter that reduced the balance would exit with the invariant false. One solution is to make the setter method for balance private. It would still need to deal with the possibility of another thread's accessing this object. Therefore, the withdraw method, the getter and setter for balance, and possibly others, will have to be synchronized to prevent simultaneous use of the balance attribute during the time the invariant is false.

6.4.1.3 Multiobject invariants   Although it is reasonable to insist that a method adhere to the rules of invariant preservations when a constraint is directed at a single attribute, compliance with these rules when the constraint affects attributes in multiple objects may be difficult and even unrealistic. Consider a savings account used to guarantee a loan; the constraint is that the savings balance must be greater than 80 percent of the current loan principle. The application allows the loan payment to be made from the savings account. Table 6-1 shows the associated loan and savings objects before and after the payment.

If the design of the payment use case is to first withdraw funds from the savings account before reducing the loan principle, then at some point the loan principle equals 100, savings balance equals 70, and the invariant is false. The control method could be designed differently, but that should not be necessary since the business rules are implemented correctly. The solution is

Table 6-1 Example of attributes that violate business rules.

		Before payment	After payment
Loan	Principle	100	90
	This month's interest	10	
	Payment	20	
Savings	Balance	90	70

to expand the time that the invariant can be false from a single method in a business object to a single method in the control object. This means that the invariant needs to be returned to true before the use case completes. Invariants that are really type restrictions are reasonable for a setter method to manage. When multiple objects are involved, the constraint becomes related to the application rather than a single class. In this case, the control method for the use case should become the focal point of constraint management, rather than a method in one of the participating objects

Now consider the next month's payment in the same example. When the transaction is complete, the loan principle is 80, but the savings balance is only 50, which is less than the 64 required by the invariant. What options does the use case have? If the only business rule is the 80 percent relationship between the savings balance and the loan principle, then the use case must reject the loan payment, and the loan goes into default status. However, it is almost a certainty that the bank has a policy (rule) that covers this situation, or it would not have allowed loan payments from savings accounts. Perhaps a backup source for the payment is required or interest and a penalty are applied and the client is notified to make an extra payment.

The problem with using invariants instead of business rules is that they leave gaps because they are not scenario specific. The constraint shown in Figure 6-1 addresses one business policy but does not cover all the rules for the loan payment use case. The rules for use case scenario correctness, given in Chapter 4, describe how to determine if a valid input state is not covered by one of the scenario pre-conditions. Convert invariants to business rules and combine them with the other business rules. In this way, the gaps and overlaps will be easier to detect and can be addressed by the client. The point is that the bank's policies should be captured and enforced as business rules in the use case description, not as invariants on the class diagram.

6.4.2 Overriding constraints

If a constraint is overridden in a subclass, it is with the restriction that it be at least as strong as or stronger than the constraint in the superclass that it supercedes. Strongly typed languages allow objects of the subclass to be instances of their superclass. Therefore, an instance of a subclass must adhere to the constraints of the superclass. A Square object is an instance of a Rectangle. If the constraint for Rectangle is: "Must have four sides and four right angles," then it must also be true for Square. However, the Square has the additional constraint: "Must have all four sides of equal length." Conversely, a Rhombus is not a valid subclass of Rectangle, since it cannot meet Rectangle's constraint that it has four right angles. When the subclass places extra constraints on the superclass, they are additive, and this creates a stronger constraint. A stronger constraint means that there are more restrictions, and fewer objects will meet those restrictions. For example, there are fewer square objects in the world than there are rectangular objects. That is because the constraint is more restrictive (stronger). Constraints in the subclass must be stronger than those in their superclass.

6.4.3 Method pre-conditions

Method pre-conditions are another form of constraint. They are managed by the users of the object instead of the methods within the object's class. For example, it is the responsibility of the user of the binary search method to ensure that the table is sorted before sending it the search message. This is an example of a method pre-condition. When documented as part of the search method behavior, it frees the search implementer of the responsibility to check for the condition and allows them to assume it is true. Pre-conditions are covered extensively in Chapter 8 on implementation.

6.5 CLASS OWNERS

Object-oriented development, while simplifying many programming tasks, has created a few new issues to address. One of these is the proliferation of methods. If several designers are working on a project and they all require new methods for the same class, there is a good chance that they might need a method with the same, or very similar, function. Someone with a class perspective of the application must resolve these design conflicts. The class owner assumes this role. The class owner is an individual who acts as a coordinating point for all the design decisions related to a single class.

6.5.1 Responsibilities

Class owners ensure that complete documentation is provided for each class. They have the last word on the attributes type, visibility, and initial values. They also define visibility for methods. They do not define method behaviors, but they may require members of the team that are defining methods to consolidate the function of multiple methods or consider using an existing method, instead of writing a new one. The definition of new methods is driven from the design of use cases, and there is a need to coordinate these requests.

Table 6-2 Responsibilities of class owners.

- Ensure that complete documentation is provided for each class.
- Determine visibility, type, and initial values for attributes.
- Determine visibility for methods.
- Arbitrate conflicts relating to duplicate or similar method names or behavior.
- Review all class design decisions.

The class owner plays this critical role and has the responsibility to review all class design decisions. A similar role discussed later in this chapter is that of the use case owner. Together, these two roles create a matrix of organizational control around the project, where the goal is to eliminate redundancy and ensure consistency across use cases and classes. Spread these responsibilities across the entire team, since they will involve some extra effort beyond that of application development. Table 6-2 summarizes the responsibilities of class owners.

6.6 OBJECT-TO-OBJECT LINKS

While designing use cases, there are specific decisions that will be made related to objects that are logically linked to one another.

☞ Which objects will contain references to other objects?
☞ Are references to be recorded as pointers or keys?

In analysis, these links are recorded abstractly as an association, but design requires a decision about how these links should be implemented. There are three options:

☞ The first object implements a link to the second.
☞ The second object implements a link to the first.
☞ Both objects implement a link to each other.

This decision is reflected in the *design class diagram* by adding an attribute in the object that refers to the other.

  If that link is to be implemented as a pointer, its type will be that of the object it points to. This implies that the object containing the attribute has a direct reference to the other object. Direct references would be named as the type prefixed by *a*, *an*, or *the* such as aVideo, anAccount, or theCustomer.

  If the link were implemented as an identifier (or foreign key), the attribute's type would most likely be string or numeric. This identifier would be used as a parameter in a *find(identifier)* message sent to a collection object to retrieve the associated object reference. To make it easier for the reader of

ANALYSIS

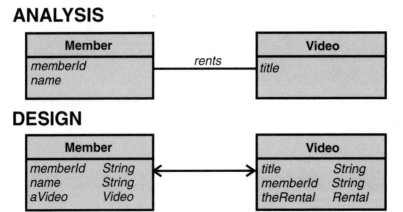

Fig. 6-2 Design representation in the class diagram.

the class to determine which design approach was taken, consider naming keys with the object name and a suffix of "Id," or "Number," like videoId, or copyNumber. Figure 6-2 shows an example of these conventions.

6.6.1 The class diagram and the data model

All data decisions must be recorded in the class diagram as well in the class specification. This means that the class diagram is transitioning from abstract to concrete, as it now represents what will be the implemented data structure of objects in the class. When the next increment or maintenance update begins, the team should work from this concrete *design class diagram* and enhance it as necessary to include the feature of the classes in this new increment. The abstract class diagram no longer exists, and there is no value in keeping it, since it is now incomplete.

While it may be the case that there is a data model to represent the database, and a separate class diagram to represent the application class, this is not a desirable situation. There may be a need to have an application object that does not map directly to a single database table. It is important to make clear which model represents the database organization. This topic is revisited in the chapter on persistence.

6.7 HANDLING DUPLICATE INFORMATION

Performance considerations often require that the same information is accessible from multiple objects, or that attributes that could have been derived from other attributes are maintained separately. When accessing the original attribute or computing the derived value requires unacceptable runtime overhead, the designer may choose to replicate that information. In some cases, only the methods of the object containing the redundant data will need its value, so the attribute can be considered private, and no getter need be provided. However, if these duplicate data are to be available for access outside this object, then a getter will be required, and a decision about how retrieval of the duplicated data will be handled needs to be made.

6.7.1 Push vs. pull

After the class designer has determined that a getter for the redundant data in the secondary object will be available, there are two implementation options.

☞ Create an event that would fire whenever the primary attribute changes. Have the secondary object register to be notified when the event occurs, and use the primary object's setter as the event trigger to notify (*push*) registered objects whenever the original attribute changes.

☞ Write a getter for the duplicate attribute that would retrieve (*pull*) the latest value of the primary attribute or recalculate the derived attribute's value, as required. In this case, the secondary object would not be required to have an attribute containing the duplicated data, except in the case where the algorithm for computing the derived attribute is so complex that it is worth the overhead to cache the derived result. Many of these decisions and tradeoffs can be deferred until and/or revisited during implementation.

6.7.1.1 An example Consider a design that has an object for each video title and a separate object for every copy of that video. Information about the movie (title, cast, runtime, etc.) would be kept in the video object, whereas information about the physical medium (VHS, DVD, copy number, status, current rental info, etc.) would be stored in the copy object. Assume that it is required that there be an attribute in the video object that maintains a count of non-rented copies. A nonzero value would indicate that at least one copy of that title is available for rent. One design choice is to update this value whenever a copy is added, removed, rented, or returned. The other option is for the video class's getAvailableCopies() method to compute the number of available copies when it is called, by checking the status of all copies. In this case, there is no need for the video class to have an attribute *availableCopies*. When the getAvailability use case invokes getAvailableCopies(), it is doing so without knowledge of which design was chosen.

6.7.1.2 Deriving attributes within the same object Similar options apply for a derived attribute like Member's eligibilityStatus, whose value is derived from the other Member attributes copiesRented and overDueFineAmount. In this case, the information required to compute the derived attribute eligibilityStatus is contained within the Member object. If a getEligibilityStatus()

method for Member is provided, it has the same options as described for duplicate attributes in multiple objects, except that it is not necessary for Member
to create an event when the push option is chosen. The business rules for
determining eligibility are defined during analysis, but the decision to have an
eligibilityStatus attribute is made during design.

6.7.2 Redundant data rules of thumb

The decision as to whether to maintain duplicate information or compute it on
request is summarized in the following rules.

- ☞ If the primary attribute's value changes less frequently than it is used
  (videos are rented less often than their status is reported), put the overhead in the use case that changes the primary attribute. That means
  that whenever the status of any copy changes, so will the availability
  count of the title object.
- ☞ When the primary attribute's value changes more frequently than it is
  used (that means that the clerk makes an availability request of a title
  infrequently, compared to how often a copy is rented or returned), it is
  more efficient to wait until availability is required and calculate it at
  that time.
- ☞ When it is more efficient to wait and calculate the value only when it is
  needed, but the calculation is complex and this overhead would occur at
  a critical time, it may be necessary to use the first rule and update the
  duplicate information as the primary value changes to guarantee a fast
  response later.

This last rule would not apply in a video store, but consider the case of a
program that monitors the values of several sensors in a temperature-critical
process (like a nuclear reactor). Assume that it is necessary to report the status of these sensors every few seconds to a master control application. If the
getStatus() method waits for the request to poll each temperature sensor and
perform the complex calculation on each piece of returned information, the
data may be stale when it reaches the master application. So the designer
may choose to recalculate status whenever a temperature sensor reports any
fluctuation, even though many temperature changes occur before it is necessary to report status.

Usage information may not always be obvious from a business rule, but
it may be based on how the business operates. Consider the getAvailability
use case that is used to determine whether at least one copy of a video is currently available (not rented). A reasonable assumption is that people walk in
and rent videos more often than they call up and ask if there is a copy on the
shelf, so the second rule is the better design choice. However, suppose that the
video tracking application is used by a small store that only has one or two
copies of each title. Members know through experience that the chance of

walking into the store and finding a copy of a popular video on the shelf is relatively low, especially on weekends. Given this fact, the actual environment is that most members use the telephone interface to see if a copy of the title is available before "wasting" a trip to the store. Under these conditions, the getAvailability use case becomes one of the store's most frequent transactions, so the first rule would be the preferred design.

Even though it is possible for the analyst to address most of these issues, in the cases where choices are based on runtime performance options, it may be that the designer or implementer needs to open a discussion with the client to resolve them. Sometimes a performance issue may not be recognized until after the application has reached an operational state, and the third rule may need to be applied as a maintenance consideration.

6.8 USE CASE OWNER

There needs to be an individual who is attuned to the business processes and business rules but is also aware of most design issues such as those just described. This responsibility should be assigned to the use case owner, a member of the team who follows the use case through the entire process. Although use case partitioning allows designers to work independently on their own use case, dependencies still need to be addressed as design decisions are made; these include how associations are implemented and what duplicate information is kept within the objects. The use case owner can help avert the design vs. implementation performance tradeoff from being overlooked or postponed too long in the process. The following tasks are part of the responsibilities of the use case owner.

- ☞ Write and validate the use case with the client.
- ☞ Review the test plan for the use cases.
- ☞ Be aware of how other use case designs impact theirs.
- ☞ Approve the use case design.
- ☞ Review ALL change requests.
- ☞ Approve changes impacting their use case.

One individual will usually own several use cases, so try to partition the work so that an individual's responsibility is spread over the increments. This will allow the use case owner to focus attention on a smaller number of use cases at a time.

6.8.1 Who should take on the role of use case owner?

Since the goal is that the use case owner follow the use case all the way through from requirements to implementation, the best choice for use case owner would be the person who writes the use case during analysis. However, some IT groups use one team for analysis and another team for design, or the design group may hand over its work to the implementers and move to a new project. When the analyst cannot remain as the use case owner throughout the project, the next best choice is the member of the team who designs the use case.

6.8.2 Multiple owners

When the organization is such that no individual can follow the use case all the way through, it may be necessary to have two use case owners (the analyst and the designer), even though continuity is sacrificed. The first task of the use case owner is to validate the analysis with the customer, and if possible, eliminate conflicts in design. So if no individual is available in both analysis and design phases, then splitting the responsibility is unavoidable. If possible, have the design use case owner attend the analysis reviews.

6.8.3 Use case owner vs. class owners

Since both the use case owner and the class owner have responsibilities that deal with redundant data, it makes sense to have the class owner of the class containing the duplicate data be the same individual as the one who owns the use case that is a primary user of that class. The primary use case of a class is one that the class exists to support. A class may have more than one primary use case. The video object exists to keep track of its status, so primary use cases would be rent and return. Consider having the same person own all three elements: the video class and the rent and return use cases. Another class is the rental object. It appears to exist to track renting as well, but the rental object is necessary only if there is a need to report the frequency that videos are rented. With that as a guideline, it makes more sense to assign the rental class and the use cases for reporting rental frequency to the same team member. Most of this may seem common sense, but it is worth a quick check before making these role assignments. The key point is that every use case and every class be assigned an owner, and that they understand their responsibilities with respect to that role.

6.9 DESIGNING USING INHERITANCE

Inheritance may seem out of place in the chapter on class design, since some readers may believe that it should be addressed as the application was being developed during use case design. Novice object-oriented programmers often feel the need to use inheritance because it is available. These enthusiastic, but often inexperienced object-oriented developers successfully apply the super-class-subclass relationship but may fail in achieving the benefits of such a relationship, and they can actually damage the structure and robustness of the

overall application. This regression occurs because they lack the understanding of the correct use and power of inheritance, polymorphism, and dynamic
binding. Inheritance, when misused, can actually degrade a system's overall
maintainability. The creation of an inheritance hierarchy should be considered
an extension of class design and another element of information hiding.

6.9.1 An inheritance design example

Consider the design problem of creating a generalized **SequentialCollection**
class that can do all the basic sequential functions like search, sort, insert,
delete, etc. The task is to write these functions so that they will work with any
implemented sequential data structure, like an array, or link list, or stream,
or even a sequential file.

6.9.2 Template methods

A class is created as an abstract superclass. It specifies the most general table
functionality such as search, sort, insert, and delete. Concrete subclasses will
provide the supporting implementation specific function. Example 6-3 shows
the code for the search method in the SequentialCollection superclass.

Example 6-3 A search template method.

```
Class SequentialCollection abstract{
// No Attributes
// Methods
boolean search (String item) {
    first();
    while (!last()) {
        String current = next();
         if (current.equals (item)
             return true;
    }
    return false;
}
```

Notice that the superclass uses the methods *next()*, *first()*, and *last()*.
Since SequentialCollection is generalized to work for any sequential data
organization, there is no way to implement these three methods in a way that
would support both arrays and link lists. Therefore, it falls on the concrete
subclasses to provide these functions. Smalltalk would add a comment to
these methods with a phrase similar to "implemented in the subclass." Java
would declare them as *abstract*, forcing the subclass to provide concrete implementation. Example 6-4 shows the design of the *next()*, *first()*, and *last()* methods in the subclass, which has refined SequentialCollection as an array.

Example 6-4 A concrete subclass of the abstract class SequentialCollection.

```
Class SequentialArray extends Sequential Collection {
// Attributes
    String items[] = new String[10];
    int x = 0;
// Methods
    public void first() {   x = 0;      }
    public String next() {
                return items[x++];    }
    public boolean last() {
                return (x == 10);   }
```

Methods in the superclass that provide larger functionality, but that require that the subclass provide simple functions to support them, are referred to as template methods [WirfsBrock90]. Imagine how many other template methods could be implemented in the superclass if the subclass could be counted on to provide the basic methods described here and perhaps one or two more.

6.9.3 Abstract methods

The concept of an abstract method is powerful. It is the key to the implementation of a template method. When a class specifies a method as abstract, it forces any concrete class wishing to be its subclass to supply a concrete implementation of that method.

6.9.4 Inheritance to simplify enhancement

When inheritance is applied with the appropriate use of subclassing, it can be a very productive vehicle. Even though creating the SequentialCollection superclass takes more time than just creating the array, it makes the implementation of the array subclass trivial. Experienced object-oriented designers estimate that designing reusable classes takes about three to five times the effort of implementing the concrete class directly. So while powerful, this kind of reuse will not increase the productivity of those projects that create the template methods because they will be forced to absorb the overhead of designing the template methods to be reusable. In general, reusable objects should not be viewed as byproducts of object-oriented application development but rather as their own business case and return on investment. Capabilities such as abstract methods, polymorphism, dynamic binding, and template methods are relatively new programming techniques. The move toward object-oriented development has made these features available to modern programmers. For this reason, do not expect that all programmers will immediately possess skills in these areas and defer their usage for a year or so.

6.9.5 Polymorphism using abstract methods

In strongly typed languages like Java and C++, polymorphism relies on inheritance to enable it. Notice that the SequentialCollection class, as implemented, works only with collections of strings. The Java code in Example 6-5 uses polymorphism to generalize SequentialCollection to work with collections of any type. To facilitate this, an abstract class Comparable was created, and the type of the argument of the search has been changed to Comparable. By definition, any subclass of Comparable is considered of type Comparable as well. To ensure that every subclass of Comparable will work correctly, Comparable defines one abstract method **equals**. This is required to allow the search to compare any two Comparables. Example 6-6 shows the abstract superclass Comparable and how a subclass of type MyClass would be implemented.

Example 6-5 Generalized concrete implementation of SequentialCollection.

```
Class SequentialArray extends Sequential Collection {
// Attributes
    Comparable items[] = new Comparable[10];
    int x = 0;
// Methods
    public void first() {   x = 0;      }
    public Comparable next() {
            return items[x++];   }
    public boolean last() {
            return (x ==  10);  }  }
```

Note that it is up to the subclass to define the meaning of the equals between two Comparables. In the case of MyClass, equals means that both the id and code attributes have the same value. Information hiding guarantees that the search will not care about the meaning of equals(), but only that semantically the subclass compares two Comparables.

Example 6-6 Comparable subclass Myclass.

```
abstract class Comparable {
    public abstract boolean equals (Comparable item) ;
}

class MyClass extends Comparable {
    String id;
    int code;
// Methods
    boolean equals (Comparable item) {
        if  ((MyClass)item.getKey().equals(id))
            return true;
```

```
        else
            return false;
    }
    public String getKey() {
        return id + code;        }
```

6.9.6 Bottom up inheritance hierarchies

In the first example of inheritance, the SequentialCollection class is designed to facilitate its extension. This was done by carefully choosing what methods are required to be implemented by its subclasses and then building the superclass method design around them. In this case, the superclass is designed for vertical reuse.

In the second example, there is no reuse of the superclass. Instead, it creates an additional requirement that the implementer of the subclass must write an *equals* method. The goal of the Comparable class is polymorphism. Now any implementation of SequentialCollection is capable of storing elements of any type, not just string. For the search to work, it is necessary to ensure that these elements can be compared, and encapsulation prevented the search from doing the compare directly. Therefore, a new method is required to return a boolean value indicating whether the two objects are to be considered equal. The requirement is that SequentialCollection needs to store objects of *any* type, which forces the designer to manufacture the Comparable hierarchy. These types of inheritance hierarchies are essential in strongly typed languages in order to apply polymorphism.

6.9.7 The don'ts of inheritance

Unless special care is taken, design flaws can result when creating inheritance hierarchies. There are two categories of these errors: structural incompatibility and behavior incompatibility. In both cases, the subclass causes existing methods in the superclass hierarchy to operate incorrectly on objects of the subclass.

6.9.7.1 Structural compatibility Figure 6-3 shows the class CheckingAccount with methods deposit and writeCheck, and its subclass SpecialChecking. SpecialChecking is *exactly like* CheckingAccount except that when a check amount is greater than the available balance, the check is paid, and the balance is allowed to become negative. The special checking account is now charged interest until the balance returns to positive. On first look, this appears to be a perfect application of inheritance. The subclass is "just like" the superclass "except" it does more.

The problem in Figure 6-3 is that the subclass attributes are capable of containing values (negative balance) that were impossible in the superclass.

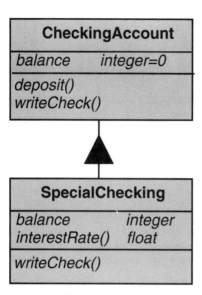

Fig. 6-3 Structural incompatibility example.

Some of the superclass's methods may have been written with the assumption that negative balances are impossible. If these methods are invoked for objects of the subclass, the results will be unpredictable. And even though the designer of the superclass could have added a constraint for balance, the CheckingAccount class is correct without it since it accurately implemented the business rules. The design flaw was interpreting "is just like, except" as the reason to subclass. The first inheritance rule is: a subclass may have no values for its attributes that are invalid in the superclass. This property is known as data compatibility.

6.9.7.2 Behavioral compatibility The second rule of inheritance hierarchies is: behaviors overridden in a subclass should return the identical values of their superclass counterpart. A violation would be to make the Circle class a subclass of Polygon. Even though a circle is mathematically a polygon with an infinite number of sides and angles approaching 180°, the implementation is impossible, since software languages do not deal with anything of infinite size. As long as the Circle class overrides all or most of the methods in the Polygon class, everything will work correctly. However, it fails the test that overridden methods must return the identical values as their superclass counterpart. In this case, the circle and polygon area methods return different values, which means that one of them is incorrect. This makes the two classes behaviorally incompatible, which will require the developer of the subclass to override every other incompatible method.

In this example, even though the circle was not a polygon, it was still forced into the hierarchy. When this happens, the only way to prevent failures is for the subclass to be made aware of every new method in the inheritance hierarchy and given the opportunity to override it. Whenever the superclass adds a new method and no override is provided, the results may be disastrous.

Another violation of this rule that is not as obvious at first glance is to define Rectangle as a superclass and a Square as the subclass. The rules of geometry specify that a square is in every way a rectangle. If that is true, then how can this hierarchy violate the rules of inheritance? Consider that the Rectangle class is defined with the attributes of length and height, but to optimize storage the Square is defined to use only the attribute of length and does not bother to initialize height. This design violates behavioral compatibility since the area method for a rectangle will not give a correct result when applied to a square object. It also violates structural compatibility, since the attribute width in the Square has a null value, which is invalid for a Rectangle. In this case, the problem arises because the rules of geometry clearly state that a square is a rectangle, and it is assumed that any programmatic implementation would respect that Archimedean principle.

Designers are free to implement a software representation of concrete reality in any way that provides a correct solution of the problem, but inheritance elicits restrictions that may not be compatible with all design alternatives. These situations arise because hierarchies are not designed but allowed to evolve. The best inheritance hierarchies are those constructed from the bottom up, after all application classes have been completed. Only then is it known for sure whether two or more classes can be safely joined in a hierarchy that conforms to the rules of inheritance. Mistakes like those described are common among novice inheritance programmers. The best way to avoid them is to avoid the use of inheritance for at least a year or two after beginning object-oriented software development. Designing for inheritance is a skill separate from learning to work with objects, classes, and messages. Do not be disappointed if its mastery takes an extra year or two. The good news is that it is a skill that can easily be deferred.

6.9.8 Reuse should also be considered a special skill

Before leaving this topic, it is appropriate to once again visit the issue of reuse. Although it is true that much of the design of a class is driven by the needs of the control objects, its functionality can be shaped to facilitate enhancement. The class design creates potential reuse, but this effort requires talents not normally found in programmers with only language skills. It takes a couple of years of object-oriented design experience before mastering reuse. That means that novice developers should generally assume that none of their classes will be reusable. Chapter 12 (Maintenance) discusses the importance of functional stability. For now, it is sufficient to remember that any class targeted for reuse should have a rock solid design, have undergone extensive multienvironmental testing, and have already been reused at least three times before making it generally available.

6.10 CORRECTNESS QUESTIONS

Having discussed the details of class design and treated it as a separate activity within OODP, it is necessary that this activity have its own correctness criteria as well. The following five questions summarize the class design correctness issues.

☞ Is every constraint recorded on the class diagram or in the class specification captured in the business rule of some analysis use case description?

☞ Does every non-getter method have a use case that requires it?

☞ Does each method specification support the use case design of every use case in which it participates?

☞ Do all subclasses preserve the valid values of attributes in the superclass?

☞ When overriding methods, do the new methods return the identical values of their superclass counterpart?

6.11 REVISITING THE INCREMENTAL AND TRACEABLE PROPERTY OF THE PROCESS

Having looked at both use case design in Chapter 5 and the details of class design in this chapter, the next activity is implementation. Before proceeding, it is appropriate to review the incrementable attribute of the process, which states that it should be possible to partition the product requirements in such a way that any increment could be implemented without requiring modifications to prior increments. The first step is to define each requirement as a use case and provide it with its own specification in analysis, its own sequence diagram in design, and its own method in the control class. When new use cases in subsequent increments are implemented, no changes are required to existing methods in the control object, since each method is dedicated to its own use case. If the business object methods are limited to getters, setters, and other primitive functions, only new methods in the business objects should be required to support new use cases. These features provide the assurance necessary that no rework of existing code is required. Naturally, if a prior requirement changes, then there will need to be changes to existing tested code. But together use case and classes have simplified the problem of adding new function. Use cases encapsulate each requirement, and the control method encapsulates the use case. Partial classes are more compatible with this approach than a partial module from the traditional structured approach. Note that capability deteriorates when the stair pattern is applied and business rules are partially implemented within one or more business classes.

Persistence

*T*his chapter deals with the storing and mapping of an object's data to a permanent (persistent) medium. The knowledge of and responsibility for this persistent mapping is encapsulated within the object. This chapter discusses persistence and some of the potential framework solution to facilitate it.

7.1 PERSISTENCE DEFINITION

Persistence is the attribute of data that guarantees its availability even when the application that created it aborts. For an object, that means that all its attribute values must be recoverable when the application is restarted after a normal shutdown or failure. Usually the object will write its data to a file immediately after it is changed. Then if the application terminates suddenly and must be restarted, the restart facility will restore the object's state by reading the information from the associated file.

7.1.1 Mapping persistent data and objects

There are three basic approaches to storing an object's data on a persistent source.

☞ One object per file

☞ Several homogeneous objects in a single file

☞ Many objects of many classes stored in a relational database

7.1.1.1 One object per file The one-object-per-file design is only practical when there is a small fixed amount of information to be stored on the persistent source. For example, an array of price categories, or a table of currently logged-on clerks would be small enough to be stored as its own file.

7.1.1.2 Several objects in a single file Storing several objects in a single file is a more common approach to data and objects. In this mapping the logical records of the sequential or keyed file are each represented as an object in the system, and a second collection object represents the file itself.

7.1.1.3 Many objects stored in a relational database For large relational databases there will be objects of many classes stored in the same database. The simplest approach is to have one table for every class. Each attribute in the class becomes a column in the table, and each row represents an object. There are an infinite number of ways to map an object to multiple tables or a subset of records in a file, but applications will operate most efficiently with a one-to-one relationship.

7.1.2 The nonpersistent object-oriented design

Although persistence is not unique to object-oriented design, most object-oriented languages mask the problem from the application. Object-oriented training and texts that teach programmers how to write an object-oriented program will have them create their objects with the attribute values stored only in the volatile memory allocated to the object. For programs that are written based on this approach, everything will work correctly as long as it recreates all the objects every time the program is run. However, in a real application, like the video store, the rental objects from one session must still be available even if the program is shut down and restarted. That requires persistence.

7.1.3 Persistent design

Consider how the rent video design would look if its objects were to manage their own persistence. Figure 7-1 shows the sequence diagram for the rentVideo use case.

Since the goal is to encapsulate persistence and have the application independent of it, the discussion that follows will focus on the design of the methods that either access an object in a collection or change the attributes of an object. In Figure 7-1, that includes find() in listOfVideos and listOfMembers,

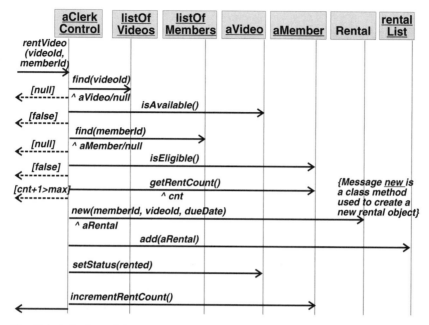

Fig. 7-1 A design of the rentVideo use case.

new() in the Rental class, add() in rental List, setStatus() in aVideo, and increment() in aMember. There are only four basic operations to consider.

- ☞ Retrieving an object from a collection as in the find() method being sent to the listOfVideos and listOfMembers objects.
- ☞ Changing the value of an attribute, which several of the methods in Figure 7-1 do. The example will explain the persistent function of just the setStatus() method for the aVideo object.
- ☞ Creating a new object, which is what the new() method in the Rental class and the add() method in rentalList denote.
- ☞ Removing an object from a collection of which there are no examples in this use case design.

Case 1: Retrieving an object from a collection: Consider the message find() sent to listOfMembers. It takes a memberId as an argument and returns a Member object if one exists with that name. The method must search all the records in the persistent file, database, or data set looking for one that has a memberId attribute equal to the find parameter. If no record exists, then the method returns null. However, if a record with the specified member name is found, the find() method must create a new Member object, initialize its attributes with the associated information from the database, and return the new Member object to the sender of the message.

Case 2: Changing the value of an attribute: The setStatus() method uses the message parameter to change the video from available to rented. Although the method returns no object, setStatus() must ensure that the data record in the persistent file that was used to create this aVideo object is retrieved from the database, updated, and written back. This implies that when the object was created and initialized by the find() method, it stored within the object a way to determine which physical/logical record on the file or database contains the object's persistent counterpart.

Case 3: Creating a new object: When the new method for the Rental class is invoked, it creates a new instance of Rental and initializes it based on the parameters. The add method must create a data record with the same information and insert it in the appropriate place in the persistent collection.

Case 4: Removing an object from a collection: Consider a method delete(anObject) that is part of some collection class. The object-oriented convention is to use strings, numbers, or some other primitive key as the argument of a search and then to use the object itself when doing add or delete operations on collections. This design ensures that the object to be deleted is the one that is referenced outside the collection and eliminates any ambiguity associated with deleting collections with duplicate identifiers. In the case of a persistent collection, the concept of deleting the object specified by the delete() method argument is less precise. The database, unlike the internal object-oriented language collection, does not have a pointer to the object that it can compare for identity. So a persistent delete can *only* compare the keys to determine identity. For this reason, it is logical to take the same approach for the design of the delete method. Instead of passing an object as the argument and forcing the delete to extract the predefined attribute to use as the basis for selecting the record to be deleted, have the delete argument be the database record key. In that way, the correctness of the delete method, and that of the other methods that use delete, can be based on the way the persistent database package actually works.

When persistent data are shared, there are two additional design considerations.

First, it may be necessary to retrieve the current persistent object before retrieving any information, even if the object is already cached in memory. In those cases, each getter in the class would refresh the object before each access.

Second, when writing an updated object's data to a shared database, it may be necessary to retrieve the persistent data and ensure that it has not been changed in the interim, before writing the memory resident object to the file. This may require that each record (object) in the database have a timestamp representing when it was last written.

7.2 PERSISTENCE CONSIDERATIONS

7.2.1 Keys vs. pointers

Object-oriented programming languages are typically taught using direct references from within one object to another. This type of design allows very fast access to the associated object. However, traditional database design uses identifiers (foreign keys) to reference an associated object (table/row). This requires that an identifier (or key) be supplied as the search argument for the collection to be able to find the actual data record/object. Once the logical record in the database has been found and instantiated as an object in memory, then a reliable pointer reference can be established. This method is slower, but when objects are persistent, there is no guarantee that when one object in memory is referenced by another the first object will always be allocated to the same address when it is instantiated from the database. Therefore, the pointer reference stored in the referencing object is almost guaranteed to be invalid the next time these objects are used. For that reason designers should plan on using object identifiers instead of pointers to reference one object from another.

7.2.2 Collection classes

When objects are retrieved and instantiated, updated and replaced, or created and added, the most logical place to perform these tasks is in the collection rather than in the individual objects. This design allows for some generalization of the collection classes so that several persistent collections can be implemented with the same object-oriented collection.

7.2.2.1 Business objects   Business objects need only have enough persistence awareness to notify the collection when they are changed and ready to be added or replaced in the database. The business objects may also need to communicate with the collection before modifying attributes when the persistent data is shared. In this case, the setter would request that the collection refresh the object attributes from the file before updating the object's attributes.

7.2.2.2 Encapsulation   One of the benefits of encapsulation is that the programmer can initially create the business objects to be nonpersistent tables and arrays. This will simplify testing, and when the object is redesigned to use persistence, errors and bugs can be assumed to be related to the persistence design since the application logic will not have changed. The important part of persistence mapping and management is that it should be accomplished without the knowledge of the application. It should be encapsulated within the object exactly as any other data design decision. The exception to this rule is when it is necessary to allow the application to have control over rollback and commit of complex transactions. When using autocommit mode, these decisions can be masked from the application.

7.3 PERSISTENCE CLASSES

Many existing software products can manage all or most of the persistence management discussed on behalf of the collection classes and their members. Most fall into three categories and are specific to the object-oriented implementation language.

7.3.1 Relational frameworks

Relational frameworks are products that allow the object-oriented application to map every attribute in an object to a column in a table within a database. The business objects are defined as subclasses of the framework's collection and member objects. The framework handles all the SQL for retrieving data and creating the objects including joins when the mapping is one to many from objects to tables. In some cases, the object will need to manage the complex logic required to perform an update on these objects. When the object-to-table mapping is one to one and the updates are set to autocommit, the framework handles all the persistence management.

7.3.2 The JDBC model

JDBC is a set of Java interfaces that database vendors may elect to implement. The syntax is a subset of SQL, but there is no requirement that the databases be relational. The business or application objects are responsible for creating and executing the SQL commands. The advantage of JDBC is that the same command will retrieve information from any database, from any vendor, that supplies the interfaces.

7.3.3 Object-oriented databases

Object-oriented databases integrate objects and persistence. The application creates business objects within the framework, and the databases do the rest. Originally, object-oriented database products could not be used with existing databases and had to be built from scratch. The advantage of object-oriented databases is the seamless way they link objects and persistence. They will even manage the use of pointers as object-to-object references on behalf of their instance.

7.4 MAINTENANCE

Persistence raises another issue regarding encapsulation, which is the restructuring of data without affecting the application and this could include adding new attributes. When an attribute is never used as part of any existing application, should it be deleted and not included until the application is updated to require it? The strict interpretation of encapsulation would say yes, but the fact is that there is more to altering a persistent object's data structure than changing a few getters and recompiling. The persistent shadow of the object must be restructured as well, and adding a few bytes to a database table or the records in an enormous inventory file is not a simple recompilation. So when it is clear that attributes will be required in planned but unspecified applications, it may be more efficient to add them now with null values and save the database redesign effort later. This issue of managing the redesign of databases that are fronted by an object view is discussed further in Chapter 12 on maintenance.

CHAPTER 8

Implementation

This chapter describes the details and issues associated with implementing the use case designs and class specifications. Many of the items discussed are language specific. This book uses Java as its language for examples.

8.1 IMPLEMENTATION TASKS

The implementation activity topics are divided into three parts.

☞ Creating the classes and the attributes required to support the use case designs in the current increment
☞ Implementing the methods specified during design or required to support the use case design
☞ Other implementation-specific considerations

8.2 DEVELOPING NEW CLASSES

If the use case design is patterned after Jacobson's fork, most of the details of business classes can be developed from the class diagram. For each business class object, define its attributes and a getter for each attribute. These will be the majority of required methods. All remaining methods will be created based on the needs of the use case control method design. The implementation of the control method itself is based on either the sequence diagram developed during design, the analysis use case description, or the requirements use case specification. The decision table if available should be included or referenced in the control method, since it can also serve as the method's specification, description, and documentation.

8.3 IMPLEMENTING NEW METHODS

New methods in an increment come from two sources: control methods that implement each use case and the methods that collaborate with the control methods.

8.3.1 Implementing the use case from the sequence diagram

When implementing the use case control method from the sequence diagram, the messages can almost be copied directly from the design. Only the details of algorithms and the use case's control flow will need to be added. The control method's collaborating methods had their behavior documented when the method was conceived during design, and these methods must be implemented first. If they do not exist, implement them as they are encountered in the coding of the control method.

8.3.2 Implementing the use case from the decision table

Implementation based on the analysis decision table presumes a design that is obvious from the business rules of the decision table. When writing the messages based on the analysis decision table, follow the same flow that was described in design for developing the sequence diagram from the decision table, and implement collaborating methods as required.

8.3.3 Implementing the use case from the requirements

The steps to implement from requirements are a combination of selecting the strongest pre-condition scenarios combined with the rules for implementing from decision tables. The implementers are actually doing specification design and coding as a single activity, but mentally each activity is being performed as a separate step.

8.4 IMPLEMENTATION-SPECIFIC CODING CONSIDERATIONS

There are three items related to coding issues that were not discussed during use case design. They are identified here and discussed over the next few topics.

☞ Storing and accessing duplicate information

☞ Platform- and coding-specific issues

☞ Handling runtime exceptions

8.4.1 Duplicate information in multiple business objects

The decision to supply a getter for the attribute in the secondary object is part of use case design, but the management of the duplicate data is deferred until implementation. The developer must either create the event processing logic and methods in the associated classes to maintain the duplicate data or modify the getter method in the secondary object to retrieve or compute that data dynamically.

8.4.2 Platform- and coding-specific issues

Several decisions that are language- or platform-specific must be deferred until the code is written. These include numeric data representation, file naming conventions, asynchronous threads, and data access.

8.4.2.1 Handling runtime exceptions   Some nonbusiness rule errors will not have been identified and, therefore, not specified during analysis or design. These errors are related to the runtime platform and include memory allocation, input/output (IO), synchronization, and errors related to other software. During implementation, the developers need to detect and handle these conditions. In a language like Java, they will be trapped as exceptions. When they occur, implement the defined recovery and, if necessary, abort the use case. When an existing return code number has not been defined, create a new value or use a default return code value accompanied by an explanatory message.

8.5 CORRECTNESS

The correctness questions for the implementation activity are based on either the sequence diagram, the analysis use case description, or the requirements definitions, depending on which intermediate deliverable is available. Always perform validation from the most detailed level available for a given use case.

8.6 CORRECTNESS QUESTIONS USING A SEQUENCE DIAGRAM

☞ Is every message in the sequence diagram implemented as a method in the appropriate class? *(Is there a method for every design message sent?)*

☞ Do the parameters of the messages in the sequence diagram agree with respect to type and order with the implemented message? *(Was the message transcribed into code correctly?)*

☞ Is each method's implementation correct?

✗ When a method is implemented from its design specification, is the implemented method correct with respect to that specification?

✗ When no method specification was created during design, does the implementation of the method agree with respect to parameter type and order, and return type, with the message recorded on the sequence diagram?

☞ Does the logic of the control method's implementation (loops, conditions, algorithms) agree with the business rules of the use case's analysis specification? (*Does the control method implement the use case business rules?*)

Note that the last correctness question does not use the sequence diagram but uses the less detailed model from analysis. That is because the sequence diagram will usually not contain sufficient detail on the pre-condition and post-condition of the use case scenarios.

8.6.1 Correctness from the decision table

The correctness questions are the same no matter what is used as the guide for implementation, but when the sequence diagram is omitted, the correctness becomes more subjective.

☞ Does the logic of the control method implementation (loops, conditions, algorithms) agree with the business rules of the use case's analysis specification?

☞ Does the control method implement the use case business rules?

☞ Do the methods used by the control method support the implementation of the use case? When these are simple getter methods, the answer is usually a trivial yes.

8.6.2 Correctness from the requirements

When a use case's implementation correctness is determined directly from the requirements, it is assumed that

☞ There are no more than two or three outcomes.

☞ The number of scenarios equals the number of outcomes.

☞ Each business rule has a single simple condition.

☞ If a scenario exists that changes state of an object, its rule is algorithmically trivial.

If these conditions are not met or the following correctness questions are difficult to answer, the implementer may wish to "rough out" a quick sequence diagram or decision table and review it with the designer. It can be discarded after the use case verification is complete, or it can become the property of the designer and retained.

Correctness questions:

☞ Does the number of paths through the code match the number of outcomes in the requirements?

☞ If returned information is required for a scenario, is it included in the return object?

☞ Does the implementation for each scenario logically and reasonably agree with the stated outcome?

8.7 LANGUAGE IMPLEMENTATION CONSIDERATIONS

If the design is written and reviewed with no specific language in mind, the programmer will have to address some deferred items. These include typing, polymorphism, private methods, global variables, and inheritance structure.

> ***Author's Note:*** *Although there are many object-oriented languages, this book uses Java syntax when giving examples. Java has the most robust set of object-oriented and software-engineering features. It enforces strong typing and supports private attributes and methods, which Smalltalk does not. It uses the single-rooted inheritance structure and the variable to object reference model, which C++ does not. It uses pure abstract classes (interfaces) for multiple inheritance, and its event model is the most robust available. If the implementation language of the project is not Java, some conversion will be required.*

8.7.1 Typing

Every language has its own implementation of primitive types like integer, decimal, floating point, string, character, and boolean. The programmer must decide how to implement these to best support the design. In some languages these primitives are combined (Java has no decimal, but uses float). In other languages they may appear as classes (in Java and Smalltalk a string is a class). The programmer will need to adapt the coding to the language-supplied types and the user-defined types, but these types may not supply all the features assumed during design. For example, the design may have used Date as type and assumed the capability to compute the number of days between two date objects. If this feature does not exist, the implementer will need to include this function, perhaps by extending the Date class.

8.7.2 Defining access to attributes and methods

Every language has its own interpretation of encapsulation. Smalltalk has no facility to prevent access of instance variables from the subclass and no way to make a variable completely public. Java cannot duplicate Smalltalk's attribute access without exposing the variable to the entire package, so implementers must deal with encapsulation when the classes are created.

UML allows for the specification of such attributes as private, public, or protected. The UML meaning of public and private, while not available in all object-oriented languages, is at least well defined. Protected, on the other hand, is only language defined, and has a different meaning in each language. The same situation also exists for methods. The programmer may need to rethink these aspects of the solution once the language is selected.

8.7.3 Global data

Another language-specific consideration is global data. Both C++ and Smalltalk allow data that is totally unencapsulated. Global data in Java must be represented as a public attribute within a public class; these attributes are usually defined as class attributes as well. Even though it is recommended that global data be avoided in software, the decision to use global data should be deferred until implementation if it is required.

8.7.4 Strong typing

Most object-oriented languages today are strongly typed, although Smalltalk remains the most notable exception. With strong typing, the programmer can count on the compiler to do most of the type checking. However, if it becomes necessary to define a subset of the valid values of a language-defined type, that responsibility lies within the implementation of the methods that encapsulate the attribute. Chapter 6 showed how an invariant documents a constraint, limiting the legal values of an attribute. For methods that modify that attribute, here are the rules as they apply to implementation.

- ☞ It is allowable to violate a constraint/type within a method as long as
  - ✗ It is restored before exiting the method.
  - ✗ All other threads are blocked while the attribute is in its invalid state.
- ☞ The object must be created with the attributes in a valid state. This can be accomplished by providing an initial value for each attribute or using the technique known as lazy initialization. That is where the getter method performs initialization when it is first invoked.
- ☞ A method may assume that all attributes are in a valid state when the method is invoked. The first two rules essentially guarantee this one.
- ☞ When a method determines that it has created an invalid state, it must roll back all attributes to their values before the method began. It must do this while ensuring that no other thread has gained access to any altered attribute. Finally it should return a status to the invoking method informing it of the error.

This last rule only applies when a method modifies multiple attributes. For example, consider a method in an Account class that transfers some amount of funds from itself to another account that is passed as a parameter. Example 8-1 shows the method with no subtype enforcement.

Example 8-1 Transfer method of Account class.

```
void transfer (amount, otherAccount) {
    otherAccount.deposit(amount);
    balance = balance - amount;
}
```

If balance were defined to be an integer greater than or equal to zero, and if the transfer amount is greater than the from-account balance, the type would be violated. However, it is not enough for the method to simply reject the transaction when it discovers this; it must also withdraw the funds already deposited in the transfer-to account. This is only a problem for methods that update more than one attribute. An implementation of the transfer method that preserves the invariant via rollback is shown in Example 8-2. Checking for sufficient funds before doing the withdrawing from the otherAccount could optimize this design further, but the example was crafted to show the rollback requirement.

Example 8-2 Transfer methods with constraint checking and rollback.

```
void transfer (amount, otherAccount) {
    otherAccount.deposit(amount);
    if (amount > balance)
        otherAccount.withdraw(amount);
    else
        balance = balance - amount;
}
```

8.7.5 Enumerated types

A similar situation occurs when a type is enumerated. An attribute like weekday might be restricted to the integers 2, 3, 4, 5, or 6, or a video's status attribute might be limited to the string "available," "rented," or "missing." The type checking for these attributes will need to be handled in the associated setter methods of the class. Localizing this enforcement within a single method may seem practical, but it raises additional implementation issues. Assume that all changes to an attribute are performed by its setter method. When the setter encounters an illegal value, how does it communicate the error to the caller, and does that affect the coding of the rest of the application? If the fork pattern has been applied, then only the control method must check for error return codes, but if the error occurs deep within a series of method calls, then every collaborator all the way back to the interface object will need to check for and react to this error in the data.

8.8 METHOD PRE-CONDITIONS

Methods can transfer some of the responsibility of type checking by converting the subtype constraint to a method pre-condition. Pre-conditions are part of the method specification and are used to state what must be true before a method is invoked. This can be accomplished by removing a constraint such as /* **balance >= 0** */ from the attribute definition of balance, and defining a pre-condition on the withdraw method as shown in Example 8-3. This specification now requires that the input to this method be an object of type Account and a variable of type double with the additional restriction that it must be less than or equal to the balance attribute in the Account object.

Example 8-3 Withdraw method of Account class with pre-condition.

```
//Pre: amount < account.balance
withdraw (Account account, double amount){
    balance = balance - amount;
}
```

Note that most method pre-conditions are design decisions and the implementer is usually in the role of ensuring that they are true before invoking the method with the pre-condition specified.

8.8.1 Responsibilities

The pre-condition shown in Example 8-4 places the responsibility on the caller to ensure amount has a legal value with respect to balance. This is a code review issue, which must guarantee that the pre-condition be met before the method is invoked. In the example, the parameter weekday is limited to values of 2, 3, 4, 5, or 6. The pre-condition states that the method will *assume* that this is true and does no value validation of the weekday parameter.

Example 8-4 An example of a pre-condition to strengthen parameter type.

```
// Pre:  1 < weekday < 7
    public void setDayNumberToWeekday(int weekday) {...}
```

The code walk-through has the additional responsibility of ensuring that a legal value is supplied as a parameter whenever this method is invoked. Whenever invalid input values can cause serious repercussions outside the application, the implementer of the method may still need to check for invalid values, and return with no action if an invalid value is supplied. The definition of a pre-condition violation is an undefined result; therefore, no change to the attributes is a correct outcome.

8.8.2 Rules

There are two rules for pre-conditions.

1. It must be possible and reasonable for the calling method to guarantee the pre-condition.
2. If the pre-condition is not met, then any external effects should not be catastrophic.

A pre-condition like "final account balance must be sufficient to cover at least 30 days of debit activity" would violate the first rule, since there is no way for an application to predict the future account activity. A pre-condition that stated that "temperature change must not place reactor in a range that would cause reactor meltdown" would be an example of a violation of the second rule, since an invalid input could result in the loss of human life. Usually *catastrophic* will be based on the client's definition of the word, so pre-conditions will require getting them involved.

Keep in mind that with pre-conditions one does not expect violations. It is not a probability issue. Pre-condition violations are just a variation of the bug, where the application sets an attribute to an illegal value. Like any other software defect, it must be repaired. Suppose that the result of a pre-condition violation is that a utility company sent bills to its customers, overcharging them by 10 percent. Does this error represent a serious bug? Absolutely, and even though the utility company may wish to categorize it as catastrophic, it is not. First, the bug did not cause any unreasonable hardship, except to the utility company IT manager. And second, it can be reversed, repaired, and recovered.

8.8.2.1 Pre-conditions are part of a method's signature Since pre-conditions are part of the signature of a method, they cannot be added or strengthened after the fact without potentially negative effects on code that is already using them. Code that was reviewed as correct when the pre-condition required that the value of the withdrawn amount must not be greater than the account balance will be incorrect when the pre-condition is changed to require that the withdrawn amount not exceed the current balance less $200.00. This type of change is as dangerous as changing any other part of a method signature. On the other hand, removing or weakening a method pre-condition will not affect the correctness of the application. For example, if the withdraw method's implementation is changed to allow overdrafts, which means that the pre-condition is no longer required on the amount, all existing applications will still be in compliance.

8.8.3 Advantages

Pre-conditions can simplify a program's design and readability. Simplicity facilitates enhancements and reduces the probability of injecting new errors, which should offset any inconvenience owing to their failure.

Consider the message flow shown in Example 8-5, and suppose that sufficient funds are not available to complete the transaction. The Account class's withdraw method must include extra code to test the available balance and additional code to report if the withdraw was unsuccessful. The withdraw method in the customer object must have an extra three or four lines of code to check on the response from account and to report it to its caller, which requires the withdraw method in the Control class to add extra code to process the response from the Customer class's withdraw method.

Example 8-5 Error checking without the use of pre-conditions.

```
//Control class
ReturnCode withdraw(amount, cust, account) {
    int r = cust.withdraw(amount, account)
    if (r != 0)
        rc.set("NSF");
    else  rc.set("OK");
    return rc;
}

//Customer class
int withdraw(amount, account) {
    boolean b = account.withdraw(amount);
    if (b == true)
        return 0;
    else  return 1;
}

//Account class
boolean withdraw(amount) {
    if (amount > balance)
        return false;
    else {balance = balance - amount;
        return true;     }
}
```

Example 8-6 shows the simpler code within the account methods for customer and account, when using a pre-condition. Notice that pre-conditions make the methods not just smaller but simpler to read and comprehend.

Example 8-6 Error handling deferred using pre-conditions.

```
//Control class
ReturnCode withdraw(amount, cust, account) {
    double bal = account.getBalance();
    if (amount > bal))
        rc.set("ISF");
    else
        cust.withdraw(amount);
        rc.set("OK");
    return rc;
}

//Customer class
//Pre-condition: amount <= account.balance
void withdraw(amount, account) {
    b = account.withdraw(amount);
}

//Account class
//Pre-condition: amount <= account.balance
void withdraw(amount) {
    balance = balance - amount;
}
```

8.8.4 What pre-conditions are not

The goal of a pre-condition is not to allow invalid input. Method pre-conditions defer the responsibility to exclude bad data to that point in the application that is responsible for implementing the business rules. This allows validity checking to be done only once, keeping to a minimum the amount of code that must reject legal data values.

It could be argued that it makes more sense for the validation code to be placed only in the setter method, rather than have every part of the application that updates the associated attribute check its validity. This would be a good approach except for two things.

☞ If the application does not check the message argument for valid values before sending the message to the setter method, it needs to check for an error response after the method returns, so there is no real savings.

☞ The application quite often knows the value it is using is valid, so frequently no additional checks are required.

Another argument that favors performing data validation inside the object that owns the data is, as the rules of encapsulation suggest, that it is the object's responsibility to understand its own data. That argument is actually false; valid data values are part of the business rules and, therefore, belong to the application rather than the business objects.

8.8.5 Overriding pre-conditions

Recall that when overriding an invariant in a subclass, the new invariant had
to be stronger than its superclass counterpart; otherwise, the subclass would
violate the structural compatibility rule. However, a method pre-condition is
the exclusive property of the method that defines it, and new methods, including those created as part of specialization, can determine their own restrictions. Subclass methods are free to extend, reduce, or eliminate the overridden
method pre-condition without affecting the correctness of the superclass, or
the applications that use its objects.

As an example, assume an airline has a policy that only 80 percent of
available seats on a given flight will be sold in advance. One possible design,
to implement this rule, is to add a pre-condition on the sellTo method of the
Customer class.

```
//pre: seats + seatsSold <= .8 * seatsAvailable
sellTo (seats, flight, date)
```

Now consider a subclass of Customer called PreferredFlier. These
objects represent customers with special privileges, one of which is when they
buy a ticket, they will be allowed to purchase seats up to 95 percent of capac-
ity. So the PreferredFlier class overrides the sellTo method and changes the
pre-condition.

```
//pre: seats + seatsSold <= .95 * seatsAvailable
sellTo (seats, flight, date)
```

This presents no problem. If the business rule had been implemented as
an invariant, the override would have been illegal, since it defined a weaker
state. However, for an application to use the new sell method, it must first create an instance of the PreferredFlier subclass, and it is reasonable to assume
that the developers of the application are aware of the new business rules for
PreferredFliers. Unlike invariants, pre-conditions are design decisions and
are the exclusive property of the method designer. Here is one last point before
ending the discussion of pre-conditions: whenever a pre-condition modification
is the result of changes to business rules, it may be necessary to update the
use case description that is affected.

8.9 INHERITANCE

In Chapter 6, the discussion on strong typing showed how an object-oriented
design using inheritance and polymorphism could circumvent some problems related to strong typing. Joining several classes with a common superclass allows them to be viewed by the compiler as the same type. The
following example illustrates a design requirement solved with subclassing.
In Figure 8-1, VHS, DVD, and Game are all kinds of objects that can be
rented in the video store. By giving them a common superclass, any variable

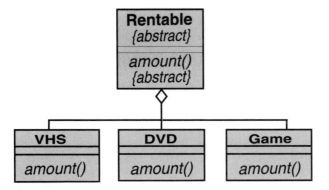

Fig. 8-1 Class hierarchy to facilitate polymorphism.

or parameter that needs to be able to operate on all these objects needs only declare its type as Rentable; then, it may use VHS, DVD, and Game objects interchangeably.

8.10 ABSTRACT CLASSES

In Figure 8-1 Rentable is an abstract class, which means that it cannot be instantiated, only subclassed. Abstract classes are a key feature of robust inheritance hierarchies for two reasons.

First, abstract classes are not business objects, but rather tools of the designer, and will not be affected by changes to the business rules. If the VHS or DVD class changes, it may be necessary to override methods in Rentable, but it is not necessary to change the Rentable class itself, since it is abstract and not part of the client's view of the data.

Second, abstract classes can have abstract methods, which can direct the implementation of their subclasses. The method amount() in the Rentable class is an abstract method. All concrete subclasses of Rentable are required to implement amount as a concrete method. This allows users of Rentable object to know for certain that they will be able to send the Rentable instance the amount() message.

When the class is pure-abstract, it has no concrete methods and no instance data (a Java interface is an example). Pure-abstract classes are the safest kind of superclass because there is nothing to change, and they can participate in a multiple inheritance hierarchy without the traditional problems multiple inheritance can cause. The example that follows explains this dilemma.

Consider the case where, in addition to having several items in the store that can be rented, there is a separate set of items that can be sold. Assume that there is some overlap of these items but that neither is a subset of the other. Without multiple inheritance, there would be no way to construct a hierarchy such that all sellable items have a superclass different from the one for rentable items and that any particular item could be a subclass of either sub-class or both. Using multiple inheritance, the new hierarchy allows a class to become a subclass of both Sellable and Rentable. But a multiple inheritance problem appears when both superclasses contain an identical method like computeProfit(). When the message computeProfit is sent to an object that shared these two superclasses, the message handler would have to somehow be given special instructions as to which computeProfit method to run. A simi-lar situation exists in the compiler when the two superclasses share an identi-cally named attribute. For this reason, many object-oriented languages have chosen not to implement multiple inheritance. Java solves the problem with pure-abstract classes (which it calls interfaces) that have only abstract meth-ods and no attributes. Since only interfaces may participate in multiple inher-itance hierarchies, the problems just described are eliminated. Any inherited method must be overridden in the concrete subclass so the message handler never reaches the point of having to choose a method amongst its two super-classes, and attributes only exist in the subclass.

8.11 REUSABLE HIERARCHIES

Many inheritance hierarchies are built not to support the design of an appli-cation but to be a product in and of itself. The feature of a class that makes it most reusable is to be designed independent of a single application and capa-ble of being adapted for use in many applications. These classes are best developed as part of their own project, and not as a byproduct of another application.

When a project is provided a specification, its primary goal is to create an application that will meet that specification. It is unreasonable to expect that the class designer will be able to see the bigger picture required to generalize a class's capabilities. Even if the designer is successful in this endeavor, general-izing the classes for reuse requires at least three times the effort. Because of this added cost, it makes more sense that this effort be funded as an indepen-dent IT activity, or that the classes be purchased rather than built in-house. When considering investment in this type of reuse, there are two major cate-gories of hierarchies to consider: class libraries and frameworks.

8.12 CLASS LIBRARIES

A class library is a collection of generalized classes with a broad range of uses across several applications. Many are provided as part of an object-oriented language and include utility classes that essentially define the language. Within an IT organization, a few classes may be developed and added to these libraries to provide projects with classes that can be used in multiple applica-tions across a common problem domain. Another source of reusable classes is independent vendors that offer libraries that provide extensions to the object-oriented language.

8.12.1 Features of class libraries

Classes packaged as part of class hierarchies tend to

- ☞ Be stable
- ☞ Be generalized
- ☞ Be intended for instantiation rather than subclassing
- ☞ Have utility function
- ☞ Come with deep hierarchies
- ☞ Have only minor use of aggregation and inheritance

They are classes that a developer might use across several applications. Examples include collections, date, time, numeric parse functions, scientific, geometric, statistical, trigonometric, physical science subroutines, and extended user interface objects. In a class library, most classes are part of small independent groups that only occasionally interact with each other, but they are appropriate for use within many diverse applications. A few classes may be related by aggregation, and classes related by inheritance are usually a case of simple specialization. There are relatively few abstract classes, and those that exist are refactored from their subclasses.

8.13 FRAMEWORKS

Frameworks are class libraries as well, but frameworks are specific to a particular domain. This domain may be technical, or the domain may be industry or application specific. Frameworks will have a much higher percentage of abstract classes. Framework classes will be high in functionality, and rely on their subclasses to implement abstract methods. Within a single IT organization, application frameworks may have a lower reuse rate than class libraries, but they will make up a larger part of the application in which they are included. Therefore, they are almost always purchased rather than built in-house. Class libraries are also purchased, but when the possibility of reuse is high, some elements may be developed within the IT organization. Frameworks are usually built and sold as a single unit, but class libraries are more likely to evolve over time. Java's Swing user interface classes act as a framework, whereas the original Java Advanced Windowing Toolkit (AWT) package behaves more like a class library.

8.13.1 Type of frameworks

Frameworks fall into three general categories.

☞ Application Frameworks: These include advanced collection hierarchies and some database front ends.

☞ Technical Frameworks: These are the sophisticated user interfaces like Java's Swing, relational database wrappers for persistence support, and in some cases low-level classes that support existing business objects.

☞ Industry Frameworks: These are specific to a problem domain. There are frameworks for banking, insurance, retail, etc. Developers use industry frameworks as their base, and develop applications as a refinement of them.

Frameworks rely heavily on abstract classes, with perhaps as much as 80 percent of their total classes being abstract, and their abstract classes contain a large number of abstract methods. A banking application framework might have classes like Account, Customer, Loan, Transaction, and even SavingsAccount and CheckingAccount, many of which are abstract. These classes would contain basic banking methods like deposit, writeCheck, makePayment, withdraw, transfer, and getPayment, many of which might be abstract. Application designers would then implement the details of these methods to customize the application for their environment.

8.14 ENCAPSULATION

8.14.1 Preserving encapsulation

Implementation is an appropriate place to discuss encapsulation, since it is the time when the programmer, for both good and bad reasons, chooses to break the rules of encapsulation. Some situations require that the class expose what should normally be private information about its state. There are also cases where the implementation architecture takes the control of encapsulation out of the hands of the programmer. For example, when an object-oriented application shares a database with non-object-oriented applications, it is impossible to maintain the constraints that encapsulation made so simple. The important thing to remember about encapsulation is that the decision to violate object orientation's prime directive should be deferred until as late as possible in the process, usually during performance testing. Here are the guidelines to follow when considering breaking encapsulation.

☞ Do not use public attributes as a convenience. Force the team to justify each use of a public attribute.

☞ Never anticipate the need to override encapsulated data. Wait until the problem arises. Avoid the temptation to design around encapsulation.

☞ A public attribute is not an excuse to bypass the get/set interfaces. When a public attribute is created to circumvent a performance problem in one part of the application, do not treat it as a public attribute in another part unless that part of the application can also justify the need to access the attribute directly.

☞ Record the name of methods using direct access to an attribute adjacent to the public attribute in the class specification. This will allow you to identify potentially broken code if the design of the data within the object containing the public attributes changes.

8.14.2 Getters and setters

In every other case, make all of an object's attributes private and supply getter and setter methods to access them. These methods should be used even within the object itself. Since private variables do not require that the methods of its class use these accessor methods, it will require discipline on the part of the team. Enforcement of this discipline will usually fall on the shoulders of the class owner and project manager.

Beyond the benefits of encapsulation that getters and setters support, there are other advantages to the process of using the get and set methods exclusively as the means of accessing an object's attributes.

8.14.2.1 Value change management Having exactly one method that changes an attribute means that there is only one place to include notification code when its value changes. It also means that a debug trap can be set in just one place when trying to find how and when an attribute acquired a specific value.

8.14.2.2 Advanced typing When the attribute's language-defined type is not strong enough that the compiler will be able to guarantee its legal values, the setter can be used to check for and reject those values outside the required subtype. In languages like Smalltalk that have no typing, unless the setter performs type checking, there will be none.

8.14.2.3 Simple invariants Invariants are a special case of attribute typing, except that the legal values of an attribute may be dependent on current values in other attributes. For example, the value of day of the month is dependent on the values in the attributes month and year. If inconsistent values are considered an error, the setter for day of month can perform this check.

8.14.2.4 Managing redundant data A getter method allows encapsulation of the decision to retrieve or calculate redundant data on request in lieu of maintaining a copy of the information and returning it as needed. As the business processes change and it becomes necessary to change the way redundant data are managed, only the setter method of the attribute in the primary object and the getter methods of the attribute in the secondary object will need to be changed.

8.14.2.5 Pre-conditions   When pre-conditions were discussed earlier, it was
stated that one of the rules for allowing a pre-condition was a violation would
not be considered catastrophic. Suppose after implementation of the application, it is determined that the pre-condition should have been an invariant
and managed by the object. The setter can be changed to check for illegal values and reject the update. This same technique can be used during test, to
temporarily check for constraint violations. After testing is complete, that
debug code needs to be removed from only one place.

8.14.2.6 Synchronization   If it becomes necessary to restrict access to an
object or its attributes to a single thread, the getters and setters can act as the
serialization point. This is not a general rule, and there are many cases when
serialization needs to be at a higher functional level.

8.15 PUBLIC VS. PRIVATE METHODS

During design most of the methods detailed are public. It is normally the case
that private methods, even if specified during design, may have their detail
deferred until implementation. It should be a project default that all new
methods created during implementation will be private. Given the choice, it is
always preferable to make a method private. Private methods are easier to
maintain, since they have the flexibility of changing their signature while only
impacting the other methods in the class when they do. It is always possible to
promote a private method to public. On the other hand, after a method is public, changing either its signature or semantics, or converting it to private, will
have an impact on code that is not easily identified, and may affect the project
schedule.

8.16 SUPPORT OF THE TEST AND USER INTERFACE (UI) TEAMS

Two special implementation responsibilities of the development team must be
completed before beginning use case design. The first is the creation of the
skeleton control class, and the second is to provide getter method access to the
business objects and their attributes in support of test case validation.

8.16.1 Skeleton control object

When the use cases are "agreed to" at the end of requirements, one of the first
tasks the developers must complete is the creation of the skeleton control
class with a method for EVERY use case in the application, not just the current increment. These methods have no body other than a return of a null
object. The classes are provided to the use case testers and the UI team to
allow them to compile their programs. Having the application development

team supply these methods rather than letting the testers and interface developers write their own version guarantees that all the teams are working from the same set of requirements. That is, they are all writing or using methods with the same signature. These classes will change as requirements change and must be updated and redistributed whenever

☞ A new use case is added,

☞ The order, number, or type of a parameter of a use case changes,

☞ The returnCode content changes.

The skeleton control object embodies requirements definition in a way that makes it clear if one or more of the teams are out of sync. When a requirement does change, either a test case or a user interface class will no longer compile, and the teams will recognize it. Since the control class is owned by development, it is their responsibility to maintain and distribute it as quickly as possible after changes have been "agreed to." If the development team delays getting this package to the other teams, the completion of their task will be impacted.

8.16.2 Test getter methods

The test planners identify attributes within the business objects that need to be accessed to validate that the use cases being tested correctly update the state of the business objects. The developer must provide getter methods that give the test cases the ability to access the business object collections, their members, and the attributes within the business objects. Many of these getters will have already been provided when the class was defined. For the remaining attributes, this access must be provided as soon as possible and should be one of the first tasks performed during implementation.

8.17 RUNTIME SCENARIOS

During coding, developers will often identify scenarios that were impossible to predict during requirements. They are related to specifics of the language, hardware, operating system, or peripheral software like database systems. They include errors like "insufficient memory," "device IO errors," and runtime logic errors such as exceeding the bounds of an array. Some of these errors will be handled as exceptions; a few may require changing the requirements to add a new scenario.

8.17.1 Error recovery and reporting

Since most of these runtime errors and exceptions were not foreseen until code, the user interface will not expect them, and the testers will not have created test cases for them. Therefore, the implementers need to communicate these conditions by having the control method return a unique return code, with an explanatory message. When the test case logs the discrepancy, the message will identify it as a non-business-rule error. If the user interface does not recognize the return code, it will display the default message provided and correctly assume that the use case failed.

Note that when the implementation language supports exception handling, the control method will act as the collection point of these failures. It is not advisable to allow the interface to process exceptions directly; instead the returnCode object that is returned from the control object should provide this information.

Test Planning

*T*his chapter discusses use case testing in general and the test planning activity in detail. It includes an explanation of all the elements of the test plan. It describes the reasons that test planning and test case development are separate activities in OODP.

9.1 TESTING USE CASES

Use case testing is not system, integration, stress, or acceptance testing. It is functional testing. It is the use case version of an application's unit test, and since the application is independent of the user interface, the goal is to completely test the application without involving the user interface.

Use case testing is not just testing a use case, but testing using use cases; that is, each test case will use other use cases to establish the pre-condition of the scenario to be tested. Every scenario will have one or more test cases and only use cases will be used to create those tests. The reasons for using use cases to test use cases are, first, if there is not at least one sequence of use cases that can create the scenario pre-condition, then either there is a missing use case, or the use case to be tested has an impossible outcome. Second, creating the pre-conditions by means other than using use cases may create an invalid test.

As an example, assume that the application has a defect in that no use case currently exists that changes a member's status from "eligible" to "ineligible" when videos that he or she has rented become overdue. The plan for the scenario *"member with overdue videos is attempting to rent another video"* is to rent a video and allow it to go overdue, and then attempt to rent a second video. The test will fail because the member's status was never set to "ineligible," and the member will be allowed to rent the second video.

Contrast this with the test plan that modifies the customer's status to "ineligible" before running. With this approach, the test of rentVideo will succeed (that is, the rent use case will reject the rental), but the flaw in the application is missed, and the missing use case may never be detected until perhaps late in the process.

9.1.1 Use case test plan

A use case test plan is developed from the basic use case definitions recorded during requirements and is more narrative than procedural. It identifies the set of use cases that establish the scenario pre-condition and the validation steps to determine whether the scenario post-condition is correct. Even though the pre-condition state is achieved by running other use cases, post-condition validation must access the business objects directly. For example, the plan to establish the pre-condition and test the scenario "successfully rent a video" might be

> Add a video and a member and have that member rent the video. The response should be okay.

However, for validating the post-condition, it is more efficient and effective to examine the business objects directly. So that part of the plan might state

> Check to see that the video is rented to the member and marked unavailable and the member count of rented videos is equal to 1.

Since there are other ways to achieve an equally valid pre-condition state, the test plan should show at least one or two alternatives that will be used. For example, other tests would be

> Add two members and two videos and have each member rent one of the videos.

> Add a member and a video. Have the member rent the video, return it, and rent it again.

Professional testers usually have insight into what makes for the best test cases.

9.1.2 Initializing the test case

Every test must be run from a well-defined state. That means the exact value of every variable that is part of the pre-condition or changed by the post-condition is known. If this is not assured, two problems will arise during the testing process. First, failed tests may be impossible to debug because it will not be possible to recreate the exact state of the system when the test ran previously. Second, if the values of all attributes were not precisely known before the test is run, there would be no way to know for sure if the post-condition state was accurately attained.

In order to guarantee a known state, every test must start with no objects in the system, other than empty collections. The test case will create and initialize all the objects required for the test case pre-condition. Although this may seem like an unnecessary burden on the tester, the value of this approach far outweighs any extra work. There are ways to simplify this setup that will be discussed in the next chapter.

9.2 THE USE CASE TESTING PROCESS

Testing in OODP has four phases.

- ☞ **Test planning.** This phase occurs immediately after requirements. Its input is the list of use cases and their outcomes.

- ☞ **Test case design.** This phase, which begins during analysis, uses the business rules documented in the decision tables to define the pre- and post-conditions more accurately.

- ☞ **Test case development.** This phase starts as soon as the development and test teams agree that the test cases, as designed, will test all the business rules. The deliverable is the code that runs and evaluates each test case.

- ☞ **Test execution, evaluation, and correction.** This phase of testing, which begins sometime during application implementation, runs all the tests and determines whether the tests were successful. If necessary, corrections are made to either the test case or the application, and the test is rerun. This cycle of execution, evaluation, and correction continues until all tests have run successfully against the same version of the application.

The following topics provide a more detailed description of each of the test phases. The details of the steps in creating and reviewing the deliverables for the test planning phase are covered in this chapter. Chapter 10 covers the details of the other three test phases.

9.2.1 Test planning

The test plan is the definition of how use cases will be verified. It specifies the process and, at a high level, how the pre-conditions of each scenario will be established. It accomplishes this by identifying a sequence of use cases that will create the desired state. The test plan also describes the post-conditions that will be validated. For scenarios that change the state of the system, this usually means checking every changed attribute. For scenarios whose business rules reject the update, this may involve checking one or more attributes to see that they have not changed. The test plan should also specify whether any returned information is expected as part of the ReturnCode object.

9.2.2 Test case design

The test case design is a rework of the test plan based on the business rules that were defined during analysis. The design records the details of the messages required to invoke the use cases that establish the test's pre-condition. Another message is defined with input values that will elicit the correct scenario in the use case to be tested. Finally, the design records the test case post-condition validation by defining code that will interrogate the business object's attributes and compare their values to the expected values. Test design is complete when the test design details for all test cases for this increment are reviewed and approved.

9.2.3 Test case development

The difference between test case design and development is that the former is a textual description of the programming required whereas the latter is the program code that will run the test. Combining these into a single activity is a common practice when the same team is doing both tasks. Test case development creates the test object that contains all of the test cases. Test development is complete when all the test cases compile correctly. This requires that all the business object classes, with the test support methods included, be delivered to the test team before the end of this phase of testing.

9.2.4 Test execution, evaluation, and correction

The test object and its main method automate execution of test cases. The more critical task in test execution is, when failures occur, determining whether the failure was the fault of the test or the application. This phase is a combined effort of test and development, and it may require several iterations before all tests run error free and uninterrupted. Uninterrupted means that the entire test suite in the test object runs without a single failure. If a test failure requires a change to an application object, the entire set of tests is rerun.

The details of these last three steps are explained in Chapter 10.

9.3 CREATING AND REVIEWING THE TEST PLAN

This section explains the details of the test plan. As mentioned earlier, a test plan contains the specifics for each planned test case. A test case has three parts:

☞ Identify the use case and scenario to be tested.

☞ Describe how the scenario pre-condition will be established using available use cases.

☞ Describe how the scenario's post-condition will be validated.

Test plans are written only for the use cases in the current increment. That means that they may assume that only the current and the previous increment's use cases are available. For example, a test plan that stated it would test "add a video successfully," by first adding it and deleting it, is assuming that the delete video use case is available in this increment, which may not be true. Even when the use case is available, it is better to base post-condition tests on direct examination of the data rather than the success or failure of a use case.

One of the problems uncovered by test planning occurs when a use case required to establish the pre-condition for a scenario is not available. For example, suppose increment one contained only the use cases add video and remove video. There would be no way in this increment to test the scenario remove a rented video since rent is not included. This design of the test plan will require that the entire use case be retested when rent is eventually added in a later increment. Try to avoid these partial increments because they are inefficient. If they are absolutely necessary, then create a section of the test plan that refers to future increments and document it there. In this way, the required retest of this use case will not get overlooked. Otherwise, the use case may incorrectly be considered tested and complete since all the tests ran correctly. The problem is that all the scenarios were not tested.

9.3.1 Establishing the pre-condition

The test plan should say in words how the pre-condition will be established. These sentences should reference the use cases used to achieve this state. A test plan description for the OK scenario of the returnVideo use case might be written as

> Add a member and a video, have the member rent the video and return it two days later.

Since there are an almost limitless number of ways to establish the pre-condition, the test plan's objective is to identify which ones will be used. This allows the client an opportunity to see how closely the test mirrors real business scenarios. A test plan for return overdue, which has the member renting a video and returning it 60 days late, while possible, may not represent the typical user environment situation, and the client may insist on a more realistic test where the video is returned a day or two late. The reason for planning test cases before writing them is that changes can be accommodated while the test details are still informal. The test plan should attempt to provide at least two ways to establish pre-conditions for each rejection scenario and three

ways to test the scenarios that make modifications to the object's state. Once
reviewed, the decision may be made to not implement all these tests, or the
team may decide to add more.

9.3.2 Validating the test

Part of the test plan is describing the attributes that will be checked to ensure
that the use case correctly established the post-condition of the scenario. In
the case of successfully return a video, the test plan post-condition might be

> Ensure that
>> video is marked available,
>> member rent count is decreased,
>> member fines are not increased.

Even though the business rules have not been completely spelled out during requirements, some obvious state changes need to occur to support the
other use case scenarios. It is already known that two of the outcomes of rent-
Video are "member has maximum videos rented" and "video is already rented."
Therefore, the business objects will need to remember that a video was successfully rented or returned. This planning is not infringing on either analysis
or design by assuming that there will be ways to make these checks. Later in
test design, when the business rules have been identified and recorded, the
post-condition checks will become more specific and may need to be changed.

When the initial and final states of all objects are the same, as in "renting
an already rented video," testing for the correct final state is checking to see
that nothing changed. Technically, this would involve checking every attribute
for identity, which would be unreasonable. However, experienced testers usually have an idea where to look for changes that should not have occurred, and
one suggestion is to check just one or two attributes for each identity scenario
but make it a different attribute for each scenario. For example, when
attempting to rent an already rented video, make sure that the member rent
count was not increased. When attempting to rent an invalid video, check that
number of rentals is still the same; and when trying to rent to an ineligible
member, check that the video was not inadvertently marked available. This
provides coverage for multiple attributes but spreads the identity checks over
several test cases.

Validation of state requires getter access to attributes in the business
objects and the control object. The developers will need to provide these for all
the attributes specified in the test plan. One of the purposes of test planning is
to identify these methods early so that they can be added to the classes for the
current increment. Avoid requesting methods that provide functionality for a
class that will not be used anywhere but in test. For example, consider the
testing of the "already rented" scenario of the rent use case where the test case
needs to ensure that the member object was not charged a late fee. The testers
might ask the developers to provide the method:

```
"boolean customerHasLateFees()".
```

However, if that functionality is not required anywhere else in the system, it would be better to use a basic getter for late fees such as:

```
"double getLateFees()"
```

In general, use only getters for test case validation whenever possible.

9.3.3 Approving the test plan

When the test plan is complete, it should be reviewed with the client and the use case owner. Each of these individuals will have a different perspective on what the test should accomplish. The use case owner is interested in seeing that the test is complete with respect to its validation of the post-condition, whereas the client is more interested in determining that the test is representative of the way the application will be used in the environment. Since, by definition, the business rules are not understood during requirements, avoid criticizing the test plan for accurately validating the post-condition. This facet will be reviewed in detail during test case design which will begin toward the end of analysis.

9.3.4 Test plan correctness questions

Test planning like analysis or requirements gathering creates a formal interpretation of an informal need. Correctness is a matter of asking the client, "Do we have it right?" For this reason some of the correctness questions are more informal than formal.

- ☞ Do the use cases that establish the pre-condition refer only to use cases in this or a previous increment?
- ☞ Can every scenario of every use case be tested in this increment; if not, how has the fact that a retest is required been documented?
- ☞ Has development agreed to provide the test support methods to give access to the business objects for the purpose of scenario post-condition evaluation?
- ☞ Do the clients and use case owners agree that test coverage is complete and sufficient?
- ☞ Is every post-condition check possible given pre-condition setup?

9.4 A SIMPLE TEST PLAN FOR THE VIDEO STORE

Here is a partial test plan for the video store use cases: addMember and rent-Video.

9.4.1 Test Case: addMember

Scenario—**OK**
> Add a new member.
> Try to find the added member in the member list.

Scenario—**Duplicate Name**
> Add a member.
> Add a member with the same name.
> Size of member list should be 1.

9.4.2 Test Case: rentVideo

Scenario—**OK1**
> Add a video and a member.
> Have the member rent the video.
> Retrieve the rental for this video and make sure that it is rented to the correct member.
> Member's rent count should be 1.
> Video status should be "rented."

Scenario—**OK2**
> Add a video and a member.
> Have the member rent the video and return the video.
> Have the same member rent the same video again.
> Retrieve the rental for this video and make sure that it is rented to the correct member.
> Video status should be "rented."
> Member rent count should be 1.
> Size of rental list should be 1.

Scenario—**Invalid Member ID**
> Add a video.
> Try to rent the video with any member name.
> Size of rental list should be zero.

Scenario—**Invalid Video***
> Add a new member.
> Then have the member rent any video title.
> Video status should still be "available."

Scenario—**Member has max rentals**
> Add a member.
> Add four different videos.
> Have the member rent three of these videos.
> Try to rent a fourth.
> Last Video should still be "available."

Scenario—**Video unavailable**

Add a video.

Add a member.

Have the member rent the video.

Have the member try to rent the same video.

Size of rental list should be 1.

Scenario—**Member has overdue fines**

Add two different videos.

Add a member.

Have the member rent one of the videos.

Make the date three days later.

Have the member try to rent the other video.

Second video status should be "available."

Notice that the test of a successful scenario checked every state change that was known at the time. The exception scenarios picked one attribute and made sure that it did not change. When tests for all scenarios are run, they will have checked multiple attributes for identity.

The post-condition check for the invalid video scenario of rent video* is incorrect because its validation implies that the video is still available since the rent failed. However, there was never any video added, so there is no object to check the status of. This is the most common type of error in test planning. It will be found quickly in design, but it is included here as a demonstration of the kinds of defects that are caught by correctness question number 5.

In the OK scenario test case of the addMember use case, the validation suggests trying to find the added member in the Member list. This requires that the test have access to the list of members and that a method for that class be provided to search for a member. No attempt is made at this time to name either of these methods. That will be done as part of the review of these plans with the development team.

Another way to validate that the member was added would have been to try to delete it. This is valid, but only if the delete use case is part of this or a prior increment. It is reasonable to ask the development team to enhance the business classes with getter methods not required for the current increment, but it is not productive to ask that use cases be added to support test validation of a scenario. Whenever possible, use getter methods to validate scenario post-conditions.

Notice the OK2 scenario of rent video. The plan is to have a member rent, return, and rerent the same video. This is a situation where the client might ask to change the plan to have a different member rent the returned video to get a more realistic event captured by the test case.

9.5 WHY TEST PLANNING IS A SEPARATE ACTIVITY

OODP defines test planning as an activity separate from test case development. Even though all the testing activities could be lumped together under a single task referred to as test, there are five important reasons why it is identified as a step that is prerequisite to test case development.

- ☞ Test case development must wait for the business rules to be well defined and agreed to before it can know how to validate that the use case is correct.
- ☞ Developers need to be made aware as soon as possible of the test support methods required.
- ☞ The skills required to develop a test plan differ enormously from those required to develop test cases.
- ☞ Test planning can help identify missing requirements.
- ☞ Test plans written using informal sentences are more conducive to changes.

9.5.1 Writing test plans before the business rules are available

The business rules that define the pre- and post-conditions of use case scenarios will not be available for some time. If the test team waits for this detail before beginning the test planning process, too much valuable time will be wasted. There will usually be sufficient information in the requirements to make inferences about how to establish most scenario pre-conditions and validate their post-conditions. The outcomes of deleteVideo already specify that it cannot be deleted if it is rented. In this case, the pre-condition is pretty well understood, and since pre-conditions are established by running other use cases, it is not necessary to know how the rent will alter the state of the video object. It is sufficient for planning just to know that it will. Even validation of post-conditions, which is more dependent on attribute values, can be stated abstractly, and the detail can be added in test case design. Based on the outcomes in the use case definition of rentVideo, it is known that there needs to be a way to determine whether a video is already rented, that a member exists, and that the member does not have more than three videos currently rented. Therefore, it is reasonable for the test plan to assume that once a video is rented, there will be a way to determine the video's status, as well as the number of videos a member has rented. The activity of trying to record these steps without the precise detail will give the testers additional insight into what is essential for these tests to be correct.

9.5.2 Notifying developers of the test support methods

When the test plan is complete, the test team provides the developers with a list of the methods required to retrieve business data for the purpose of validating the post-condition. Test development will require these methods to compile the test cases. The planning process is intended to help the tester identify these support methods very early in the process and to give the developers time to plan their implementation along with the methods defined as a result of use case design.

9.5.3 The test plan skills

Writing test plans is not a technical programming task. It can be accomplished by anyone familiar with the problem domain and its business processes. That person can be anyone who understands how systems in the problem domain are used by their actors. With a small amount of training, both the analyst and client are capable of performing this task. In cases where the analysis is done by a team other than development, this is a very practical approach. By making test planning separate from development, the project manager has the flexibility to use a different resource to staff both tasks.

9.5.4 Test planning helps identify product requirements

While the team is developing the test plan, they will find that the information necessary to write its details raises questions about the requirements. This may help identify overlooked use cases, scenarios, and object attributes. For example, it is obvious that to test the "member has overdue videos" scenario of rent video, the video must be rented. But what use case makes the video overdue? While the answer to the question is not important for this example, the fact that the test plan raised the question is.

9.5.5 Test plans are easier to change

Since these plans are informal, there will be less resistance on the part of the test case developers to consider changes. During review, simple changes can be noted as comments in the margin of the plan. Complex changes may require a rewrite of the plan for one or two use cases, but only if a rereview is required and the change is considered crucial. In most cases, the test case design will serve as the changed plan. It is not necessary to keep the test plan as a permanent deliverable since it is superseded by the tests themselves.

For all these reasons, it makes sense to separate the creation of the use case test plan from the development of the test cases.

After the test plans are reviewed and approved and the use case business rules from analysis are available, the test team can move on to the task of writing the actual test cases.

Test Case Development and Execution

*T*his chapter describes how the test plan is implemented and how to build the test object. It combines test case design and development into a single activity and discusses statistical and random testing.

10.1 TEST CASE DESIGN VS. TEST CASE DEVELOPMENT

This chapter combines the discussion of the design of test cases and their development. OODP defines each of these as separate activities since they have different deliverables and goals. Test case design is much like application design in that it provides for a more abstract approach to recording and reviewing the test cases. Test cases are normally written in the same language as the application; therefore, if an application were to be dispersed onto multiple platforms requiring different languages, it would be necessary to rewrite all the test cases for each language. In that environment, it may make more sense to have a separate test case design deliverable. However, most of the time test cases will be written directly from the revised test plan, and no test case designs will exist.

173

10.2 THE TEST OBJECT

Test case development is built around a test object. Each test case is a method within it. The Test class will need an instance variable for each control class in the increment and a static method that contains the statements to execute all of the tests. Test cases should return a boolean so that the main test method can report such information as 7 out of 140 tests failed. The details of the failures will be recorded by the test case in the test log.

10.2.1 The standalone test case

Every test case starts with an empty system (no business objects) and is independent of all other test cases. It is responsible for creating its own precondition for the scenario it tests and need not be concerned about the state of the system when it completes. The test case establishes the pre-condition first by initializing the system to empty and then by sending a series of messages to the application control object. After the pre-condition state is achieved, it invokes the method in the control object for the use case to be tested. This is followed with a series of messages to the control and business objects to validate the post-condition.

10.2.2 Advantages

Standalone tests are an important element of OODP. They have the following advantages:

☞ They are repeatable. That means that every time the test runs, it runs with the exact same sequence of messages from the exact same state. This eliminates the problem of failures that cannot be recreated.

☞ All tests are independent of each other. When the first 19 tests out of 20 fail, it does not invalidate the execution of the 20th. Each test will pass or fail on its own merit. All the tests that ran before have NO effect on the execution of the current test.

☞ Standalone tests are easier to debug. Because each test runs the exact same way every time, the programmer can set breakpoints and traps at the places in the code where the failure may have started and be certain that the test will go through those traps every time. This makes problem determination much simpler.

☞ They can easily be rerun without complex setup. When a test case is dependent on the results of the tests that preceded it, the setup is more complex because the tester must ensure that each of the other tests ran exactly as expected before execution of the final test. This can require extensive time to "set up" the test.

Even with independent testing, one failed use case can block testing of another. If the addVideo use case is not working correctly, it will prevent the testing of all use cases that are dependent on it.

10.2.3 The test object's init() method

The key to the standalone test case is the test object's testInit() method that invokes the testInit() methods in all the application control objects that are part of the system being tested. These control object methods are created by the development team. The testInit() methods are responsible for returning the system to its initial state. These methods will include some or all the following actions:

☞ Resetting every collection object to empty

☞ Setting the date to a known and expected value

☞ Seeding random numbers so that generated sequences are predictable

☞ Anything that places the system in a state that is considered its most primitive, and for which there is no other valid state that existed before it

As an example of the last bullet referring to the most primitive state of the system, consider a table that defines the reporting periods of the business year. Assume that the new application's requirements specify only changing this table, not creating it. For the application to work correctly, this table must already exist. If the table is omitted, a use case that "alters fiscal quarter report date by (qtr, days)" will not function correctly. On the other hand, a system whose use cases include a behavior such as "set fiscal qtr reporting date(qtr, date)" should assume that no table exists, since any such table can be created, and the most primitive state is for the table not to exist.

If there is a special test initialization function that is only required for a single test case, work with the development team to design and implement this capability as another testXxxx() methods. Once the application goes into production, all testXxxx() methods should be removed or at least disabled. Disabling can be accomplished by commenting out all the code and renaming the methods to errTestXxxx(). This will prevent accidental use.

10.2.4 The test support requirements

Development has the responsibility of supplying the test team with three implementation items.

☞ A skeleton control object that has the signature (but no body) of every method in the increment

☞ All the ReturnCode subclasses

☞ The business object classes with the getters required by test to do post-condition validation

These items are necessary for the test team to be able to compile the test object. This package should be created as soon as possible after analysis use cases and test plans are reviewed and agreed to as correct.

Since requirements will change, these objects will also change, and will need to be refreshed. In some cases, the control objects will be replaced with new ones that have a partial implementation of the increment's use cases. These may need to be accompanied by the latest version of the business object classes in order for the control class to compile correctly. Deferring all changes to the next increment will alleviate this problem.

When development has completed the implementation phase of the increment, this control object is replaced with one that contains the use case methods to be tested. At this time, it will be necessary to transport all the business classes from development to the test platform before running the tests. If development and test are being done on separate computers, always move development code to the test computer and not the other way around. This forces development to identify and gather up all the pieces of the increment and to leave behind old versions and stub code. It is not unusual for the test machine to have compiler errors when the test and application classes are first compiled together. The errors are usually caused by the following situations.

- ☞ The control object is not clean. That is, it still has references to items that were not included in the build.
- ☞ Development has changed the signature of a use case. This can be on the control method or information within the returnCode object.
- ☞ Development has eliminated or changed the name of a getter method required by the test team.

10.3 THE RETURN CODE OBJECT

Use case methods in the control object need a way to communicate back to the object that invoked them whether the caller is the test object or the user interface object. The object that sends the control object a message needs to know:

- ☞ Whether the use case was successful
- ☞ Specific returned data to be provided to the user

The least amount of information required is a numeric return code that uniquely identifies the scenario, and a message that explains it textually, like "$500.00 successfully deposited in account 12345." A ReturnCode class like the one shown in Table 10-1 with getters for the numeric return code and the message would suffice for most use cases. However, if the use case needs to report additional information, such as a new balance, then ReturnCode will be subclassed, and a new attribute and a getter for balance can be added. A

Table 10-1 Example of the basic ReturnCode class.

```
public class ReturnCode {
    int result;
    String message;

    public String getMessage() {
        return message;
    }

    public int getResult() {
        return result;
    }

    public ReturnCode(int rc, String msg) {
        result = rc;
        message = msg;
    }
```

hierarchy of these classes would provide a means to return any amount of information to the test and user interface objects (see Figure10-1).

Each test case will use the numeric return code in the ReturnCode object to compare to the expected value. If these values do not agree, the test case will report the discrepancy as an error. When validating a use case, the test case should be able to predict the exact value of the other ReturnCode attributes; incorrect values should be considered an error in the post-condition.

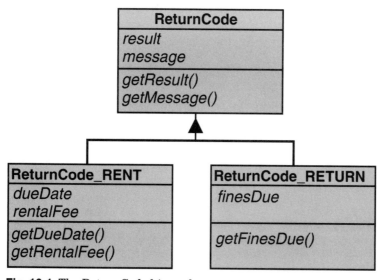

Fig. 10-1 The ReturnCode hierarchy.

10.4 WRITING THE TEST CASES

As a review, recall that each executable test case has three parts.

☞ Establishing the pre-condition. This includes the testInit() function.

☞ Running the test case and validating the return code.

☞ Validating the post-condition.

Each test case will start with a message to all the control objects to invoke their testInit methods. This is followed by a series of messages that invoke the use case methods in the control objects to establish the scenario pre-condition. Each of these messages will have specific values for their parameters that will allow the test case to predict the final system state and returned values.

10.4.1 Establishing the pre-condition

The test case establishes the pre-condition based on the test plan, but care must be taken to first review the business rules as defined in the analysis decision table for this use case description because they may have changed since the test plan was written. The values chosen for the control method parameters are based on what scenario and post-condition are desired. In some cases, the values returned from one message sent to the control method will be required as the parameter on a subsequent message. For example, suppose that the use case addMember takes arguments of name, phone, and credit card and returns to the user a member identification that must be used for all subsequent transactions for that member. Test cases for most scenarios of the rentVideo and deleteMember use cases will need to extract the generated memberId from the returnCode object provided as a result of creating the member and provide it on subsequent use cases.

10.4.2 Setup methods

Requiring the test cases to start from the "empty" state forces them to go through several identical sequences of setup before each test. For example, consider the more complex version of the video store application; all the scenarios for rentVideo, returnVideo, payFines, and one each of the deleteVideo and deleteMember scenarios must invoke the following use cases as part of their pre-condition setup:

```
addVendor(...)
addCategory(...)
addVideo(...)
defineBranch(...)
addCopy(...)
addMember(...)
createRental()
```

This could be accomplished with several cut-and-paste steps by the tester, but a more efficient approach is to create a test setup method that runs this sequence of use cases. This new method may now be invoked as part of any test case that requires the particular use case that the setup method provides. This greatly simplifies the test case itself, and saves a lot of typing as well.

To facilitate understanding and use, name the setup methods based on the state that they establish. The preceding example might be named "start-RentalAgreement."

When using test setup methods, consider having two or three versions that establish a similar, but not identical, pre-condition. For example, the preceding sequence of use cases could be augmented with a different set that adds multiple vendors, branches, and categories. It could then create several copies of more than one video title. By having several ways to create a commonly used state, the test cases stay fresh and avoid the problem of always starting from an identical state.

10.4.3 Running the test

The messages used to establish the pre-condition will have defined the legal and illegal values required to test the use case scenario. The test developer must ensure that all these values are known. In some cases it may be necessary to request the development team to provide special getter and setter methods to support establishing the pre-condition. For example, recall the use case that assigned the member identification when a new member was added. In the add member use case, the memberId was returned as an attribute in the returnCode object, but consider the case where it is not returned but e-mailed to the user for security reasons. How does the test case that needs to delete this id find the system-generated character string? The solution requires the application developer to provide a method that returns the last generated memberId. This may require that the control object remember a value that it normally would have discarded.

10.4.4 Using the return code object

The returnCode object contains the numeric return code of the scenario, and any attributes that need to be returned to the interface as part of the use case signature. The test case will compare the numeric return code for the correct value. The test code should compare every returned attribute within the returnCode object to the value expected by the test case. These checks are critical to determining the correctness of this scenario within the use case. Any differences in the expected and actual values must be recorded in the test object error log.

10.4.5 Validating the post-condition

In addition to return codes and returned values, the test case must retrieve every attribute that the business rules specified as being altered and compare its value to that expected by the test case. Much of this information is not taken from the test plan but from the details of the use case description that were not available during test planning.

10.4.5.1 Scenarios with no state changes   Some scenarios are transaction rejections and perform no changes in the business objects; others merely perform queries on the data and return information. These were never intended to alter state. For scenarios of the first type, choose an attribute that would have changed if the use case had been successful and make sure that it still has its original value. These comparisons include checking the following:

☞ Attribute values for identity

☞ The size of collections to see that they have not changed

☞ Ensuring that objects were not erroneously removed from or added to a collection

If each scenario tests a different condition, the overall use case test will have checked most attributes for identity.

Query use cases, which have no change component, are easier since there are usually only one or two scenarios and the validation is focused on the returnCode object rather than the system state. For these test cases, no special business attribute getters will be necessary.

10.4.5.2 Reporting and recording success or failure   Test methods need to report two potential pieces of information:

☞ A boolean indicating whether the test was successful or not and an indication of the failure if there was one. The success indicator boolean variable can be returned from the test method.

☞ Log the details of a failure in a way that allows them to be reviewed by both testers and developers.

The latter element means ideally that there should be a hard copy of this log available. It is not necessary to log successful tests, and doing so makes it harder to find the failures, which one can assume there should be fewer of. The logged failure should contain enough information to identify the specific test case that caused it and the details of what went wrong: invalid return code, wrong attribute final value, erroneous change to state, etc.

10.5 TEST EXECUTION AND EVALUATION

The role of the test object is to provide a medium for storing all these logically independent test cases. Its *main* method allows executing all the test methods in an uninterrupted sequence. That means that every test case can be executed and evaluated quickly, simply, independently, and as necessary. This gives the opportunity to run all the test cases without an interruption that causes the code base to change between test cases. Here are some rules for running and evaluating test case results to take advantage of this testing approach.

- ☞ Run all test cases before making changes to the code.
- ☞ Try to repair all defects before the next test run.
- ☞ If intermediate code versions are tested before all bugs are repaired, be sure to run the entire test suite when all fixes have been applied.
- ☞ Do not allow changes due to new requirements, if at all possible, until all tests have run successfully.
- ☞ The final test run should complete with no failures.

The purpose of these rules is to allow the testing phase to reach the point where every use case is correct at the same time. If it is never possible to run all test cases with no intervening code repair, there is a good chance that the overall quality of the code may be regressing with each fix, rather than improving.

Once all the test cases are written and compiled, it is not necessary to wait for all the use cases to be implemented before beginning test. If development agrees and has reached a stable point, they can send intermediate versions of the control, business, and return code objects. The decision as to what makes a stable point is whether there exists a set of completed use cases that have no dependence on those that are not yet complete. The test plan will provide some guidance here. This early testing is not a goal that should force development to alter their plan. Test should not pressure development to make an early code delivery for an increment, but if it can be done easily, use cases and the standalone test case facilitate this testing approach.

For example, suppose that increment one is composed of the following use cases:

```
addVideo()
addCopy()
addMember()
rent()
return()
```

The application development team may have completed the addVideo, addCopy, and add member use case quickly, but they are taking more time on the more difficult rent and return. If test development is complete, there is no reason not to take the opportunity to test addVideo(), addCopy(), and addMember() since they have no dependency on the other two.

10.6 A TEST CASE REVIEWED IN DETAIL

Table 10-2 is an example of a single test case for the "return an overdue video" scenario. The line numbers have been added to make it easier to reference them in the ensuing explanation.

Table 10-2 A sample test case.

```
01   boolean return_OVERDUE_1() {
02     boolean b = true;
03     vc.testInit()
04     vc.addVideo("GWTW");
05     vc.addCopy("GWTW",01);
06     vc.addMember("sal");
07     vc.rent("GWTW",01,"sal");
08     vc.testBumpDate(4);
09     ReturnCode rco = vc.return("GWTW",01);
10     if (rco.getRC() != 56) {
11        System.out.println ("return_OVERDUE _1 failed—wrong return code");
12        b = false;
13     }
14     VideoList vl = vc.getVideoList();
15     MemberList ml = vc.getMemberList();
16     Video v = vl.findVideo("GWTW",01):
17     if (!v.getStatus().equals("avail") {
18        System.out.println ("return_OVERDUE _1 failed—video not available");
19        b = false;
20     }
21     Member m = ml.findMember("sal");
22     if (m.getRentCount() != 0)
23        System.out.println ("return_OVERDUE _1 failed—member count wrong");
24        b = false;
25     }
26     if (m.getFinesDue != 3.0)
27        System.out.println ("return_OVERDUE _1 failed—no fines charged");
28        b = false;
29     }
30     return b;
31   }
```

Line 01 is the method name. One suggestion is to name each test case with the use case name concatenated with the scenario name in uppercase concatenated with a number to separate it from the other tests for this scenario.

Lines 02 through 07 establish most of the pre-condition. There is now a video store with one title, one copy of that title, and one member, and that member has rented the copy of the video. Note the real values for each input.

Now the video must become overdue. **Line 08** invokes a control method that changes the system date. This method is named using the testXxxx convention to remind the development team to remove it before the system goes into production. Code should also be included in the testInit() method of Video-Control to reset the system date back to today. When System resources like date need to be manipulated for testing, wrapper them. Then have all the applications and test methods that need these resources use the getter for the resource. Write any testXxxx() methods as necessary to manipulate these resources.

When the pre-condition is established, the next step is to test the scenario. **Line 09** invokes the returnVideo method in VideoControl to run the use case to be tested. Every control method for a use case returns a returnCode object. This returnCode object will have a numeric return code and a default message string.

Line 10 checks to see that the control method has returned the correct return code. In this case, the expected return value is "56." If this value is not returned, a failure is reported in **Line 11**.

Line 12 sets the boolean value that the test case will eventually return to the Test main method. This value was initialized to true, and any failure will change it to false (indicating a failure in the test case). Notice that even after this failure is detected, the test continues with the third phase and validates the post-condition state changes. Always check as many details of the test case for correctness as possible. Even if one fails, making additional checks will save both tester and developer some time later by uncovering multiple failures at the same time. There can be situations where a failure blocks any subsequent checks. In this case, it becomes impossible to continue with the rest of the test.

Lines 14 and 15 get the list of members and the list of videos from the control object so it can retrieve the actual video and member objects that were created. Since testInit() recreates these collections, this step needs to be repeated in every test case that needs access to an object in a collection. The testInit method could have acquired addressability to all the collections, but it is actually more efficient to retrieve them separately in each test. An alternative is to have a test setup method that stores all collection references in the test object.

Lines 16 and 17 get the "01" copy of "GWTW" and check to see that its status is available. If it is not, **Line 18** prints out a test failure message. This message has enough information to make it possible to find the test case that generated it. It should be easy to see what caused the error when reviewing the test case in the failure log. The check preceding the message can also be used to set a debug breakpoint in the test case.

Line 21 gets the object for the member that rented the video. Notice that the test assumes that the addVideo and addMember use cases are working correctly, so it does not check to see if the object returned from the findVideo() or findMember() is null. The rationale is that this test was not written for those use cases, and reporting an error here would be redundant. The down side of this approach is that in a language like Java, if the add is unsuccessful then this test will be aborted at runtime. If the test decides to make a check for null, there is no need to report the failure; merely abort the test case.

Line 22 checks to see that the member's rent count was returned to zero, and **Line 26** ensures that the renter has been charged a late fee.

Notice that a successful test case reports no status. As was mentioned earlier, this makes it easier to review the log and focus on failures. If successes were reported as well, the debuggers would need to read these messages more carefully just to find the failures. An increment may choose to rerun the tests from the previous increments as well. As the number of test cases grows, wading through all the successes just to find the failures will be time consuming.

10.7 TEST OBJECT STATE DATA

Normally there is no reason for the test object to have state data. Every Test object method is an independent test, and there is no shared information, since every object is created within the test methods. The exceptions are when test setup methods, like those that get addressability to collection objects, save references to objects that are needed in the remainder of the test.

10.8 TESTING WITH EXISTING DATABASES

When all objects and their persistent counterparts can be created within the test method, the techniques described so far will successfully support testing. When the function to create new objects is not part of the application being tested, it may be necessary to use an existing database as the initial test state. However, it will often be more efficient to add use cases to create new objects and build the database up from a null state. When even this is impractical, the safest approach is to have a function within the test object that will instantiate the database to a consistent state before every test. This usually means a copy of the data from a stable read-only file. When this is not practical and test cases must be run using the state of the previous test, the next best plan is to string test cases together and build each one's pre-condition from the planned post-condition of the previous. In this case, run the dependent tests as a single method. If one test fails, there is no reason to run any subsequent tests. Wait until the blocking test case failure is repaired. It should still be a goal to have all tests run without failure.

When the tests are run using live databases, control's testInit() method cannot alter the live data before each test. It is recommended that live data never be used with test cases but that a copy of the database be used instead.

10.8.1 Using nonpersistent object for testing

Even with a permanent database, use nonpersistent objects for early increments. Later when the application logic has been debugged, use the next increment as the cut over to persistence, then retest the use cases with the information now residing in a database. This separates the testing of the use case and the persistent access. Encapsulation makes this data redesign relatively simple and can assist in separating application and persistence-related defects.

10.9 KINDS OF TESTS

It is important to position use case testing among the other kinds of software testing within the development process. Next is a discussion of unit and functional testing, in which use case testing belongs. This is followed by an overview of other tests that can be performed after use case testing is complete.

10.9.1 Unit test

A traditional unit test is running the code through every path, condition, or branch. The intent is to exercise every possible sequence of program statements and, thereby, guarantee that no piece of the code will go untested. Use case scenarios define the code paths. By definition of the coverage rules listed in analysis for decision tables, there is no combination of conditions and hence no path through the code that is not defined by one of the use case scenarios. Test coverage that tests every scenario must exercise every code path. Therefore, use case scenario testing is unit testing.

10.9.2 Functional test

Functional testing is defined as testing all possible functions and every alternative of these functions. This kind of coverage is also included when every scenario of every use case is tested. Both function and unit test are considered to be development activities; that means that they are not tests performed on code that development considers complete but rather that they are part of the process of producing the working code.

10.9.3 Other tests

After development considers the program to be correct with respect to its specification, independent tests are performed to validate how well the product will work in the client environment. These include the following tests:

System test: Testing the product in a live operational environment with existing databases and other software products.

Acceptance test: Testing the product in the client environment, with special tests that the client feels are essential to determine application readiness.

Performance test: Testing the product under duress to evaluate whether it can operate effectively under load conditions that are typical of the day-to-day environment.

These tests and others, when applicable, are just as important as the development tests described earlier, but since their form is unaltered by OODP, they are not discussed further in this book.

10.10 ENHANCING USE CASE TESTING

Functional testing has been around for a long time. Some of its strongest criticisms have included the following:

☞ Given enough passes through the test cycle, the program can be taught how to pass all the tests.

☞ Finding bugs during test and fixing them gives no insight into the quality of the product.

☞ Errors found and fixed do not represent any usable quality metric.

The last item, which will not be addressed here, refers to the fact that all bugs are not equal. An error that prevents the system from booting cannot be considered the same as an error that misspells the heading in a yearly report. Bugs need to be converted into realized failures and weighted by their frequency and impact to the user.

10.10.1 Random value use case testing

The first criticism, which speaks to the repeatability of test cases, can be addressed by randomizing the values of the use case parameters. For example, consider a test case for an insufficient funds scenario of a withdraw use case. Assume that the inputs are the amount to be withdrawn and the account number. Example 10-1 show a typical test case for the withdraw use case.

Example 10-1 A partial test case with fixed data values.

```
returnCode = openAccount();
account = returnCode.getAccountNumber();
deposit(account, 50.00)
withdraw(account, 75.00)
(Validation is not shown.)
```

This test case will always use the same values, and eventually the application code will "get it right." An alternative is to use random values for inputs.

Suppose that a function exists that returns a random value from a range of two numbers. The revised test case in Example 10-2 shows the use of random numbers to generate the inputs to the test case's use cases.

Example 10-2 A partial test case with random data values.

```
returnCode = openAccount();
account = returnCode.getAccountNumber();
dAmount = random(0,10000.00)
deposit(account,dAmount)
wAmount =
    random (dAmount+0.01, dAmount+5000.00)
withdraw(account, wAmount)
```

The openAccount use case creates a new account and returns the identifier for that account as an attribute of the returnCode. The deposit use case is supplied a random value between 0.0 and ten thousand dollars. To ensure a test of the insufficient funds scenario the subsequent withdraw uses a random withdraw amount greater than the amount deposited.

The advantage of such an approach is that every test case is unique and that there is the opportunity to discover less obvious combinations of inputs that cause errors. The changes required to convert test cases to random values are minimal, but the advantages are enormous. However, this approach presents the debugger with the dilemma of not being able to recreate a failed test case easily. This can be solved in one of two ways. The first option is to list the details of a test case when it fails, including the specific input values used. The alternative is to make it possible to seed the random generator routine so that the tester can reproduce the random values. The latter option is more useful for the earlier phases of testing. In the later stages, the more random the random values, the better the test coverage.

10.10.2 Random test cases

The second concern with functional testing—"finding and fixing bugs give no insight into the quality of the product"—can be addressed using random test cases and making statistical inferences about the product. There are two aspects to this approach. The first is the use of random test cases to create a statistical sample of functional usage. In this model, use case tests are not predefined but are generated randomly based on probability. For example, assume that the addCustomer use case represents only 2 percent of the use cases run in a day, whereas rent and return represent 40 percent and 45 percent, respectively. Therefore, when selecting a test to run, rent should be chosen 20 times more often than addCustomer. This profile allows testing to mirror the real environment and will cause failures to appear at approximately the same rate as they would in production. If 100 tests discovered four failures, the following assertion can be made:

> When the application is used in an environment that matches this usage profile, it will fail approximately 4 percent of the time.

Note that even though these random test cases still use random values their goals are not the same. When use case testing was done using the main method and the test object, the goal was functional coverage, and every scenario was tested more or less equally. This testing was designed to discover defects in the application so they could be fixed. When test cases are chosen at random, the goal is not to discover defects but to make a statistical statement about the mean transactions to failure (MTTF) of the application.

When all defects have been repaired, the statistical evaluation can begin again, and the trends in MTTF can be plotted to predict the MTTF for the next version of the application.

While these types of test are not unique to object-oriented development, they are enabled because the use case approach to requirements and analysis is function based, and as far as the user is concerned correct function is the primary measure of its goodness.

10.10.3 An example

Consider the data from Table 10-3. During the first test phase, the test application generated 10 random tests, based on the usage profile. Of those 10 tests nine of them failed. The application, therefore, can be said to have a transaction failure rate of 9/10. Or given an environment that is similar to the one defined in the usage profile, the average transaction will fail about 90 percent of the time. Now assume that all discovered defects are repaired and the next phase of tests generates 35 random tests. During this phase, only two of the tests fail. The new version of the application can now be said to have a failure rate of 2/35 or an MTTF of 35/2. That's an average of 17.5 use cases without a

Table 10-3 Test and failure rate data with exponential regression analysis.

Build number	Tests run	Failures	Failure rate	MTTF	Regression
1	10	9	0.900	1.111	1.0
2	35	2	0.057	17.500	18.8
3	100	1	0.010	100.000	102.1
4	300	1	0.003	300.000	339.1
5	1000	1	0.001	1000.000	860.4
6					1841.4

failure. If the system is continually repaired and retested, the MTTF should continue to increase to the point where no more failures are detected. This does not mean that the application is defect free, it just means that the failure rate is so low that too many tests would have to be run to find the next error. However, using a theory called Software Reliability Growth Modeling, which states that quality software will exponentially decrease its failure rate with each new set of fixes, and a simple statistical technique called nonlinear regression, the new MTTF of the application can still be computed. Table 10-3 shows a series of test runs. Each run is followed by a rebuild of the application after the found defects are repaired. The last run required 1000 tests to find an error. Using regression analysis (the complete spread sheet formulas are not shown), the probable MTTF of the last untested version is projected to be a 0.05 percent failure rate, which would require approximately 1841 additional tests to find the next defect.

A thorough discussion of statistical software testing is far beyond the scope of this book, but it is mentioned here because the use case approach to testing enables it. Perhaps even more important, this technique allows the application to state its quality in terms of use cases between failures rather than number of bugs discovered, or bugs undiscovered. For more information on statistical software testing and evaluation, see [Poore83] or [Dyer92].

CHAPTER 11

User Interface

This chapter elaborates three of the roles of application development. They are designing the physical look and feel of the user interface, implementing the user interface, and developing the application that responds to the requests generated by the user interface.

It separates user interface design from application design, describes those elements that drive the design of the user interface, and highlights where in the process each of these drivers is most critical.

It describes the overall architecture of the interface object, the role of the return code object in user interface design, and how to test the user interface independently.

11.1 PRODUCT DEVELOPMENT ROLES

User interface design and development is a key activity in the user's perception of the usability and quality of the application. To the user, the user interface *is* the application. It is also the most volatile area of change in the application. To manage these issues effectively, OODP separates application development by defining three principal roles:

☞ The user interface designer
☞ The user interface implementer
☞ The application developer

Design separated the control and user interface objects. This chapter refines development of the user interface still further.

11.1.1 User interface designer

11.1.1.1 Responsibilities   The user interface designer is responsible for capturing the application functionality with screens, reports, menus, and on-line help; then she obtains user acceptance of the packaging of these elements. She designs all of the previously discussed objects, as well as the flow from screen to screen, and the definition of user interface behavior for all business processes. The user interface designer packages use cases with a series of windows, keystrokes, and mouse clicks to show the users how they will interact with the application to perform their day-to-day tasks. The most important and time-consuming responsibility of this person is to have the client "like" the way the user interface flows. Usually this is a long and tedious process since the customers/users/clients will change their minds often as the user interface designer walks through their proposal.

11.1.1.2 Skills   This is not a programming or an application design task. The individual in this role will need skills in graphic arts, screen design, human factors, and user interface task flow management. Far too many organizations give these responsibilities to programmer/developers who have no training in any of these areas. This frustrates the user interface design process because it is more difficult for these individuals to understand where the clients/users are coming from when they are dissatisfied with the user interface but are unable to explain why. It also frustrates the application development process because the developers are spending a large amount of their time on these user interface activities, which have nothing to do with the application. User interface design is almost a full-time job; it also does not parallel incremental development, since user interface design tends to follow the business process, and these will most likely not match up with the planned increments. The surest way to be successful with user interface design is to separate it from development and assign the responsibility to a qualified professional.

11.1.2 User interface implementer

Since the role of user interface designer requires no software skills, the task of implementing the user interface in a programming language must be performed by a separate individual.

11.1.2.1 Responsibilities The user interface implementers are responsible for bringing the user interface to life. They must populate the screens and windows with icons and the other visual artifacts that were specified by the user interface designer. They manage the flow among screens and respond to user interface stimuli like mouse clicks, screen touches, key strokes, etc. They are responsible for gathering the input, from the user interfaces, that is required for the use case. It is their task to edit this data to ensure that it conforms to the type expected by the use case and then construct and send the correct message to the appropriate control object to invoke the use case within the application. When the control object responds, the user interface implementer must examine the return code to determine the scenario and communicate the response, along with any other required information, back to the user. At the same time, they may need to adjust the user interface by disabling or enabling components, switching screens, or displaying status. Finally, they are responsible for developing the user interface test object and using it to verify that all the other tasks were completed correctly.

11.1.2.2 Skills User interface implementers are programmers with skills in the user interface aspects of the language. The do not need extensive language skills since they are focusing on building and managing the screen objects.

11.1.3 Application developer

The remaining role to be filled on the team is the application developer, which has been the topic of most of this book. They are responsible for creating the classes for the business objects and for writing the control methods for the use cases.

11.2 USER INTERFACE DESIGN DRIVERS

The user interface development team, which consists of the user interface designer and user interface implementer, work together to deliver the user interface objects. The designer is working with the customer/client to capture the look and feel while the implementer is writing and changing the methods of the interface class to enable the design. This process is parallel to the application development process and will require full-time participation of the programmer responsible for the implementation. For that reason, this individual should not have any application development responsibilities.

The user interface is susceptible to changes of a different kind than the application, and these changes will continue long after the product requirements are finalized. That is because in this area the customer is part of the design team and the user interface design is based on customer preferences. The user interface has three sources of changes:

☞ Changes to the signature of the use cases due to changes in requirements
☞ Changes brought about by the user interface designer to enhance usability
☞ Changes to the user interface look and feel requested by the client

11.2.1 Use case changes

New use cases, or changes to existing use cases based on new requirements, require new screens or redesign of existing screens. Most of this should happen early in the user interface design process, and quite often it will be the review of the prototype screen designs that triggers these changes. This suggests that the early emphasis of the user interface development team should be on user interface design and prototyping rather than implementation. As this process uncovers changes, the requirements use case definitions must be updated, and the new use cases must be communicated to the rest of the development team as soon as possible.

11.2.2 Usability changes

The second phase of user interface design is the prototyping phase where the designer, using their human factors skills, evaluates the design based on usability. Here changes to the screens are mostly encapsulated within the user interface objects. Occasionally these reviews will uncover a missing requirement, but this happens infrequently. During this phase, the user interface implementer is writing the code to bring the screens to life. They are not trying to process the input or communicate with the application but just to demonstrate the flow of work.

11.2.3 Client or user preferences

The last source of change for the user interface team is customer preference. As the customer participates in the other two activities, they will request interface changes based on what they like or don't like. The user interface designer will need to be flexible in this area since they will often have knowledge of usability factors that the customer may not see and should provide guidance. In some cases though, the customer will just "want it" changed. Caution needs to be exercised here, especially late in the cycle, that the user interface designers are not agreeing to a new function based on last-minute customer preference. The low-fidelity prototyping phases should have identified most of those; but as the customer becomes more familiar with the look and feel of the product, it is natural for them to want "more." In this area the user interface team needs to resist agreeing to new requirements that are outside the scope of the application agreed to in requirements. The rule of thumb is

> If a user interface change requires a new use case, new outcome, or new
> parameter, get the project leader involved before accepting the change.

Changing the type of a use case parameter does not fall into this category and
can be accepted. However, the user interface team also has schedules, and
eventually any changes by the client will jeopardize them. At some point, even
user interface look and feel changes will need to be deferred to a future version of the application. The team should always resist frivolous changes
throughout the process. Drawing the change is not implementing the change.

11.3 IMPORTANCE OF SEPARATING USER INTERFACE AND APPLICATION DESIGN

It is worth a few extra paragraphs in this book to itemize the many advantages of separating the interface development and application development.

☞ The skills required to do these tasks are vastly different. User interface
design is not even related to software. Even though the user interface
implementer must be an experienced programmer, they do not need the
same breadth of experience that an application developer must have. By
separating the tasks, it is easier to assign them to different individuals;
whenever the skills related to a task are more granular, it is easier to
identify a resource capable of performing that task.

☞ The user interface team and the application team have different approaches to problem decomposition. The application team is partitioning
the problem by use case (low-level functional requirements). This partitioning has its own intra-increment dependencies that, to some extent,
dictate the order in which use cases are implemented. This order will
almost assuredly differ from the order in which the user interface is
designed, prototyped, and implemented. Interface design is based more
on business processes than on use cases. A typical screen design will follow a process all the way through. A series of windows that allow the
clerk to log on, rent a video, return a video, accept payment on an overdue video, and log off will typically be designed in one pass. In that way,
the user interface designer can focus on the perspective of one actor at a
time. It is unreasonable to expect the application developers to alter
their incremental plan to match this set of use cases. It is equally unreasonable to expect the user interface design team to attempt to implement
one use case at a time.

☞ The user interface design, review, implementation, and test phases do
not partition as well as use cases. Even if partitioning were an option, it
would create an environment that would foster identification of new
requirements late in the application development cycle. The user interface team, like the application development team, wants to focus client

involvement early on in its cycle as well. Because of this, a working user interface ready to integrate with the application will probably not be available until the third or fourth application increment.

☞ The user interface look and feel requirements will continue to change after the application requirements are completed. That means that the application can be designed, coded, and tested while the user interface is still undergoing design. When these activities are combined, there will be a temptation to slow the progress of the application because the user interface is in a state of flux. By using the requirements use case definition as the contract between the user interface team and the application team, both teams may proceed at the pace defined in their individual plans. They will not need to be dependent on each other until some later increment when the integration test must be performed.

☞ User interface correctness and application correctness use different criteria. Separating them as tasks makes it easier to focus on each one's responsibilities with respect to the entire product. The application is correct if it sets the business objects into the correct state for every precondition of every scenario. The user interface is correct if it sends the correct message to the control object and correctly alters the view for every scenario.

The last bullet needs some additional discussion. It is important that the interface development and application development teams are clear on their individual correctness responsibilities and that neither one relies on the other to do part of their work. The user interface implementer should not avoid input type checking because the application will probably catch invalid inputs. For example, consider the logon use case that requires a user id, and further assume that user id must be exactly eight characters long, with the last four characters being numbers. Either the user interface will consider these restrictions and do all type checking for user id, or they will be considered business rules and the application will include a scenario for invalid user id format. However, if the user interface has this responsibility, it should not assume that no checking is necessary merely because the invalid user id will be found by the logon application.

A more critical situation is when the application ignores logical scenarios because the user interface will prevent them. Consider that the user interface for the logon use case is designed such that the users do not type in their ids but instead select them from a list provided by the user interface. If this list is created dynamically from the database of current valid users, then the user interface will never send an invalid user id as a parameter of the logon message to the control object. If the application design assumes the existence of a user interface design that does this checking, the application and user interface are now tightly coupled, and changes in one may render the other incorrect.

11.4 THE INTERFACE OBJECT

The basic interface object will have a method for every use case. As the single interface object is decomposed into several to accommodate additional windows and frames, these methods may get distributed over several objects. For example, a main window may have buttons that open a rent window and a separate return window. It makes sense that the rent and return interface methods are part of these objects. Each use case's primary methods will be tied to a user interface event, such as a mouse click, that will trigger it. It must then gather from one or more interface screens all the information required by the use case. The user interface implementer has the responsibility for editing and validating the use case input parameters for type. That means ensuring that dates are in the valid format and subtypes have values in the legal range. In general, the interface should be able to validate the values of any attributes that do not require accessing the business objects. When all attributes are validated, it should send them to the application using the appropriate message to the control object.

When the control method returns, the user interface must extract from the return code object the scenario indicator and any information that needs to be displayed or stored in the interface and adjust the user view as defined by the user interface designer. This may involve displaying a new window or new information in the current window or enabling and disabling one or more interface objects in preparation for the next event.

11.5 PSEUDO USE CASES

Often the user interface can simulate a new use case by sequencing existing control methods. This can sometimes be done without having to alter any application methods. Consider the example where the banking application has deposit and withdraw use cases, but no transfer use case. Adding the code shown in Example 11-1 to the user interface would allow the transfer capability without writing a transfer method in the control object.

Example 11-1 A pseudo use case encapsulated with the user interface.

```
//transfer (amount, fromAcct, toAcct)

rc=control.withdraw(fromAcct, amount)
if (rc.getRc() != 220)
    then .... //report error
    else control.deposit(toAcct, amount);
```

Attempting to rent a video that has not been returned requires that the clerk first get an error response back from rent, manually enter the return transaction, and redo the rent operation. Since the business process is the same in all cases, the user interface could manage the entire sequence with the code shown in Example 11-2.

Example 11-2 A pseudo use case to automatically return an unreturned video before it's rented.

```
//rent an unreturned video(title, copy, customer)

rc = control. rent (title, copy, customer);
    if (rc.getRC() = 157) {
    control.return (title,copy);
    control. rent (title, copy, customer);
    }
```

Another pseudo use case would allow the clerk to enter or scan multiple videoIds but have a single user interface rent event that would invoke the rent use case multiple times in succession until all the videos were rented. Adding several copies of a video at once would be another application of the technique. That does not mean that some of these events should not have been real use cases, but it does mean that the separation of user interface design and application design allows the development team this extra option.

11.6 TESTING THE INTERFACE

The user interface implementer has the responsibility for testing the user interface. This responsibility includes validating the use case parameters for type and order and ensuring that the user interface response for each scenario is correct.

11.6.1 The test interface control object

The key element of the user interface test is the test interface control object. When the development team delivers the skeleton control object with all of the dummy use case methods, the user interface implementer will rename the XxxControl object to be UIXxxControl. Each method can then be adapted to test the user interface correctness. There are three parts to this testing:

- ☞ Validating parameter order
- ☞ Validating parameter type
- ☞ Validating the interface response to each scenario

11.6.2 Input parameter validation

The first step in determining the correctness of the user interface is to validate input types and return the appropriate error message when an error is detected. Entering invalid data via the interface and visually verifying the response checks this logic. Whether the implementation language is strongly typed or not, or the valid type is a subtype of the language type, this validation will need to be performed under control of the user interface. Even though in languages like Java the compiler will reject invalid language types when the control method message is constructed, the user interface should still detect the error logically.

The user interface test control method should create a return code object with a default return code and a message that describes the parameters. For example, the message generated by the dummy rent use case might be "renting video *name* by member *id*" where *name* and *id* are the values of the video and customer parameters supplied by the user interface method. If the return code is not one of the reserved values, then by convention the user interface will display the default message in the return code object. This is again visually checked to ensure that the correct values arrived in the control method in the correct order. For example, if the message displayed by the user interface is "rent video Smith J to customer Gone with the Wind," there is strong evidence that the user interface reversed the order of the parameters when it generated the message to the control object. If the message is "rent video to customer Smith J," then the title parameter is not getting passed to the control object. This could be a coding error in either the user interface or its test control method.

11.6.3 Random responses

Another way to help validate the user interface is to have the dummy control method return every scenario return code along with a descriptive message. The test control object would contain code like that shown in Example 11-3.

Example 11-3 Generating random return code values in the interface test control object.

```
select (deleteVideoSwitch) {
   case (0)
      deleteVideoSwitch = 1;
      return (new ReturnCode(130, "Video deleted successfully");
   case (1)
      deleteVideoSwitch = 2;
      return (new ReturnCode(134, "Video not found");
   case (2)
      deleteVideoSwitch = 0;
      return (new ReturnCode(135, "Video is rented");
}
```

The select statement would return a different value depending on the variable deleteVidoSwitch in the control object. Assuming that its value was initialized to 0, there would be a separate variable for each use case. This code allows the user interface to see every possible response from the control object. If the user interface tester enters the same video to delete three times, they will have the opportunity to observe the user interface response to each scenario.

11.6.4 Correctness questions

User interface design has the following correctness questions:

☞ Does the user interface invoke the correct use case method in the control object?

☞ Are the parameters of the use case method in the correct order and of the correct type?

☞ Does the user interface react correctly to the scenario defining by the returnCode object?

☞ Are the correct message and associated returned information displayed?

11.7 THE RETURNCODE OBJECT

The ReturnCode class introduced in Chapter 10 is primarily for the user interface. It communicates all the information necessary for the user interface to respond correctly to the user. The numeric code defines the scenario and the default message. The user interface examines the numeric return code and determines what action to take and what message to display. The numeric return code will have reserved values for every scenario of every use case and one or more special default values that tells the user interface that a scenario other than those listed in the specification has occurred. In this case, the user interface should display the default message provided, instead of trying to determine the actions and response based on the user interface design, as with the reserved values. There may be several default numeric return codes. When the user interface is in test mode, consider always displaying the default message, perhaps in a special message area on the test console. This would be in addition to the messages generated by the user interface as part of its design. Here are some recommendations for use case return codes.

☞ Reserve a range of numbers for every use case. For example, if the values are five-digit numbers, use the first three to identify the use case.

☞ Use the last two digits as a subrange for successful vs. unsuccessful scenarios.

☞ Successful scenarios might use numeric return codes in the range 0 to 14.

☞ Error scenarios would use 15 through 89.

☞ 90 through 99 could be reserved for the default processing exception responses.

Examples of these suggested conventions can be seen in the control object sample code in Chapter 17.

11.7.1 Dealing with unforeseen exceptions

Often the application will encounter an error scenario that was not planned for in the use case specification. These errors are platform dependent like IO errors, memory problems, or language-specific exceptions. Since these errors are not related to the business rules, but generally are a fault of the infrastructure or a programmer snafu, there is no way that the user interface could have foreseen them. In these cases, the control object should use one of the default numeric return codes and supply a specific default message, which the user interface will display.

11.8 REQUIREMENTS CHANGES

All activities in the development project are affected by requirements changes, and the recommended vehicle for communicating these changes is the master list of requirements use case definitions. For most development activities, this requires that changes be made to existing code to accommodate this change. In the case of the user interface implementer, they will need to change not only their own code but that of the test control class as well. This presents a special problem for the user interface developer since they do not own that class. Suppose that the development team replaces the skeleton control object with a new version that may include application code in later increments. The user interface developer must extract only those elements of the change that apply to use case parameters or the return code object and then update their user interface test control class appropriately.

Maintenance

OODP views maintenance as a contin-
uation of development. Maintenance is additional increments that contain
new and changed use cases. Changes are either extending business objects,
creating new use cases, or changing existing use cases. This chapter considers
each of these changes and looks at the process of evaluating new requirements
for identifying unstated or overlooked changes. It also discusses how to assess
the impact of changes with respect to effort and schedule. Other topics include
maintenance with persistent objects and maintenance of the process deliverables themselves.

12.1 NEW OBJECTS AND ATTRIBUTES

The simplest maintenance involves new objects and attributes and their associated getters and setters but has no new or changed use cases. Nonetheless,
as the discussion on undiscovered function later in this chapter shows, new
objects and attributes generally lead to new use cases.

12.2 DEALING WITH ENCAPSULATED DATA

A slightly more complex change involves the redesign of the state data, which
requires that the methods of the class be rewritten to accommodate the

restructure. The goal of encapsulation is to isolate the application from impact of these kinds of changes. Public accessor methods will need to be updated to use the new data structure, but the methods must still provide the same interface and semantic behavior. Theoretically this type of change should have no effect on existing applications, but often the application will be sending messages to existing objects, invoking methods that have been changed to work with the new data structure. Some of the new methods will not work properly with the old data structure. Therefore, existing objects and their persistent counterparts must be restructured to be compatible with the updated methods in the class before these changes can be considered operational.

12.2.1 Converting data

There are two general approaches to modifying existing data. The first is to write a program that processes the data or tables directly in the database. This program would read the original data file and write the reformatted information as a new file. The second approach, which is the one recommended here, relies on the class to perform the transition. With this option, the conversion is accomplished in two steps. First, a copy is made of the old class definition, and it is renamed. Second, the structure changes, and method updates are made in the renamed class, which becomes the new class definition.

12.2.1.1 The constructor converter   The new class contains a constructor/converter that accepts as input an instance of the old class and returns an instance of the new one. A program can be written to walk through the old databases and reinstantiate each object in the new format using this constructor. There are two advantages of this approach over the one that processes the data directly from the database.

☞ Encapsulation is preserved in both the old and new objects.

☞ Constraints that are part of the class will be guaranteed since the class is building the objects.

When the data are reformatted outside of the protection provided by encapsulation, there is no guarantee that the new objects will contain data that adhere to the internal rules of the class. This means that it is possible that an object of this class may violate its constraints and perhaps cause an application to fail because it contains data that the class's methods were not designed to handle.

12.2.1.2 The converter use case   The program that converts the data can be a standalone application, or it can be built as a use case. The use case can be written to process the entire file or to handle a single element. The latter design would require it to be invoked from another use case that steps through every record. This approach is more appropriate if instances of the objects exist in multiple places. For example, consider a Date class that was only capable of handling years that were two characters long. After this class was renamed to NewDate and altered to use four characters for the year, whenever an application needs to convert to the four-digit format, they would invoke the use case that used the converter. Of course, each application could have used the constructor directly.

12.2.2 New or changed use cases

Another category of change occurs when a new use case is being added or an existing use case is being changed. A new use case is simply another use case. It can be added to a subsequent increment with no special handling. Changed use cases are a special case. These are either new scenarios or changes to existing scenarios. This category of change is slightly more complicated than new use cases, but when the fork design pattern is used, only the single control method is affected by the change. That means that the worst case is the original use case, and its associated control method is discarded and replaced by a new one, which makes the changed use case a new use case.

12.2.2.1 Orphaned methods   When the control method is completely redesigned and rewritten, the possibility exists that methods with rich function, with which it collaborated, will need to be redesigned as well. Since method redesign in most cases is discouraged, quite often the collaborating methods may need to be abandoned and their function shifted to new methods that can correctly support the redesigned control method. In some cases, it may be that the original methods have become orphaned methods. Orphaned methods are those that no longer collaborate with any other objects. When the business objects use single function methods, like getters and setters, the likelihood of orphaned methods is very low. In all cases, it is the responsibility of the class owner to address this issue.

12.2.2.2 The update increment   A big advantage of incremental development was the ability to defer a change request to a later increment. This allowed the change to be redesigned rather than just re-coded. This works fine as long as there *is* another increment. What choices are there if the change is presented while developing the last increment? There are two solutions. The first is to plan for an update increment, that is an increment with no function allocated to it. Its only purpose is to serve as a placeholder for last-minute changes. Hopefully there will be a small number of changes, and the increment will be completed in a very short time. This should avoid having to deal with even more changes. An alternative is to plan the last increment to be very small and very low in complexity so that changes can be added to it without overwhelming its design. This approach may necessitate revisiting requirements.

12.2.2.3 Changing existing methods   Consider a class with methods a(), b(), c(), and d(). Assume that this class has been around for a long time and has been well received and reused in several applications over several months. Then one day a developer, while implementing a new application, discovers a bug in method c(). As far as anyone knows, this is the first error ever found in this class. The question is what should the owner of the class do? There are three options.

- ☞ Do nothing and wait to see if anyone else detects the bug.
- ☞ Fix the error in c() immediately.
- ☞ Provide a workaround for the application that is affected by the bug.

Option one is certainly a reasonable approach, except for the fact that it forces the developer who discovered the defect to abandon the design strategy of using the defective class. Option two seems to be the choice that most programmers would elect, but in this environment it is the most dangerous. Because this class has been in use for a while, it is likely that other users may have encountered the bug as well. It is possible that they have adapted their applications to work around the method's incorrect behavior. In this case, repairing the defect may harm more applications than it helps. Consider a programmer who, using an obscure trigonometric function like hyperbolic secant, has discovered that it returns a value with what is apparently the wrong sign. Since he is not an expert in trigonometry, he assumes that his knowledge of the function is wrong and simply negates the result, which makes the code work fine. He passes this little technique around to about a hundred of his friends who have been having the same problem. Then one day six months later, after the installation of a new version of the class, the rocket ships start plunging into the ground immediately after takeoff. Do you think that he and his friends will be pleased that the defect was repaired. Perhaps he should have tried to get the defect repaired when he first discovered it, or chosen a different method to solve his problem, but he didn't; and one thing is for sure: he will most likely avoid reusing any classes in the future.

If the class owner can be sure that they can identify EVERY user of this class and notify them of the change, then this may be a safe alternative, but otherwise it is a violation of the prime directive of reuse: "Never change the signature or semantics of an established public interface."

That leaves only option three: "create a workaround." The easiest way to do that is to write a new method c1() that works correctly. This allows those who find the bug to bypass it while not affecting other users of the same code who are satisfied with its current behavior. Even here there is the possibility that this will not correct the bug for every user. If an application in need of the new method happens to be using a subclass of the defective class, and that subclass already has a method c1(), it will block access to the fix. The probability of such an occurrence is, of course, very low.

This lesson in reuse can be expanded to explain additional dangers in implementing use case with a stair design. It implies that one of the most touted advantages of rich object methods, inheritance, and object-oriented reuse, may be a significant problem when it comes to maintenance. This is the exact opposite of the benefits claimed for programs that reuse, when they list simplified and reduced maintenance of the reused code. Instead of confidently knowing that all changes to a reused artifact will be applied without impact to their application, the reuser will lie awake in fear of what a random change might do to her correctly functioning applications. How would the owner of a reusable class know that the change they are about to make will apply to every application that is currently using it? The answer is that they will not; and given the choice, almost every programmer would elect to have the opportunity to review the change before accepting it into his or her application. Reuse, which applies to most classes widely distributed within an organization, has one simple rule:

> Unless you can identify every user of your class and can guarantee that they need, or will be unaffected by, the change you are about to make to its public interface or semantics, DON'T DO IT.

12.3 UPDATING PROCESS DELIVERABLES

The OODP process produces deliverables in one activity that are used by other activities. When the business rules, design, or implementation changes, it is important to update and reissue the associated artifact. An earlier guideline stated that only about 30 to 40 percent of the use case will have analysis descriptions and that only about half of those will have a sequence diagram to record the design. These percentages are not mathematical constants, but rather guidelines based on experience and use case complexity. Some use cases are simple enough that recording their business rules in a decision table adds no additional understanding. The same can be said of the design with respect to the sequence diagram. Apply the same common sense rules when an artifact is changed. When the new business rules are well understood by everyone and the deliverable is no longer considered essential to the next activity, then it is not necessary that it be updated. The only rule is: if it is not updated, then destroy it.

12.3.1 Requirements use cases

The exception to the foregoing rule is *always* update the use case definitions. This is the only record of the product requirements. It is used by the analyst, UI developer, tester, and project planner; therefore, it must be kept accurate, current, and complete.

When the requirements are recorded, they are turned over to the individual teams. The analyst begins gathering the business rules, the tester will develop the test plan, the user interface team will begin design of the UI, and the project manager will attempt to develop a schedule and resource plan.

The members of these teams will be interacting with the client to gain approval for their individual deliverables. Each task has the potential to stimulate the client to recognize previously overlooked requirements, the details of which are critical to the project's success. The requirements use case definitions are the logical vehicle for recording these changes and communicating them among the teams.

12.3.2 Analysis decision tables

The rule for deciding whether a decision table should be created was "Does the entire team understand the business rules well enough to skip a formal recording?" If it is omitted, then the implication is that it will be possible to create a correct design directly from the requirements use case definition. This is likely to be true as long as

☞ Error scenarios are rejections of invalid inputs due to missing objects and not complex state violations.

☞ The OK scenarios business rules are obvious from the use case name.

Consider a use case that has neither a decision table nor a sequence diagram and must be coded directly from the requirements. If the use case complies with the preceding rules, the developer should be able to write a series of input validation messages followed by an unconditional trivial algorithm. If these implementations are not possible, then the design and analysis definitions may have been prematurely discarded.

12.3.3 Analysis class diagram

The analysis class diagram is the object-oriented version of the data model and contains important information about the organization of the database. It is important that this model accurately reflects the data design especially when it maps to a relational database. Often an application will create a class diagram that is independent of the database. In this case, the class diagram reflects the application, but a model that shows the database design still needs to be kept as well. It makes sense to use the data model as the object model whenever possible. In that way, only one artifact will need to be maintained. During increment one, the class diagram is refined into the object design diagram; that model now supercedes all prior class diagrams, and from then on it represents the analysis, design, and the implementation view of the system objects. This model should be maintained throughout the life of the application.

12.3.4 Design sequence diagram

The rules for omitting or discarding the sequence diagram are similar to those for the analysis use case description.

☞ Does the team feel that an understanding of how the use case should be designed is not appreciably improved by reading the sequence diagram?

☞ If a decision table exists, can the control method and supporting business object methods be implemented directly from it?

☞ If the use case description was not created during analysis or subsequently discarded, can a correct implementation be developed directly from the requirements?

In some cases, it may be that the business rules are simple enough to allow omitting the analysis use case, but the design is extremely complex and the sequence diagram may be required to understand it.

Some analysis and design artifacts will be created by the designer or analyst simply as a vehicle for recording thoughts. In these cases, it may have been obvious that there will be no need to maintain the deliverables after completion of the current activity.

> Do not resist creating any intermediate deliverable because there is concern that it must be maintained forever.

12.4 IDENTIFYING THE REAL SCOPE OF CHANGES

Maintenance begins with the first new or changed requirement after the start of increment one and continues until the application is retired or replaced. Change management includes not only deferring nonessential changes but also evaluating the requests to ensure that they are within scope and reasonable. It also must determine the true extent of the change and its cost in terms of time and people to include it in the project.

Given a change, there are three assessments to be made.

☞ Determine the true scope of the change by identifying "hidden requirements." There are guidelines that follow that can help in that process.

☞ Present all discovered new and changed use cases to the client to ensure that they are required. Some will be needed based on dependencies, but others may be deleted or deferred at the client request. The analyst will need to provide guidance in this area since there may be functionality that the client considers unnecessary but is absolutely essential for other required functions.

☞ Evaluate changes for cost. Using the list accepted by the client calculate the extra cost (effort) and schedule slip.

Never accept a change without going through the process of evaluating the real costs. Without an impact estimate, the project is headed for disaster. Even if it is clear that no additional time or manpower will be provided, the project leader should at least send a memo billing the change to the project file for documentation. If the project is seen to be overrunning its cost or schedule, this detail will be invaluable.

Although the incremental process is designed to defer changes to later increments, the evaluation and estimate should be done immediately. It is recommended that the client be billed for the cost of doing the estimate even if it can be shown that the change should have been included as part of the original application. If billing as you go for estimating new requirements is not feasible, the alternative is to keep track of the time spent estimating changes; and when the number of hours exceeds the threshold, either stop all new change requests or have the client pay for additional resources. The project leader and the client can decide how much effort for estimating changes should be included free of charge with the project before signing the contract. This threshold can serve as a warning to the client that changes have become excessive. With each change that brings the total to some significant percentage of the allotted budget, a note that warns the client of the change budget status could accompany the change estimate. For example,

> To date 50 percent of the change estimating budget has been spent.

A similar message could be sent at the 75, 80, and 90 percent points. When the dollars approach a point that there is money left for fewer than four change requests (this would be based on averages), change the memo to report dollars and change requests remaining.

> The change request budget has been depleted to $xxxx. Based on historical averages, there is enough money to handle approximately three additional requests. If you would like to discuss changing the contract to include more funds for changes, contact me this week.

12.4.1 New use cases

As an example of the change evaluation process, consider the modification to the simple video store application shown in Figure 12-1. One way to better understand changes is to create decision tables for them. Table 12-1 is the decision table used to capture the business rules for the logon use case.

> *It is now necessary for a clerk to log on to the system before performing any transactions. They must provide their user Id (cashier name) and a password.*
>
> *Once an employee has logged on, he or she will be allowed to perform most day-to-day tasks such as e-mail and time recording. If the employee is designated as a sales clerk, he or she will also be enabled to perform customer service transactions, such as enrolling new members and renting or returning videos. The system can only accommodate a limited number of logged on clerks.*

Fig. 12-1 A new requirement for the video store.

Table 12-1 The decision table for the proposed logon use case.

Logon(cashierName, password)						
Conditions						
Cashier name found	F	T	T	T	T	T
Max users currently logged on		T	F	F	F	F
Cashier is already logged on			T	F	F	F
Password is valid				F	T	T
Cashier is sales clerk					F	T
Actions						
Reject with explanation	X	X	X	X		
Mark cashier logged on					X	X
Increment number of logged on users					X	X
Display default user interface					X	X
Enable video store application						X

The following topics provide the details on the guidelines for identifying requirements beyond those stated. This process is iterative and essential when new requirements arrive frequently.

12.4.1.1 Inverse rule The inverse rule states that "Most use cases have another use case that provides the effect of reversing the original." When considering the new logon request, there is the possibility that a logoff use case will be required as well.

12.4.1.2 Parameter attribute rule The logon use case has inputs of id and password. The parameter attribute rule states that every use case parameter should map to some attribute in a business object. This is not a one-to-one relationship, but it is a many-to-one. More than one input parameter will possibly map to the same attribute. Based on this rule, since no existing attributes currently represent password and id, they will need to be added to one of the classes. The logical choice would be to store them in a Clerk class, *if* there was one.

Although this process may seem trivial with such a small change to a small problem, it is a logical thinking process that can help with larger problems. So far the questions have identified at least one more use case, one additional class, and two additional attributes.

12.4.1.3 New object use case rule   When a new class is defined, there are two questions to ask. First, are there use cases to create and destroy new objects in this class? In the current example, this will lead to the identification of addNewClerk and deleteClerk use cases. The second question is Does the object need a unique identifier attribute? In this case the assumption could be made that clerk name plays that role; however, a discussion with the client is required for a definitive answer.

12.4.1.4 Attribute use case rule   Every attribute needs a use case to set its value, and another use case to use that value. Many attributes will require a third use case to change its value. Clerk password and id can be set when the object is created, and they will be used for validation when the clerk logs on. That satisfies the first two parts of the rule. Is it possible that either of those attributes may need to change? The answer is, of course, up to the client, but they will most likely want a use case to change password.

12.4.1.5 Parameter scenario rule   This rule's question, while seemingly trivial, is still worth asking. Is there a scenario that validates each use case input? For logon, that would be invalid password and clerk id not found. For logoff, it would be invalid clerk id. The createClerk use case with inputs of clerkId and password would have similar scenarios. The deleteClerk use case would only validate that a clerk with that id existed. The change password use case's inputs would be clerk id, old password, new password, and confirm password. The related scenarios for these inputs would be clerk id not found, invalid password, and perhaps a scenario where the new password and the confirm password do not match. The client is free to select a change password use case that has only two inputs (clerk id and new password). While analysts should caution about the dangers of such an approach, the final decision remains with the client. Based on change analysis, so far, the potential new use cases identified are as follows:

```
Use Case:    logon(clerkId, password)
Outcomes:    OK
             ClerkId does not exist
             Invalid password
             Max users

Use Case:    logoff(clerkId)
Outcomes:    OK
             ClerkId does not exist

Use Case:    addNewClerk (clerkId, password)
Outcomes:    OK
             ClerkId already exists

Use Case:    deleteClerk (clerkId)
Outcomes:    OK
             ClerkId does not exist
```

```
Use Case:    changePassword(clerkId, oldPW, newPW, verifyPW)
Outcomes:    OK
             Invalid old password
             ClerkId not found
             New and verify passwords do not match
```

12.4.1.6 Scenario and state rule The scenario state rule applies except when the use case is a simple query reporting information back to the user. Every successful scenario of a nonquery use case must be remembered as a modification of one or more attributes. The use cases that add and delete the clerk are remembered by adding or removing the associated clerk object. The changePassword use case is remembered by assigning the new password to the associated clerk. But so far there is no way to record a successful logon or logoff. One option is to add a logged on attribute to clerk; there are others, but this will do for both use cases.

There is a corollary to this rule that says, "Scenarios and input states should map as well." This means that there must be a way to know that there are max users on the system, and logon and logoff must somehow affect this state. The solution is two more attributes that track the current number of logged on users and the maximum number of users that may be logged on at the same time.

With the additional attributes uncovered, the process can iterate back to the attribute use case rule and define a use case to change the maximum number of user attributes.

```
Use Case:    changeMaxUsers ()
Outcomes     OK
```

This brings the total number of use cases for this change to 6, with a combined number of scenarios equal to 14. In addition, there is one new class (Employee) with five attributes (id, password, logged on status, max users, and current users). The attributes max users and current users will be static/class attributes, shared by all employee objects.

12.4.2 Changes to existing use cases

The hardest part of estimating the impact of a new requirement is finding the changes to existing use cases. The rules stated earlier will help developers to find most of them, but without knowing why the original change was required, others may go undetected. For example, consider that the reason the client requested this change was to be able to track a rental transaction back to the clerk that performed it. If the reason for the change had been known, it might have been possible to speculate that the rent use case would require another input parameter, that of the currently logged on clerk. That would imply the application needed to maintain clerk id as part of the control object. Walking through the changes with the clients and asking them "why?" will sometimes find additional changes.

12.4.3 Estimating changes

After presenting the proposed complete list of changes to the client and having the client agree on which ones will be included in the package, the next step is to estimate the impact of these changes in terms of effort and schedule. This can be done by basing the cost on the size of this change with respect to the size of the entire application. In the simple model described here, size is equated to scenarios.

12.4.3.1 Scenario-based method   This calculation, while based on scenarios, could be based on other metrics. The guiding principle should be that there exists a correlation between the metric and the amount of effort required to implement the change associated with it. The simple estimation model that is developed in Appendix C explains how to ascertain correlation between metrics.

12.4.3.2 A simple model   Assume that the original requirement was 50 use cases and 150 scenarios. Further assume that the effort estimated for this project was 40 person-months spread over 8 calendar-months. The ratio of effort per scenario is 40/150. Multiply this times the newly discovered scenarios (10) to get a new additional effort of 2.6 person-months. The ratio of calendar-months to effort is 8/40. Multiply the additional effort by this ratio to get schedule slip: 2.6 * (8/40) or approximately 0.5 months.

Other models could have included use cases, classes, attributes, or combinations of all three as part of the size metric. The recommendation is to start with use case scenarios. Chapter 13 (Project Management) elaborates on how to gather your own project metrics and construct a local estimating model based on them.

Project Management

*T*his chapter covers the management considerations of the process, the technology, and the projects using OODP. Its emphasis is those special considerations that a project manger should give because of the new technology, but it also reviews some of the basics of project management from the perspective of object technology, especially in the areas of metrics and project planning and control. Throughout this book, many chapters refer to the discussion of project management. Now there is nowhere left to defer these items. It may seem at times that there is a hodgepodge of topics thrown together for this discussion, but in actuality it is an epilogue of the considerations that project mangers must be aware of as they forge into this new technology built around objects and use cases.

13.1 PROJECT MANAGEMENT AND THE TRANSITION TO OT

Managing a software project is not all that different because of object technology, but because object technology introduces so many new elements to the project and process, project managers may find that they need to apply the project management techniques that they already know and use, but with a little more rigor. The next few topics discuss some of these new elements and what their impact on project management might be.

13.1.1 New process

Whether the organization chooses to adopt a complete process like OODP or apply elements from several methodologies to their object-oriented development, the way they measure progress and the things they do to understand requirements, record product specifications, design, implement, and test will be different. That means that the project team must become skilled in new methods, so initially everything it does will be more difficult and take longer. This means that the staffing will be harder and that the project leaders will need to be more specific about the skills required when requesting human resources. It is no longer enough to request a programmer who can do design, or even object-oriented design. The new job description must reference capabilities based on deliverables such as "an individual who can record object-oriented design using a sequence diagram." Additionally, even though we once assumed at least a level of proficiency that allowed programmers to perform without guidance, projects may need to accept individuals with less skill in a particular area, since insufficient resources are available to meet the full qualification. These factors will requires that the plan be adjusted for lower productivity, mentored time, and additional training. When skill levels are significantly less than would be expected for programmers doing more classical development, it may be necessary to acquire the services of an expert to act in the role of mentor to support these individuals.

13.1.2 New deliverables

New methods mean new deliverables, which in turn means that the way that a project measures progress will change. Lines of code or modules complete, no long have a meaning. Even the obvious metrics like objects and methods will provide no evidence of project progress. Instead use cases and scenarios will become the predominant metrics, with business objects having a small value. That means that tasks must now be described in these terms.

> **Task:** *Record the specification for use case rentVideo*
>
> **Skill:** *Define the business rules for a use case using a decision table*
>
> **Reporting metric:** *Use cases complete (reviewed and agreed to by client)*

In the past it may have been acceptable for a project to report that analysis was complete. Detailed tracking was based on implementation deliverable, which began to appear fairly early in the process. With so many unknowns related to the new technology, the project leader must plan with more detail, even when the deliverable is more abstract. This is essential now, so that the project manager can see that the analysis phase is on schedule. Even with an incremental process, where the activity's duration may be measured in days, the project manager and the rest of his or her team must estimate the planned effort for these low-level tasks, and report status at the same level, so that everyone involved will begin to develop a sense of how long it takes to do these new things. Meanwhile, the project manager needs to be able to state with confidence when the activity will be complete based on progress that the team is making against the planned completion dates for the low-level analysis tasks. Most project managers will be surprised how much longer than expected things will take initially, but these new deliverables will allow them to measure the eventual increases in productivity, as the team grows in experience from increment to increment.

13.1.3 New metrics

Estimating as well as tracking will be based on new metrics. In object-oriented languages that combine multiple messages in the same statement, and invoke methods, which invoke methods, the concept of a line of code is no longer relevant. Work must be measured at the functional level. Use cases are one good way to measure the size of a product, scenarios are better, but during requirements gathering, when scenarios are not available, outcomes will most likely be used as the predictor of effort. It is unlikely that classes or objects will be of any value in estimating project size, since once the business classes have been developed, future applications may require no new classes. Appendix C provides instructions on how to identify the best metrics for predicting effort and how to construct a model for estimating projects and increments based on that metric. This process, while statistical, is not difficult, and the instructions are based on doing this work in a spreadsheet. However, it does require that the organization begin to collect and record information related to these metrics and the associated effort. The amount of work to do this is minimal, but it is new work and must be planned. An organization committed to migrating toward object-oriented development may wish to develop an entirely new estimating infrastructure based on these new metrics. In that way, individual projects will not be required to duplicate this effort every time. At the very least, the project manager must educate the organization in the new terms that will represent the way resources are estimated and the way progress is tracked for object-oriented projects. In some cases, this may require special education for executives before the project is underway. If everyone does not understand how significantly things may change, then there will be the temptation to assume that projects using the new technology are in trouble because no "lines of code" are being written. If the project leader can show that progress based on the new metrics is exactly what was expected and planned for in the analysis phase, then the organization's executive will be more likely to believe that the remainder of the plan will be delivered as well in the later phases. Likewise, if a project's tracking data shows the first increment taking longer than expected, it is reasonable to assume that the project was underestimated. Another project's data show productivity (per use case) increasing in later increments, and the actual data in increment one agree with the plan. For this project, it is much easier to make the case that everything is "on schedule" and that the project will complete on time.

13.1.4 New tools

Most of the tools and all the compiler-related software from the time when the organization was doing structured analysis may no longer work. Even the tool vendors that have included an object-oriented option will require that its users learn how to operate in this new mode. In some cases even personnel with non-technical jobs that provided tool support for the organization must be trained in the ways of objects. If you are fortunate enough to be using a tool that supports both the structured analysis and the object-oriented approaches, most of the configuration management issues may be minimal, but some organizations may find that they have no choice except to revise the way information related to software development is stored. Furthermore, this impact is not limited to tools that create structure charts and data flow diagram. It also includes tools that measure test coverage and manage version control and changes in source code, data model generators, and those that reverse engineered design from code.

Many organizations will be better off delaying the migration to a new tool set as long as possible, but obviously not indefinitely. Meanwhile, time will be spent in evaluating the tremendous number of tools available, to find the ones that best fit the organization's needs. For the project the best course of action is to learn using hand-drawn artifacts for at least a couple of the early increments and pilots.

13.1.5 The learning curve

It has already been explained that things will take longer the first few times, but the impact of the learning curve must be viewed from two perspectives. First, how much of an impact can the project expect as a result of using these newly acquired skills. Second, what side effects are likely when the learning curve is not managed properly.

When teams are using a significant new set of methods for software development, the estimate should include a minimum additional contingency of 25 percent for the learning curve. This is based on the assumption that all members of the team have had at least two weeks of training in the language and object-oriented methods and that no one on the team has completed a project using these methods. The 25 percent number also assumes the availability of an expert (someone with at least five years and three projects worth of experience) to act as a mentor to the team. This individual would not be responsible for performing any of the tasks for the project but instead would answer questions raised by the team, review the deliverables produced, and give guidance to the project manager. If the mentor has delivery responsibility as well, the project may succeed, but the team members will be no better off, in terms of experience, than they were before the project. The mentor needs to be available about 30 percent of the time, so need not be committed full time to a single project. This gives the organization the option of hiring a part-time mentor or using a full-time mentor to assist on two or three projects at the same time. More time will be required during requirements and analysis, less time during design, and the least participation in implementation.

If a part-time expert is not available, but 25 percent of the team consists of developers who have at least one project's experience, the 25 percent contingency still applies, but work should be apportioned such that the experienced programmers have at least half their time available to review the work of the inexperienced members of the team.

If neither of these experience mixes can be achieved, it is strongly recommended that projects with critical paths be avoided. The best environment for developing object-oriented software with a lack of real experience is a pilot project. Pilots are discussed later in this chapter, as is a plan that allows the first increment to act as the pilot.

When an inexperienced team is forced to work in an environment where there is no expertise, it will likely abandon the object-oriented process and approach. People recognize very quickly when they are incapable of performing a task, and they revert to the skills in which they have confidence. In these instances the tendency is to blame the process, object technology, its methods, and its tools. So organizations that sincerely wanted to convert to the new technology end up, not just abandoning it, but believing that it is totally ineffective, and may never revisit it again. Organizations need to understand the investment aspect of new technology and give it the full measure of time required to evaluate fairly its value and appropriateness to the organization. Some IT shops are not suited to object technology in some areas, but failure due to reckless application should not be allowed to create an atmosphere where the potential benefits are never understood.

13.2 MANAGING THE LEARNING CURVE

Having discussed the learning curve, it is necessary for the project management team to understand how to manage its progress and effects. Three aspects of the learning curve must be considered.

☞ What is the learning curve?

☞ What is its effect on the project?

☞ What are the ways to manage through it?

Later in this chapter, a discussion on skills identification and development will elaborate on many of these points. The topics that follow are intended to provide a high-level view of the issues related to skill development and the learning curve.

13.2.1 What is the learning curve?

The learning curve is the lapse between the time information is presented to an individual and the time that he or she is capable of correctly applying that information confidently without assistance. The learning curve is shown graphically in Figure 13-1. Its vertical axis is the skill levels discussed later in this chapter. They are "0—cannot use the skill, 1—can use with assistance, 2—can use without assistance, 3—can assist others, 4—can teach the skill to others." The horizontal axis is time, but with the condition that it is time spent in practicing the skill.

13.2.2 What is its effect on the project?

The learning curve initially lowers team productivity dramatically. Most of this is based on loss of confidence. As the team members begin to be able to operate without guidance, they regain the courage to explore and experiment on the job. This leads to an acceleration in learning. When the developers find that they are under pressure to make unrealistic dates, they abandon the technology and fall back on the skills that they are sure of. This suppresses growth in the learning curve and may cause the team to completely give up on the new technology as viable. This abandonment happens because the pressure suppresses the growth of learning, and frustration over lack of skill

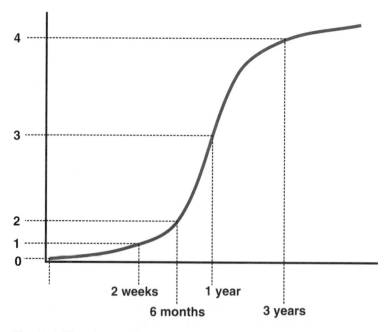

Fig. 13-1 The effect of the learning curve on skill development.

development causes the teams to look elsewhere for relief. The organization needs to recognize the impact and benefit of the learning curve and to be tolerant of it.

13.2.3 Overcoming the impact of the learning curve

There are three ways the project or organization can manage and overcome the impediments of the learning curve.

☞ Pilot projects

☞ Skill development through practice

☞ Use of mentors

13.2.3.1 Pilot projects Pilots are low-risk, short, less-complex projects that are not mission critical with sufficient schedule slack to allow them to progress at a more relaxed pace. One of their goals can be to accelerate learning by providing a nonthreatening opportunity to try out new methods, tools, and processes.

13.2.3.2 Practice When new technology training preceded actual usage by more than a few weeks, it is recommended that the team set aside time at regular intervals to practice the skills that they were introduced to in the training sessions.

13.2.3.3 Mentors Projects new to object technology can lessen the impact of the learning curve on live projects by acquiring the services of a mentor to guide the project and the project team through its first application of the methods.

Each of these topics will be discussed in greater detail under skill development.

13.3 PLANNING AND ESTIMATING

Estimating and scheduling with OODP is broken into five pieces.

☞ Other metrics and their use in planning and estimating

☞ Inappropriate use of metrics

☞ The raw estimate of the total people resources required, which was discussed earlier

☞ The distribution of the time and effort over the increments

☞ Distribution of effort among the three major roles in software development

13.3.1 Metrics

13.3.1.1 Objects   Earlier it was stated that objects are not a good predictor of effort. Even though this statement was mostly true, it assumed that the product being developed was a complete application. If the project is attempting to create a class library or framework, where there are no functional requirements, and hence no use cases, classes are a good measure of the work to be done and, therefore, represent a potential metric.

13.3.1.2 Use cases   Use cases are a good metric for doing a high-level application estimate and for tracking progress during Analysis, as well as Design, Implementation, and User Interface design. Any place where work is related to functional capabilities, use cases will work as the unit.

13.3.1.3 Scenarios   Scenarios provide more detail than the use case, so final estimates should use them as the metric. If scenarios are not available, outcomes are an excellent approximation. Scenarios are also the preferred metric for test case planning, design, and development, as well as user interface implementation.

Whereas use cases are based on pure application capability, scenarios are a reasonable measure of the complexity of the use cases. All complexity is not captured in the number of scenarios. Some design complexity will be based on the details of the scenario post-conditions. This detail will still be based on the subjective opinion of the individual designing the use case.

13.3.1.4 Process   Process metrics are most often based on defects discovered and where those defects were inserted into the product. The process is evaluated on two points: how good the process is at discovering the defects and how well it prevents them from being inserted into the application. Assume that two similar applications both create 200 defects, and through the life of the process they both remove all of them. One process successfully removes 100 of these defects during design, whereas the other only removes 50 during design and the rest during tests. The first process is considered superior since it removed more defects sooner. Similarly, if two processes can eliminate all their defects before the application is placed into production, but one process inserted fewer defects, it would be considered the superior process.

When an organization sets out to make giant improvements in quality, it needs to examine its software development process, and search for ways to decrease both error insertion and the time that an error remains after insertion. Adding more testing at the end of the process accomplishes neither of these goals. OODP does not focus on process improvement as a deliverable, but it does provide for improvement by specifying both entrance and exit criteria for each activity. When errors are discovered in a phase later than where they were inserted, the exit criteria should be reviewed. When too many errors are inserted in a given phase, the method itself, and the rigor with which it is applied, should be scrutinized.

13.3.1.5 Risk Risk was defined in Chapter 1 as an element of process activities that describe the rules for declaring an activity complete before all correctness criteria have been satisfied. However, the experienced project manager knows risk as the probability that a particular task will not be able to complete as planned. This metric is most often recorded as high, medium, or low, and means that the risk that some event will impede the task's completion has a high, medium, or low probability of happening. That translates into the risk of failure. The number of risk events is directly related to the number of unknowns in a project plan. With object technology introducing so many new variables to the process, the number of unknowns is likely to increase dramatically. The recommendation is that risk be recorded as the probability that a given task will not meet its committed schedule. This metric should be a percentage rather than the low-medium-high described earlier. This evaluation is not usually a problem for the risk evaluator, and it further allows for some differentiation among several medium or high risks. The percentage allows the project manager to combine risks of dependent tasks mathematically to compute the risk of the project. Consider a project with four tasks A, B, C, and D. Assume B is dependent on A, C is dependent on B, and D is dependent on C. Table 13-1 shows each task, its dependencies, and its individual risks. Note that task B has a probability of success of 1.0, which means that it has no associated risk.

Once the individual probabilities are defined, the probability of the project completing on time is the product of the probabilities of the dependent task, or in this case 57.4 percent. When high-risk tasks are not dependent on other high-risk tasks they do not multiply, so if all of the tasks shown in the table above were independent of each other the total project risk would be 25 percent (1 – minimum probability of success). Note that risk must first be converted to probability of success to use the foregoing technique. The project risk is of most concern to the project manager, rather than the risks of individual tasks.

13.3.1.6 Tracking Tracking progress is best accomplished using the deliverables associated with the assigned task. As stated earlier, tracking progress in a project high in new technology content is essential. If possible, attempt to

Table 13-1 Combining the probabilities of success.

Task	Dependency	1 – Risk of failure
A	—	0.75
B	A	1.00
C	B	0.85
D	C	0.90
Project		0.574

establish a completion date for each deliverable and then plot that against the actual completion, using the actual dates and simple linear regression to forecast the completion of the entire activity. Figure 13-2 shows how this would appear graphically. Notice that the trend line accounts for the rate at which the project is falling behind, rather than just the current lag in the schedule. These plots can be done easily on a spreadsheet.

13.3.1.7 Design complexity   Many have suggested metrics for measuring design complexity. These metrics are most often based on items like method fan-in or fan-out, number of attributes, method parameters, or even methods per class. The problem with most design metrics is that although they may have some relationship as an indicator of complexity, they have no quantitative interpretation. That means a class design with metric of 10 may indicate more complexity than one with 5, but it does not necessarily indicate that it is twice as complex. In fact there is no data that specifies at what values the design begins to become too complex.

13.3.2 Estimating models

In estimating, there are two problems to address. The first is deciding on the best metric, and the second is defining the best model based on that metric. The spreadsheet exercise in Appendix C incorporates both of these goals, but it is appropriate to discuss them here as well.

13.3.2.1 Finding the best metric   To determine what metrics should be considered for a particular model, the approach is to consider all available metrics

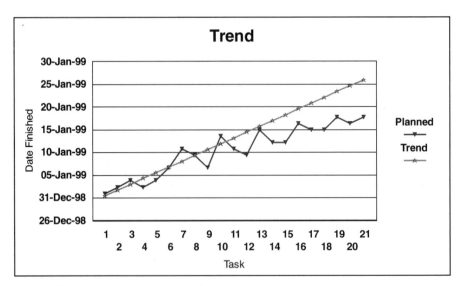

Fig. 13-2 Using regression to predict project completion.

and statistically evaluate those that have the best correlation. This means that if the goal is to build a model that converts classes into latent defects, then data must be collected from several products on number of classes and number of defects discovered after the project completed. Use the spreadsheet technique to compute the linear, and optionally the nonlinear, relation between the values. This will not only yield a regression slope and intercept but a correlation value as well. Correlations closer to 1.0 indicate that the model has some significance. Values closer to 0.0 indicate that there is no significant relationship between the metrics.

13.3.2.2 Finding the best model   Linear models are of the form $y = A + B * x$, where A and B are solved for using the regression technique. x represents the counted metric and y, the computed value. In the previous example, x would be the number of classes and y, the expected number of latent defects. When the model involves multiple input values, the model is $y = A + B * x + C * z....$ In these cases, the regression calculation will yield $n + 1$ values for n variables, and again each computed value will have its own correlation. This calculation allows for further evaluation of which metrics should remain as part of the formula and which should be discarded.

Nonlinear models are similarly computed, except that the algorithm is

$$y = A * xB + zC$$

The correlations here are based on logarithms, but are just as simply computed. After comparing the correlations of several models, choose the most promising ones.

13.3.2.3 Building the model   When one set of variables stands out as the most promising, use them to build the final model. If no one appears to be the best, but several show some promise, then base the estimate on the average of those with the best correlation.

13.3.3 Guidelines for incremental scheduling

The project manager has, as part of the planning process, responsibility to estimate not only how long it will take to build the entire application but also what percent of the total effort should be allocated to each increment. The sample project metrics that follow provide some guidance in this area.

13.3.3.1 Sample metrics for a small project   Table 13-2 shows metrics for a small three-increment sample project that was developed to train teams in the use of OODP. The project is a subset of the video store. It includes the following use cases. The outcomes are shown in braces.

```
Add Member (memberId, creditCardNumber)
    {OK, memberId exists}
Add Video (videoIdentifier)
    {OK, videoIdentifier exists}
Rent Video (videoIdentifier, memberId)
    {videoIdentifier not found, memberId not found, video already rented,
        member is ineligible}
Return Video (videoIdentifier)
    {OK, video overdue, videoIdentifier not found, video not rented}
Pay overdue fines (memberId, amount)
    {memberId not found, member has no fines due, OK, amount exceeds fines
        owed, amount less than fines owed}
Delete Member (memberId)
    {OK, member not found, member owes fines, member has videos rented}
Delete video (videoIdentifier)
    {OK, videoIdentifier does not exist, video is rented}
```

This experiment was conducted with novice object-oriented programmers, some with no object-oriented programming experience. On average, about two of each six-programmer teams had some experimental experience with Java; none had any project experience with an object-oriented language. The team distribution was as shown for six-member teams.

Application developers	2
User Interface designers/developers	2
Testers	2

The effort, elapsed time, and other project metrics are as indicated in Table 13-2. Although this data represents a project too small to be useful in producing a schedule for a large complex system, it can be representative of the time and effort required to do a small increment or pilot. In any event, each organization needs to develop its own database of estimating metrics.

13.4 METRICS AND THE SEI CAPABILITY MATURITY MODEL (CPM)

13.4.1 How metrics can improve the process

When metrics are considered in the context of process maturity, it is easier to see which metrics the organization new to object technology should be examining to support its process.

Level 2 of the CPM emphasizes validation of estimates. This implies that organizations migrating to this level should be most concerned with metrics that help the project manager predict total project effort and duration. Therefore, gathering data on scenarios, use cases, and effort expended should be the top priority of these organizations.

Level 3 of CPM focuses on project tracking and planning based on deliverables. This implies that the focus of IT shops progressing to this level should

Table 13-2 Schedule and effort data for a small training project.

	Number	Effort	Elapsed time
Use cases	7		7 hours
Scenarios	23		
Requirements		9 hours	1.5 hours
UI design		2 hours	1 hour
UI implementation		4 hours	2 hours
Increment 1 use case	3	4.5 hours	2 hours
Analysis		1 hour	0.5 hour
Design		1 hour	0.5 hour
Implementation		2 hours	1.0 hour
Test planning		2 hours	1 hour
Test development		4 hours	2 hours
Test		4 hour	1 hour
Increment 2 use cases	1	8 hours	2 hours
Increment 2 use cases	2	4 hours	1 hour

be building plans based on the deliverables of OODP and tracking to determine how close to schedule these elements are completed.

Level 4 of the SEI model suggests the ability to predict results based on measured results. This suggests that the next step is to create regression graphs to forecast the completion dates of activities based on the current actuals. This phase of process maturity is intended to bring the organization to the full realization of project management.

The final maturity level switches the focus from project management to process improvement. The goal is to improve the process to improve the product. Metrics include defects discovered and removed. If complexity measures have a place, it is here in the move to level 5, when all the other project management techniques have been mastered, and the organization is trying to fine-tune the process.

It is certainly a continuing goal to improve the process, no matter what level of the CPM the organization has achieved, but the message should be that when there are insufficient time and resources to attack all levels of process maturity, a project should focus on those that are the most in need of attention. So if estimating is ineffective, put the organization effort into improving that before trying work with design complexity issues.

13.4.2 Gathering data

An organization involved in technology advancement needs to gather data. Too much money and time are being invested in education, training, pilot projects, consultants, tools, and new processes to not spend some resources evaluating their benefit. Even though the IT budget may accept the fact that productivity will drop and costs will rise over the initial months of adoption, if some effort is not made to measure eventual improvement, how can anyone know that the investment was worthwhile.

In addition to measuring productivity, these metrics provide the opportunity to create meaningful models that can be used to predict effort, duration, and even defects on future projects. Do not waste the opportunity to gather this data. Below is a partial list in priority order of the metrics that an organization should be compiling.

Total project effort

Use cases

Scenarios

Effort by major activity (analysis, design, etc.)

Percent of duration of activity vs. entire project

Average time per deliverable (e.g., average days to develop a use case in analysis)

Defects inserted by activity

Defects removed by activity

That is enough for now. The grouping represents the priority, and it is recommended that all the items in a group be considered at the same time.

13.4.3 Manpower distribution test/development/UI

In the small training project, the distribution of manpower was 2 developers, 2 testers, and 2 user interface designer/implementers. Experience has shown that fewer application developers and user interface developers would be better. The user interface team was also doing some screen design that would have been done by the user interface designer, and when students were reluctant to take on any serious programming, they generally opted for the user interface team. Likewise the strongest members of the team chose application development, and generally found that there was not enough work for both members, so the recommended ratio is 1 tester, 0.75 user interface implementer, and 0.75 application developer. This is logical since the test team must write a method for every scenario, while the interface and application interface teams are writing methods proportional to the number of use cases.

13.5 PILOT PROJECTS

With so much new technology and an uncertainty about the schedule created by the learning curve, the advantages of a pilot project cannot be overstated. Pilots allow an organization the opportunity to evaluate how well the technology and the software development projects work together. When searching for the ideal project to sample object technology, look for a project with the following characteristics:

- ☞ Small enough to be completed within 4 months or less.
- ☞ Large enough to exercise most of the aspects of the technology.
- ☞ Simple enough to not overwhelm the developers to the point where they cannot pay adequate attention to the way they are developing the software.
- ☞ Complex enough that the organization will have the sense that "it will work" on the rest of their projects.
- ☞ Focuses on a single technology.
- ☞ A team with some experience with the technology, or if that is not possible, make sure that they are recently trained, enthusiastic, and augmented with an expert mentor.
- ☞ A project, or subproject well off the critical path.

Consider each of these as a goal, not a must. The important thing is that everyone understand the goals of the pilot should be

- ☞ To evaluate the technology
- ☞ To give experience to the team in using the technology in a risk-free environment
- ☞ To provide feedback to the organization on what works well and what does not

13.5.1 Project size

If the project is too large, the real goals get superimposed with the objective of just getting it done. There is a considerable amount of review and reflection that is required as the pilot proceeds. When there is too much project, the important stuff gets skipped. Assuming that an organization can find a small project with enough meat, an ideal pilot would be about two months in length.

13.5.2 Pilot complexity

There will be enough new "stuff" for the team to learn, and try, without further taxing their intellect with a complex problem. It is assumed that your programmers already know how to design programs that are difficult. The purpose of the pilot is to determine whether they can design regular programs using the new technology. To put it in perspective, try to find a program that could be developed by a small team (four to six developers) in about a month, then use that for the two-month pilot.

13.5.3 Single technology

Object-oriented languages, methods, processes, and deliverables are considered the single most important parts of the new technologies. Other technologies that may need to be considered by a later separate pilot are

- ☞ Reuse
- ☞ Inheritance design
- ☞ Tools

When a pilot attempts to integrate more than one technology, the negative productivity effect is multiplied, and often everything is abandoned, and one or all the technologies are blamed. Limit the pilot to just one or two new things at a time.

13.5.4 Team experience

Ideally an organization would like to staff the pilot with three of the six team members having worked on an object-oriented project before, but most of the time if an organization can find individuals with those qualifications, they may not need a pilot. A more practical approach may be to prepare a small team of enthusiastic programmers, with basic education in object-oriented analysis and design, as well as the process and the programming language to be used. Then supplant the team with a mentor who understands the process as well and use the pilot as a part of the team's overall training. The basic education should be completed between two and three weeks before the project begins (this means that it is not part of the two months). The lag is to give the team a little time to experiment with their new skills before the pilot begins.

13.5.5 Project criticality

Critical projects have a deadline, and when one of the goals of a project is to meet a date, by definition all other goals become insignificant. That is not to say that the pilot cannot produce a usable piece of code, it is just that it cannot be required until a date at least two months after the pilot was scheduled to complete. This gives the organization time to do the work over from scratch, if it turns out that the pilot produces no usable code. It should be noted that a project that produces no usable code could still be considered an enormous success as a pilot. That is why it is called a pilot and not a project. Think of a pilot as a technology transfer prototype.

13.5.6 Evaluating the technology

To be effective in evaluating the technology, the pilot and the organization need to know in advance what they expect the technology to do for them. In the case of object orientation, that pretty much eliminates productivity as one of the items the pilot plans to demonstrate. The technology to be demonstrated should be limited to evaluating the process, the methods, the language, and the deliverables. Evaluation will vary from organization to organization, but here are some guidelines.

☞ Process

  ✗ All elements are applicable.

  ✗ Entrance and exit criteria are acceptable to all parties.

☞ Development methods and techniques

  ✗ Techniques and skills required to perform are learnable.

  ✗ Methods work well within the process selected.

  ✗ Methods are not counterproductive,

☞ Deliverables

  ✗ Deliverables support the process.

  ✗ Deliverables were found useful in reviews.

  ✗ Deliverables were found useful in subsequent activities.

☞ Language

  ✗ Language is learnable in a reasonable period of time.

  ✗ Language is capable of implementing most applications for this organization.

  ✗ Language can meet performance need of organization's applications.

13.5.6.1 Gaining experience   If the pilot is well selected, it becomes an excellent vehicle for giving the team experience, and more importantly confidence, in the new technologies. Although the primary goal is to evaluate the technology, the pilot as a training vehicle is ideal, since when the pressure is off, technical individuals will automatically allow themselves to fall into experimentation mode, which accelerates the learning curve. Often a pilot where the team has the opportunity to push beyond the immediate goals of evaluation will learn as much as if they had participated in two separate year-long projects with deadlines and no time to "play."

13.5.6.2 Organization feedback   The final goal of the pilot is to provide feedback, most likely in the form of a report, to the organization on the highlights and the low points of the project. This feedback should be treated like a project post mortem and identify not only all the good and bad things that happened but also what the team would do different the next time, if there were a next

time. This type of information is invaluable to the groups that were not fortunate enough to participate in the pilot, which allows for an important comment. It's okay to give many groups within an organization their own pilot.
The advantages just identified need not be isolated to just one area of the
organization. However, keep in mind that pilots are a technology investment
expense, just like education, tools, computers, etc.

13.6 TRACKING AND CONTROLLING THE NEW PROCESS

Project tracking and control, while clearly basic project management activities,
have their importance elevated considerably with the introduction of new technology. Experienced project managers are able to sense the progress of their
teams based on day-to-day status and amount of running code available. Object
technology, incremental development, and a formal process like OODP that has
several deliverables may make this style of project control more difficult, not
just for the project manager but also for other stakeholders in the organization
dependent on the activities of their project. The major reasons why the project
manager will need to exercise greater control over project progress are

☞   Increments do not distribute work evenly.

☞   Deliverables that are not executable may seem a waste of time.

☞   The learning curve associated with new technology will initially deterio-
      rate productivity.

This section considers how these items have an impact on the ability to
be in control of the project and then describes techniques for maintaining control and tracking progress.

13.6.1 Increments do not distribute work evenly

Consider a project divided into five increments, each with the identical number of use cases, and assume that the use cases are distributed such that each
increment has use cases of approximately the same complexity. The effort
required to complete the first increment is perhaps as much as twice that to
build the last, even if the team is already experienced with the technology.
This means that if the project is evaluated at the end of increment one, and
the metrics are extended to estimate the duration of the rest of the project, the
resulting schedule may appear so unacceptable that the project will be can-
celled. Table 13-3 shows a more likely distribution of effort, given an equal
number of scenarios in all increments.

13.6.2 Some deliverables may seem a waste of time

Organizations that are used to tracking progress with metrics like code completed or modules tested will become uneasy as the new deliverables delay the

Table 13-3 Sample effort distribution over increments.

Increment	Percent of scenarios	Percent of effort
1	20	30
2	20	25
3	20	20
4	20	15
5	20	10

traditional ones. It may seem that a project is not making progress when it reports use cases defined, followed by decision tables completed, and sequence diagrams reviewed. The benefit of doing a good job in analysis and design can prove to be a bit frightening when these phases burn up half of a total schedule for a project without yielding a single line of code. This new pace, if compared to a project operating in the old waterfall rush to code style, can make it appear that the new object-oriented methods are ineffective as compared to the "old way," and this perception may cause an organization to put pressure on the object-oriented project to stop spending so much time in these early phases and to get on with the job of developing some code.

13.6.3 The learning curve will initially deteriorate productivity

As was mentioned earlier, the effect of new technology on a project will require at least 25 percent more resources. If the organization chooses to attempt this conversion without proper training and experienced mentors to guide the novices through the initial phase of the learning curve, the impact will be even greater, perhaps as much as double the time to build the same system, using the organization's traditional languages, methods, and processes. Again, this sharp decrease in productivity can be erroneously interpreted as what is to be expected whenever this new technology is used.

13.6.4 Planning and tracking

To give everyone confidence that the project is still on schedule, even with the slowdown in progress caused by the elements just described, it is important that the project manager be able first to predict the productivity drop in advance and, second, to show that the overall plan is based on productivity increasing as the project proceeds.

To accomplish this, create a plan based on an overall increase in effort of 25 percent (assuming that you have brought in the appropriate level of technology expertise). Then either distribute the effort evenly across all increments, but remove about 25 percent of the use case from the first increment and move them to the third or fourth. Optionally, distribute the work (the number of scenarios) evenly across all the increments but move some of the effort from the latter increments to the first and second. Given the distribution of increments and use cases, create a schedule for increments showing the beginning and ending dates for each activity from analysis through test. Keep in mind that testing and user interface development overlap with application development.

At the start of each activity, rough out the date by which each individual deliverable would have to be completed for the activity to meet its schedule deadline. Once the plan is complete, track the actual dates for each completed deliverable, and project the completion of each phase based on the observed trends. When analysis is complete, update the schedule to reflect the deliverables and their planned completion dates in design, and once again track actuals and forecast phase, increment, and project completion dates.

This tracking will yield one of three results:

☞ The project will be on schedule, or very close to on schedule.
☞ The project will be ahead of schedule by some number of days.
☞ The project will be behind schedule by some number of days.

The first option is an indication that the overall project will most likely finish on time. The team's estimates were reasonable, and so far they are pretty accurate. All that remains is to continue to plan and track the remaining activities and increments, to ensure that things don't go wrong. In this scenario, you can request that the organization maintain confidence in your existing plan and IT schedule, since you have shown that the target dates for the deliverables that precede code were met. It is therefore reasonable to assume that all other targets will be met. If the plan continues this way through the end of increment one into the first few activities of increment two, everyone's confidence will soar.

The second result, while at first seemingly good news, is not the same confidence booster as being right on schedule. It offers you two choices. The first is not to report the early finishes but to hold back until the trend is extended for two or three more checkpoints. The second choice is to replan immediately. When available, the first option would be preferred, but in either case look for the bad assumptions in the planning. If planning were merely done too conservatively, then the project will continue to move ahead of schedule at a steady rate, and it will become more likely that the project is really ahead of the plan and an adjustment can be made. On the other hand, if the planning were just done poorly, then the project may fall back or even lurch ahead or back by an amount inconsistent with any trend. In this case, you need to regroup and figure out what is wrong.

The last case is just a variation on the second; the only difference is that the initial data shows the project behind. Continue to track and look for reasons for the variance and try to determine whether the plan was poorly done or just laid out too aggressively. In all these cases, the team and organization can watch as the project tracks on or off the plan, and if adjustments to resources, function, or schedule need to be made, they can be done much earlier in the process because the tracking data are available so much sooner.

13.6.5 Managing the 10 percent overlap

The waterfall model discussed in Chapter 2 describes an overlap in the phases, which in some projects is so great that coding is beginning before requirements are completed. The recommendation was that this overlap should be no more than 10 percent. This means that if a project is assumed to have 100 use cases, analysis can begin as soon as 90 have been identified. The problem with this tack is that you don't know how many use cases there are in total, you only know how many have been found. So how does the team plan on finding 90 percent? There are five steps to attaining this goal.

☞ When you stop finding use cases, applying the discovery methods described in Chapters 3 (Requirements Definition), 9 (Test Planning), and 12 (Maintenance), assume that you have found the planned 90 percent. The assumption is that the effort to find the next few use cases is greater than that required to deal with them as they turn up later in the process.

☞ Keep track of how many were found and how many were discovered subsequently.

☞ At the end of the project, this number can confirm or refute the hypothesis that 90 percent were found with the planned activity. A sanity check must be applied here to ascertain whether the additional use cases were within the initial project scope or not. Do not count the ones that were not. However, do count use cases that were considered in scope but rejected because they were discovered too late and were not considered critical.

☞ Investigate what caused the team to not be able to discover the remaining use cases. Some possible reasons are

✗ Lack of diligence in applying the rules of discovery

✗ Insufficient initial detail to start the requirements process

✗ Lack of cooperation or motivation on the part of the client

The real reasons are whatever the team believes they are. Your list will be different than the preceding one, but make a list. Look at a missing requirement, review each of the discovery questions, and ask should this have uncovered this one. If the answer is yes, then the first reason applies. Use similar criteria for other causes.

☞ Finally, ask how the requirements activity might be changed in the future to unearth more of those use cases. It is this step that will move the process closer to the objective of finding 90 percent of the use cases. Without the analysis described here, achieving that goal is a mere matter of luck.

13.6.6 Dealing with risk

The 90 percent target was a risk associated with the requirements activity in OODP. Other activities have similar risks that should be evaluated post-project in a very similar way. These include items like

- ☞ Did coding errors result from detailing too few use case designs?
- ☞ Were too many changes allowed into the product after analysis?
- ☞ Did changes not get reflected in the requirements use case definitions and, therefore, were not communicated to the rest of the team?

In each case, the step to reevaluate the risk and its impact are almost identical.

- ☞ Make the assumption about how much is enough, and the resulting impact.
- ☞ Compute the error in the assumption and the real impact.
- ☞ Review the reason why the process was not as effective as possible.
- ☞ Attempt to adjust the process to improve the results of the next iteration.

13.7 IMPROVING THE PROCESS

Managing the 10 percent activity overlap describes an example of process improvement. The same model can be applied to any area of the process where results do meet expectations, such as defects discovered, or average time to complete tasks that produce the same deliverable. In all cases, the process improvement goals and activities are the same. The goal of process improvement is to produce a deliverable that has one or all the following attributes:

- ☞ More reliable
- ☞ Better quality
- ☞ More accurate
- ☞ Less costly

Process improvement, as a strategy, assumes that the defects in the deliverable are not the fault of the producer as much as they are the fault of the process, and it is more efficient and effective to repair the process rather than the deliverable. As an example, assume that programs historically complete development with 0.01 latent defects per use scenario. The organization has decided that there is a financial benefit to reducing the number of latent defects. They have roughly three choices on how to proceed.

- ☞ Assume that their programmers are doing sloppy work and try to motivate them to do better.
- ☞ Enhance the testing process and try to find more of the remaining faults before committing the application to production.

☞ Attempt to improve the process so that fewer errors are inserted into the product.

Process improvement always takes the last tack, and possible approaches would be to provide more skills training or development, enhance the review and inspection activities, use expert consultants and mentors, or enhance the exit criteria of activities that seem to be introducing the most defects. This may seem a round-about way to eliminate the defect, but in the long run it is far more effective because, by changing the process, the improvement is permanent.

13.7.1 Steps of process improvement

Process improvement is a journey, which involves examining the flaws, determining where the flaw originated in the process, and asking if it could have been avoided or removed before the activity ended. There are four actions to accomplish this.

☞ Examine the final work product for the most serious defects. Serious is relative, and as the more sensitive flaws are eliminated, the less important ones move up in seriousness. That is why process improvement is a journey. Until all flaws have been permanently eliminated, the process of improving the process continues. Finding defects is relatively easy—they seem to show up where they are not wanted—but it is important to categorize a defect's severity based on its impact to the user of the deliverable that contains it and avoid the temptation of basing seriousness on how difficult it will be to eliminate the flaw in the future.

☞ Try to determine where in the process the defect was inserted. If the program has a compiler error, it is most likely a coding defect. If it has a logic error, it could have been introduced during either design or code. If the final application behaves incorrectly with respect to the specification, the error could have been created almost anywhere in the process. If the use case description is determined to have been incorrect, then the flaw was inserted during analysis. If the decision table was correct, but it was the sequence diagram that had the error, then the error slipped in during design. The same logic can be applied if the sequence diagram was correct as well. That would imply that the flaw was created when the design was implemented. If the use case containing the defect had no decision table or sequence diagram, then the coder incorrectly interpreted the requirements and introduced the error.

☞ Given the insertion point of the defect, review the methods of that activity to see if they could be improved to create fewer defects in the future. A less desirable choice is to ask if the correctness question and the review at the end of the activity could be elaborated to catch the error before the deliverable is turned over to the next activity. Perhaps the design activity can be made less error-prone by requiring that designers have at least one increment where they work with an experienced leader before they are allowed to design on their own. Or it is decided that each design will be reviewed by two team members instead of the usual one. Another possibility is that too few designs are being formally recorded as sequence diagrams. In all these cases, it was the procedure that was modified, and if effective may produce fewer errors in many products to come. Part of this step is to weigh the impact, in terms of time and money, of changing the process. Although having the design reviewed by one extra person may be cost effective with respect to the time saved in handling this error later in the process, or after project completion, adding 10 additional reviewers is most likely not cost effective. Even though this latter option may be disregarded, that does not mean that there is not another solution that is cost effective.

☞ Finally, evaluate the effect of the change by examining the deliverables created from the modified process. Process improvement can be tricky. If too many changes are made at once, then there is the possibility that they will cancel each other out and a good process change will be lost because of it. Likewise, an improvement may make a difference, but if not examined closely enough, it will be missed. Suppose that the old design method produced an average of one error for every five use cases. When the new process is put in place, that ratio improves to one out of every six. If enough detail is not available, the improvement may not even be noticed, and yet it was effective. The new products coming out of it have 20 percent fewer defects because of the change.

Table 13-4 summarizes the steps for improving the software development process..

13.7.2 Lessons learned

Process details often get lost or forgotten in the "heat of the schedule." That information is required to make the process improvements described earlier. After that project is completed, it may not be as easy to recall where the defect was inserted or what may have caused it. Consider holding a short review at

Table 13-4 Process improvement activities.

- Examine the final work product for the most serious defects.
- Determine where in the process the defect was inserted.
- Review the methods of that activity to see if they could be improved to create fewer defects.
- Evaluate the effect of the change by examining the deliverables created from the modified process.

the end of every activity, or at least at the conclusion of every increment, where the team reflects on where it felt there may have been problem areas, and where there were some exceptional high spots. Record these very informally in the project file. This meeting should last no longer than an hour if it is held at the end of an activity, or perhaps three or four hours if held at the end of an increment. This will provide the stimulus for the project wrap-up meeting, when the real process improvement work can be given the time it needs.

The project and process highlights and lowlights recorded informally at the end of each phase can be scrutinized and converted to either changes to the process to be applied immediately or suggestions that may need to be considered as potential changes by future projects. Categorize these latter changes by activity and make them available as a lessons-learned resource that future project managers and group leaders can review at the beginning of each new project or at the start of a process activity. They can then be selectively applied depending on the specifics of that project. This information may facilitate small improvements to the process that would have otherwise never been considered, or perhaps they will act as warning signals for pitfalls to be avoided. In either case, since the information was not considered essential to all future projects, it may have never been available, if it were not documented in the lessons-learned file.

13.8 SKILL ACQUISITION AND DEVELOPMENT

The last topic to be discussed in Part I of this book may seem a bit out of place, but it is intended to be a reflection, on the part of the project leaders, of all the new skills that may be required to implement new technologies and how to manage their acquisition. This chapter has already discussed the new talents required for OT and provided guidance on identification of these skills by ensuring that tasks are tied to deliverables, which in turn are linked to skills. The details of the preceding chapters provided specifics on what artifacts should be produced and how to create them. What has not yet been discussed is how to acquire these skills. Perhaps this topic should have been the first one in this chapter, or included in requirements, where planning was first discussed. However, it is the belief that after the details of OODP and its management have been explained, the suggestions that follow will be able to be better explained in the context of the process.

It should be clear to the reader that the placement of the details of this topic is not related to when it should be performed within the process.

13.8.1 Skill identification

Skill identification is based on the assumption that skills are directly related to the deliverables to be produced. The following bulleted items review the steps of skill identification.

☞ Define the activities.

☞ Define the deliverables.

☞ Define the tasks associated with each deliverable.

☞ Describe the skills required based on creating that deliverable.

Create a work breakdown structure that is granular enough that at its lowest level the task to be completed will produce a single deliverable. For schedules that are describing activities over the next two or three months, these will reflect one instance of that deliverable. For example, task A1 would be to create the decision table for the use case rentVideo. This allows assigning the task to an individual. For tasks that are not to begin in this time frame, it is enough to identify a higher level task that describes the creation of several of these deliverables. Task A—create decision tables: This task could also be broken down in smaller chunks, to allow for resource estimating. The task could identify several use cases that need to have decision tables created. Since the deliverable is the same, the skill required to produce these deliverables is the same. Once the project manager knows how many deliverables are required, the time required, and the time available, the manager is in a better position to estimate the number of individuals with this skill that will be required and during what time periods they will be needed.

When identifying skills, be sure to specify the level of performance as part of the requirement. These fall into four of the five skill categories.

☞ Perform the task with guidance from others.

☞ Perform the task with no guidance.

☞ Guide others in performing the task.

☞ Teach others to perform the task.

13.8.2 Skill acquisition

Skill acquisition is probably the most important and most difficult task that project managers face. It is the most difficult because it is often based on the subjective opinions of the person being considered, the individual making the recommendation, and the team or project leader making the selection. The most effective tools available (in order of least to most) to help in the decision making are

☞ A resume with references to where and when the individual has performed this task in the past

☞ Direct interrogation on the ability of the individual to create the required deliverable

☞ Testing to see if the individual is capable of creating the deliverable as required by the task

☞ First-hand knowledge based on observation of the individual on a prior project

13.8.2.1 Observation   Clearly, having worked with someone who has performed the task before, or knowing a person that has, is the best confirmation of his or her ability to perform successfully in the future. In many organizations, this is accomplished by having the same team move from project to project. Both the team member and the project manager understand everyone's capabilities, which in some cases may create a situation where everyone agrees that no one has the required skill.

13.8.2.2 Testing   Testing is the next best option, and it is actually a simple matter to prepare a short exercise to see if the candidate can develop the necessary deliverable given the requirement. For example, suppose that an individual claims to be capable of doing use case design given a specification in the form of a decision table. If the prospective team member were handed a decision table for a use case and asked to create a sequence diagram that reflected a correct design, the results could easily be evaluated to determine whether the person had the skills he or she claimed or not. If there is a problem with this approach, it is that many believe that tests exert unnatural pressure on those to be tested, and may not fairly evaluate their skills.

13.8.2.3 Interrogation   When no other data are available to support the individual's ability to perform the task required, it may be necessary to ask the candidate a few direct questions. Have you ever worked with use cases before? Did you use decision tables or sequences diagrams. What specific deliverables did you create on your last project? Did you ever act as a mentor to someone else learning these skills?

13.8.2.4 References and resumes   The last level of resource evaluation is subjective. When candidates list experience and references as the only evidence of their ability to perform a task, you can contact the references, or have them describe in their own words the details of their assignment.

13.8.3 Skill development

As important as it is to understand the skill requirements, it is just as important to be prepared to adapt to the skills set that is provided. That means assessing the team skills and determining where the shortfalls are. It is unlikely that you will get all the skills you need in the time frame you need them, so any skills definition plan must be converted to a skills development plan as soon as the actual skills of the actual team members are ascertained. Skill development can be accomplished in four ways.

Formal classroom education

Self-study, reading, personal experimentation

Mentoring

On the job learning—trial and error

13.8.3.1 Classroom education   The most readily available skill development medium is classroom training. This venue brings together a subject matter expert and the development team. It should provide a mix of prepackaged lecture and exercise, as well as educational interaction where the student can affect the direction of the learning. Hands-on training is a good technique to jumpstart the self-learning process, but it should not be considered a substitute for it. Classroom-acquired information has a half-life of only a week or so, if it is not applied or renewed, and usually only provides skills that can be applied with assistance from others.

13.8.3.2 Self-study and practice   Most self-study alternatives require that time be allocated in the plan for these extra activities, where the developers will stop being productive. Education is easy because it is obvious when they are in the classroom that they are not working on their assignment, but self-study is trickier because managers are reluctant to let an individual go into goof-off mode on the job when there is work to be done, even though this time may be a very cost-effective way of increasing the team's skill level. One way to formalize this learning time is to make it a group activity. Let the group structure how they will spend the time allotted. The most effective way to schedule these sessions is to slice out an hour and a half or so, on the same day every week. During non-periods, the developers would be working on projects using the methods and skills that they have been applying for years. The playtime would be for practicing new skills. Here are some guidelines for these sessions.

☞ Add the activities to the work plan for their current project so that everyone will know that they are not supposed to find the time themselves.

☞ Do not require any reports or ask for status from the group in these meetings. This will make it seem like there is some specific measurable objective to be achieved. This is not productive. Skills development is hard work, and it CANNOT be rushed by providing checkpoints.

☞ Do not assign work to the group that is related to current responsibilities or current projects. The best stuff to practice on is requirements from completed projects. In that way, they do not get bogged down in complexity issues and can focus on the new skills that they are trying to develop.

☞ Always apply the methods and skills in as formal and complete a way as possible. Do not cut the corners that you might on a real project. Cutting corners is an easy skill to learn later. This means that they should use all the theoretical as well as the practical methods.

☞ Avoid the use of tools, unless the tool is the critical skill that you are trying to master. Tools tend to get in the way, and any method that cannot be applied without a tool should be avoided.

☞ Leave some time at the end of every session to review what was done, and ask, How else could it have been done? Sometimes the answer may become the topic for the next week's sessions.

13.8.3.3 Mentoring Mentors can be an extremely effective way to facilitate technology transfer. They allow the development team to do all, or practically all, of the actual work in creating the deliverables, and then reviewing the work products and providing feedback on their correctness and goodness. In this way, the team has ownership of the products, but the project has the confidence that it is being done correctly. The mentor can also help with the planning and estimating so that the project tends to stay more or less on schedule. An effective mentor should also be able to provide some supplemental training to the team, as it is required.

13.8.3.4 On the job learning The most effective and most time-consuming approach to skills development is to let the teams flounder about and learn completely on their own. A simple pilot project that should have taken three or four weeks with a mentor can easily take several months with no assistance. Even preceding this activity with a couple weeks of classroom training will not make an appreciable difference. In some cases, there may be no other assistance available in the new technologies. However, care must be taken that the team understands the frustration they are taking on, or they will abandon the new approaches very quickly.

It is appropriate to end this chapter and this part of the book with a summary of the activities that project managers, working for the first time in object technology, should focus on.

☞ Identify skills based on required deliverables.

☞ Be prepared to adapt the plan when available skills fall short of those required.

☞ Do not ignore or underestimate the learning curve.

☞ Use a rigorous and robust process to guarantee that each deliverable is a precise refinement of the requirements.

☞ Track the actual completion dates of each deliverable compared with the plan, and use the data to forecast project progress and completion date.

☞ When evaluating new methods and processes, attempt the first use of the new deliverables without tools.

☞ Consider using a pilot to lessen the effect of the learning curve and to evaluate new technology before integrating it into the organization.

An Example Creating OODP Deliverables

This section walks through the development of the complete set of deliverables for the video store, using four increments. Code is shown for a few test cases, a control method, and one interface method. These are included just for demonstration. A complete set of source code for the application, business objects, test cases, and the user interface test case can be downloaded from ***http://www.obps.com/downloads.html***. The other deliverables begin with the statement of requirements, and as each new deliverable is encountered, a narrative briefly reviews the activity that creates that deliverable.

Chapter 14 introduces the textual requirements and develops the use cases, the incremental plan, and the project plan. Chapter 15 presents the deliverables for each activity in increment one. Chapter 16 presents some coding sample for test cases, use case control methods, and user interface test methods. Chapters 17 through 19 are the deliverables for increments two, three, and four. Chapter 20 includes details of the user interface development and test object and examples of state diagrams.

Requirements and the Incremental Plan

*T*his chapter describes the complete video store requirements and shows all of the requirements deliverables.

- ☞ Vocabulary
- ☞ Actors
- ☞ Use case definition
- ☞ Input types
- ☞ Incremental plan
- ☞ Project plan

14.1 REQUIREMENTS STATEMENT

14.1.1 Overall

Customers should be able to browse the store's video catalogue via a kiosk in the customer floor area. This would allow for customers to make queries like "show me a list of films directed by Woody Allen" or "show me movies in which Tom Hanks appears." The system must be able to administer the renting and returning of videos, using a graphical user interface. The clerk should be able to find out if a copy of a video is available, rented, or missing (meaning it is lost). It should also be possible to determine when a title will become available, if it is rented. If the title is not available in this branch, it should be able to determine whether it is available at another store. Each morning have the program print and flag all customers who have overdue movies, which movies they are, and how overdue they are. The system should be able to provide how many times a movie has been rented and report on the most popular rentals and the "poor performers." It should be possible for customers to call and make reservations for movies, whether they are available or not. If the movie is not rented, then the clerk should go out to the shelf and remove the video so that no one else can claim it (this is currently done today). If the movie is currently rented, then the customer is added to the wait list for that movie. When the movie is returned, the system should check the reservations and notify a clerk to call the customer who is first on the waiting list.

14.1.2 Customers

The system must be able to add, update, and remove customers from the system. Customers must become a member and provide a credit card. Members only need to show their membership card at the time of rental. A customer who has not returned a movie that is due will not be allowed to rent or reserve additional movies until the overdue movies are returned and any late charges are paid.

14.1.3 Videos

The system must maintain information on every title carried by the stores and be able to add new titles as they arrive and remove titles if they become damaged, lost, or stolen. It should handle categories of movies (e.g., action, comedy, and children's movies). Each movie can only belong to one category. Each movie should have a rating (G, PG, PG13, R, NR) and an age limit. Anyone younger than the age limit for a movie will not be allowed to rent that movie. Each cassette should be marked with a bar code, which contains a system-recognizable identifier for that copy of a movie. Each movie has a title and a suggested rental price. A copy which is already rented cannot be rented again until it is returned. A copy of a movie can also be recorded as "missing."

14.1.4 Vendors

The company buys movies from vendors. The vendor charges a royalty based on the number of rentals. This is either a fixed fee per rental or a percentage of the rental price. The application must maintain information on what movies are purchased, from which vendors, and the royalties that are owed the vendors based on rentals. It must be able to produce a list of vendors and how much money each one should receive for a given time period.

14.1.5 Rentals

Members can currently rent a maximum of three videos. A printed rental agreement should contain information on who rented the films, the titles of the movies, when they were rented, when they should be returned, and the total amount charged.

14.2 REQUIREMENTS DELIVERABLES

14.2.1 Nouns

Scan the raw requirements text for nouns. Identify each one as either object/ attribute, actor, alias, event, or N/A. For aliases include the original noun. All of the foregoing classifications except for N/A will become the candidate vocabulary. During requirements these terms will be used to write the use case definitions.

Noun	Type	Noun	Type
Customer	Actor	Credit card	Object/attribute
Store	Alias (branch)	Deposit	Object/attribute
Kiosk	N/A	Time of rental	Object/attribute
Video catalogue	Object/attribute	Late charges	Object/attribute
Floor area	N/A	Paid	Object/attribute
Query	Event	Category	Object/attribute
Film	Object/attribute	Rating	Object/attribute
List of films	Object/attribute	Age limit	Alias (rating)
Movies	Alias (film)	Anyone	Alias (Customer)
System	N/A	Cassette	N/A
Video	Object/attribute	Bar code	N/A
User interface	N/A	Identifier	Object/attribute
Clerk	Actor	Title	Object/attribute
Copy	Object/attribute	Rental price	Object/attribute
Rented	Object/attribute	Rented	Object/attribute
Missing	Object/attribute	Returned	Object/attribute
Title	Object/attribute	Missing	Object/attribute
Branch	Object/attribute	Shop	Object/attribute
Morning	N/A	Vendors	Object/attribute
Overdue	Object/attribute	Royalty	Object/attribute
Times...rented	Object/attribute	Number of rentals	Object/attribute
Popular	Object/attribute	Fee	Object/attribute
Enough (rental)	Object/attribute	Database (vendor)	N/A
Rental	Object/attribute	Purchased	N/A
Poor performer	Object/attribute	List of vendors	Object/attribute
Reservation	Object/attribute	Money (due)	Object/attribute
Not rented	Object/attribute	Time period	Object/attribute
Wait list	Object/attribute	Max rentals	Object/attribute
Next	Object/attribute	Rental agreement	Object/attribute
Reservation	Alias (wait list)	Who rented	Alias (customer)
Discount	Object/attribute	When rented	Object/attribute
Membership	Object/attribute	When return	Alias (due)
Identification	N/A	Amount charged	Object/attribute
Membership card	N/A		

14.2.2 Actors and use cases

For each actor, list the associated use cases. The same use case may appear with more than one actor. However, this has not been done in this example.

14.2.2.1 Actors

Clerk
Customer
Manager
Administrator

14.2.2.2 Use cases

Clerk

Get video availability—Reports if video is available, rented, or not carried.

New rental agreement—Initiates a sequence of rentals for the same customer.

Rent a video—Adds a single video to a rental agreement.

Rental override—Allows renting to an ineligible customer.

Reserve a video—Adds a customer to the wait list if no copies are available.

Cancel rental—Cancels the entire rental agreement.

Collect rental fee—Closes out the rental agreement.

Return a video—Marks a video as available and checks for late fees.

Pay fine—Reduces the amount of fines owed by a customer.

Customer

Search a title—Scans movie database for information on the title.

Find videos for actor—Scans a list of videos for those in which this actor played a part.

Find videos for director—Scans a list of videos for those that this person directed.

View cast—Shows the main cast for this film.

View video clip—Shows a clip, if available, for this film.

Manager

Add new video title—Adds a new title to be carried by the stores.

Add a new copy—Adds a copy of an existing title for a given branch.

Set copy status—Used to mark a copy as missing or restore it to available when it is found.

Remove a copy—Removes a copy of a title from stock.

Remove a video—Removes the tile from all stores.

Add a customer—Adds a new customer.

Remove customer—Deletes the customer.

Run usage report—Reports on how often videos were rented in a given period.

Run overdue report—Identifies overdue videos.

Administrator

Add video category—Adds a new category for videos.

Add a vendor—Adds a vendor for movies and assigns an id.

Remove a vendor—Removes the vendor.

Run vendor royalty report—Itemizes how much royalty is owed a vendor for a given period.

Define a branch—Creates a new branch for assigning copies.

Remove a branch—Removes the branch.

14.2.3 Use case definitions

For each use case, record its inputs and its outcomes. Include along with the outcome any returned information. These will become the formal statement of requirements that will last throughout the project and into maintenance. The project manager will use these to create an estimate and a plan. They will be used by the user interface team to define the interface between the user interface and the application and by the test team to develop the test plan. The return code associated with each scenario is shown preceding the outcome.

Use case	defineBranch
Inputs	branch number
Outcomes	10100, OK
	10114, Branch exists
Use case	addCategory
Inputs	category
Outcomes	10200, OK
	10214, Category exists
Use case	addMember
Inputs	memberId, credit card number, phone number
Outcomes	10300, OK
	10314, MemberId exists

Use case	addVideo
Inputs	title, category, rating, vendor id, rental fee, late fee, rental days
Outcomes	10400, OK
	10414, Title exists
	10415, Invalid category
	10416, Invalid vendor id

Use case	addVendor
Inputs	vendor name, address, royalty, type
Outcomes	10500, OK(vendor id)
	10514, Vendor exists

Use case	addCopy
Inputs	title, copy number, branch number
Outcomes	10600, OK
	10614, Title not found
	10615, Copy number already in use
	10616, Branch not found

Use case	newRentalAgreement
Inputs	None
Outcomes	20100, OK
	20114, Rental agreement active

Use case	rentVideo
Inputs	title, copy number, member id
Outcomes	20200, OK
	20214, Title reserved
	20215, Member ineligible
	20216, Copy not available
	20217, Title not found
	20218, Copy not found
	20219, Member not found
	20220, No rental agreement
	20221, Copy belongs to another branch

Use case	collectRentalFee
Inputs	amount paid
Outcomes	20300, OK (Change due)
	20314, Insufficient amount
	20315, No active rental agreement
	20316, No videos rented

Use case	returnVideo
Inputs	title, copy number
Outcomes	20400, OK

20401, Overdue (days)
20402, Next reserved (customer)
20414, Title not found
20403, Overdue (days) and next reserved (customer)
20415, Copy not found
20416, Copy not rented
20417, Wrong branch
20418, Member not found

Use case	reserveVideo
Inputs	title, member id
Outcomes	20500, OK
	20501, Title available
	20514, Title not found
	20515, Member not found
	20516, Member ineligible

Use case	runOverdueReport
Inputs	None
Outcomes	20600, OK

Use case	rentOverride
Inputs	title, copy number, member id
Outcomes	30200, OK
	30214, Title not found
	30215, No rental agreement active
	30216, Copy not found
	30217, Member not found

Use case	payFine
Inputs	member Id, amount
Outcomes	30100, OK
	30114, Member not found
	30101, Change due (amt)
	30102, Still owes (amt)
	30115, Member has no fines outstanding

Use case	getAvailability
Inputs	title, branch
Outcomes	30300, On shelf (category)
	30301, Due back (date)
	30302, Available at (list of branches)
	30314, Title not found

Use case	runRoyaltyReport
Inputs	from date, to date
Outcomes	30400, OK

Use case	runUsageReport
Inputs	from date, to date
Outcomes	30500, OK

Use case	cancelRentalAgreement
Inputs	None
Outcomes	40100, OK
	40114, No rental agreement active

Use case	unreserveVideo
Inputs	title, member id
Outcomes	40200, OK
	40214, Video not found
	40215, Member not on list

Use case	setCopyStatus
Inputs	title, copy number, status
Outcomes	40300, OK
	40314, Title not found
	40315, Copy not found

Use case	removeBranch
Inputs	branch number
Outcomes	40400, OK
	40414, Branch does not exist
	40415, Branch has copies

Use case	removeCopy
Inputs	title, copy number
Outcomes	40500, OK
	40501, Last copy
	40514, Title not found
	40515, Copy not found
	40516, Copy rented

Use case	removeVideo
Inputs	title
Outcomes	40600, OK
	40614, Copies exist
	40615, Title not found

Use case	removeMember
Inputs	member id
Outcomes	40700, OK
	40714, Member id not found
	40715, Member has videos rented
	40716, Member owes fines

Use case   removeVendor
Inputs   vendor id
Outcomes   40800, OK
            40814, Vendor not found
            40185, Vendor has titles

Use case   transferCopies
Inputs   old branch number, new branch number
Outcomes   40900, OK
            40914, New Branch not found
            40915, Branch has no copies

Use case   reassignVendor
Inputs   old vendor id, new vendor id
Outcomes   41000, OK
            41014, vendor not found
            41015, Vendor has no videos

Use case   search
Inputs   title (abstract)
Outcomes   50100, OK (List of movies)
            50114, Title not found

Use case   findAllMovies
Inputs   director, mode
Outcomes   50200, OK (List of movies)
            50213, Invalid mode
            50214, None found

Use case   findAllMovies
Inputs   actor, mode
Outcomes   50300, OK (List of movies)
            50314, None found
            50315, Invalid mode

Use case   viewCast
Inputs   title (List of Actors)
Outcomes   50400, OK
            50414, Title not found

Use case   viewClip
Inputs   title
Outcomes   50500, OK (MPG file)
            50514, No clip available

14.2.4 Input type information

For all the attributes that were shown as input to one or more use cases, show the details of their validation. It is assumed that the user interface will reject all values that fall outside of these subtypes and will only pass valid parameters.

title	string(1..30)
copy number	string(3)
member Id	string(8)
amount	decimal(10,2)
director	string(1..20)
actor	string(1..20)
category	string(1..15)
branch number	string(3)
vendor name	string(1.20)
vendor Id	string(4)
phone	string(10)
address	string(1..20)[4]
from date	date(yyyymmdd)
rating	{G, PG13, PG, R, NR}
to date	date(yyyymmdd)
mode	{new, add, sub search}
status	{avail, rented, lost}
royalty	decimal(8,2)
type	{percent, amt}
rental fee	decimal(8,2)
late fee	decimal(8,2)
rental days	integer > 0

14.2.5 Incremental plan

The increments are defined in terms of use cases. An increment may contain only use cases that are dependent on the use cases in this increment or a prior one. The use case dependency graph is shown in Figure 14-1. Normally only the plan for the current increment is required. We have chosen to show the details of all five increments, realizing that increment two will need to be replanned at its inception. We will reshow it there as well. Each increment includes a strategy statement. That is the rationale used to choose the use cases in this increment.

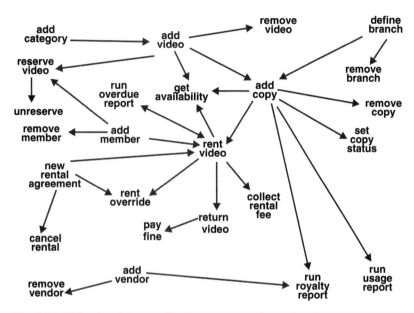

Fig. 14-1 Video tracking application use case dependencies.

Increment One (Strategy—Do easy use cases first, make a small first increment to lessen the impact of the learning curve)

> defineBranch (branch number) {OK, Branch exists}
>
> addCategory (category) {OK, Category exists}
>
> addMember (memberId, credit card number, phone number) {OK, MemberId exists}
>
> addVideo (title, category, rating, vendor id, rental fee, late fee, rental days) {OK, Title exists, Invalid category, Invalid vendor}
>
> addVendor (vendor name, address, royalty, type) {OK (vendor id), Vendor name exists}
>
> addCopy (title, copy number, branch number) {OK, Title not found, Copy number already in use, Branch not found}

Increment Two (Strategy—Deliver sufficient function to train users and evaluate system capability)

> newRentalAgreement () {OK, Rental agreement active}
>
> rentVideo (title, copy number, customer id) {OK, Title reserved, Customer ineligible, Copy not available, Title not found, Copy not found, Customer not found, No rental agreement, Copy belongs to another branch}

collectRentalFee (amount paid) {OK (Change due), Insufficient amount (amount still owed), No active rental agreement, No videos rented}

returnVideo (title, copy number) {OK, Overdue (days), Next reserved (customer), Title not found, Overdue (days) and next reserved (customer), Copy not found, Copy not rented, Wrong branch, Member not found}

reserveVideo (title, member id) {OK, Title available, Title not found, Member not found, Member ineligible}

runOverdueReport () {OK}

Increment Three (Strategy—Continue with increment two strategy—now include all use cases except those that do simple cleanup)

RentOverride (title, copy number, member id) {OK, Title not found, No rental agreement active, Copy not found, Member not found}

PayFine (member Id, amount) {OK, Member not found, Change due (amt), Still owes (amt), Member has no fines outstanding}

GetAvailability (title, branch) {On shelf (category), Due back (date), Available at (list of branches), Title not found}

runRoyaltyReport (from date, to date, vendorId) {OK}

runUsageReport (from date, to date) {OK}

Increment Four (Strategy—Add the rest of the main system functions; this is the last increment of the first release; keeping it simple allows for last-minute changes)

CancelRentalAgreement () {OK, No rental agreement active}

UnreserveVideo (title, member id) {OK, Video not found, Member not on list}

setCopyStatus (title, copy number, status) {OK, Title not found, Copy not found}

removeBranch (branch number) {OK, Branch does not exist, Branch has copies}

removeCopy (title, copy number) {OK, Last copy, Title not found, Copy not found, Copy rented}

removeVideo (title) {OK, Copies exist, Title not found}

removeMember (member id) {OK, Member id not found, Member has videos rented, Member owes fines}

removeVendor (vendor id) {OK, Vendor not found, Vendor owns titles}

transferCopies (old branch number, new branch number) {OK, New branch not found, Old branch has no copies} reassignVendor (old vendor id, new vendor id) {OK, New vendor not found, Old vendor has no videos}

Increment Five (Strategy—Defer kiosk implementation to a later release to accommodate aggressive schedule)

search (title) {OK, Title not found}

findAllMovies (director, mode) {OK, None found, Invalid mode}

findAllMovies (actor, mode) {OK, None found, Invalid mode}

viewCast (title) {OK, Title not found}

viewClip (title) {OK, No clip available}

14.2.6 The estimate and the plan

Using the use cases for the entire project and the incremental plan, create an estimate of work for each increment. This should include elapsed time and total person-days required. The example uses the model that was developed in Appendix C to compute raw person-days from scenarios. The details of the effort and schedule by increment are in Table 14-1. Table 14-2 shows similar information for the user interface design and development. The spread for effort across the activities is based on the guidelines from the project management chapter (13). The plan assumes that the team will consist of six individuals: two for UI development, two for application and class development, and two for test. Because the model is nonlinear, the effort for the individual increments exceeds the effort for the total project. If the linear model had been chosen, that would not be the case.

Scenarios = 90

Effort = 203 person-days

Duration = 34 work-days

Table 14-1 Planned effort and duration by activity by increment.

Increment	Scenarios	Effort	Duration	Analysis	Design	Code	Test
1	17	41	7	2	1	3	1
2	25	62	10	3	2	3	2
3	16	45	8	2	3	1	2
4	32	55	9	3	1	3	2
Total	90	203	34				

Table 14-2 Planned effort for each phase of user interface design.

Design	Walkthroughs	Development	Review	Test
7	6	14	2	5

Increment One Deliverables

*T*his chapter shows the deliverables to be created for increment one. Each deliverable is preceded by a brief review of the steps to produce the artifact. The deliverables shown are

☞ Use case list
☞ Increment one plan
☞ Use case descriptions
☞ Data dictionary
☞ Analysis class diagram
☞ Use case design
☞ Class specifications
☞ Design class diagram
☞ Test plan

15.1 INCREMENT ONE—PLAN/SCHEDULE

Table 15-1 shows the plan work distribution for the delivery of increment one.

Table 15-1 Increment one activity plan.

Day	1	2	3	4	5	6	7
Test	Plan	Plan	Write	Write	Write	Test	Test
Development	Anal	Anal	Des	Impl	Impl	Impl	Test

15.1.1 Use cases

Increment One (Strategy—Do easy use cases first, make a small first increment to lessen the impact of the learning curve)

Use case	defineBranch
Inputs	branch number
Outcomes	10100, OK
	10114, Branch exists

Use case	addCategory
Inputs	category
Outcomes	10200, OK
	10214, Category exists

Use case	addMember
Inputs	memberId, credit card number, phone number
Outcomes	10300, OK,
	10314, MemberId exists

Use case	addVideo
Inputs	title, category, rating, vendor id, rental fee, late fee, rental days
Outcomes	10400, OK
	10414, Title exists
	10415, Invalid category
	10416, Invalid vendor id

Use case	addVendor
Inputs	vendor name, address, royalty, type
Outcomes	10500, OK (vendor id)
	10514, Vendor exists

Use case	addCopy
Inputs	title, copy number, branch number
Outcomes	10600, OK
	10614, Title not found
	10615, Copy number already in use
	10616, Branch not found

15.2 INCREMENT ONE—ANALYSIS

15.2.1 Use case descriptions

For nontrivial use cases in this increment, record the business rules by scenario in terms of pre- and post-conditions. Indicate if the use case is part of the increment but the decision table is omitted.

The decision tables in Table 15-2 through Table 15-7 are all inclusive for the purpose of this example. Normally several of these would have been eliminated.

15.2.2 Data dictionary

For each term from the domain used in the use cases for this increment, create a definition. For objects, state the purpose of the object in this application. For attributes, give their semantic definition. For attribute values, give the meaning. For state idioms, define the associated attribute(s) values. For verb phrases that are algorithms, define the formula in terms of attributes. For all

Table 15-2 Decision table for addMember use case.

Use case: addMember(memberId, phone, creditCardNumber)								
Conditions								
Member with memberId already exists	T	F						
Actions								
Reject	X							
Create newMember with information supplied		X						
Add new member to list		X						

Table 15-3 Decision table for addCategory use case.

Use case: addCategory (category)								
Conditions								
Category exists	T	F						
Actions								
Reject	X							
Create new category		X						
Add new category to list		X						

Table 15-4 Decision table for addVendor use case.

Use case: addVendor (vendor name, address, royalty, type)								
Conditions								
Vendor exists	T	F						
Actions								
Reject	X							
Create new vendor with name, address, royalty, and type		X						
Add new vendor to list		X						
Generate and return new vendor Id		X						

Table 15-5 Decision table for defineBranch use case.

Use case: defineBranch (branch number)								
Conditions								
Branch number exists	T	F						
Actions								
Reject	X							
Create new branch with branch number		X						
Add branch to list		X						

Table 15-6 Decision table for addVideo use case.

Use case: addVideo (title, category, rating, vendorId, rentalFee, lateFee, rentalDays)								
Conditions								
Title exists	T	F	F	F				
Category exists		F	T	T				
Vendor with vendorId exists			F	T				
Actions								
Reject	X	X	X					
Create newVideo with supplied information				X				
Add video to list				X				

Table 15-7 Decision table for addCopy use case.

Use case: addCopy (title, copyNumber, branchNumber)								
Conditions								
Video with this title exists	F	T	T	T				
copyNumber for this title exists		T	F	F				
Branch with this branchNumber exists			F	T				
Actions								
Reject	X	X	X					
Create a new copy for this title and branch				X				
Add copy to list of copies for this title				X				

others, use your best judgment at what information will help the developers and the clients understand the problem that will be solved. For increment one, only those attributes that are part of the increment have been identified. Additional entries will be added as each increment requires them.

Category—Details of categories that the video store uses to distribute videos, for easy location by customers.

> **name**—Company assigned name (e.g., Action, Comedy, Mystery, Drama, Science fiction, etc.) Store must use categories created by business for all videos.

Vendor—Information about the companies that wholesale videos to the company.

> **id**—Unique application assigned vendor number.
>
> **name**—Video wholesaler name.
>
> **address**—Wholesaler's street, city, state, and zip. Used for ordering new videos.
>
> **royalty**—Amount of royalty paid to vendor per rental. Amount represents either a dollar amount or a percentage of rental fee, depending on type attribute.
>
> **type**—{amount, percent} Indicates the interpretation of the royalty attribute.

Branch—One branch object exists for every store that rents videos.

> **number**—The unique branch identifier. The company assigns this number at the time the branch is created.

Video—Information about each movie title carried by one or more branches.

> **title**—Commercial title of the movie. (Sometimes shortened version is used, but every attempt is made to make these unique.)
>
> **category**—Category where video will be shelved in the video store.
>
> **rating**—Letter rating assigned by producers of the movie {G, PG, PG13, R, NR}.
>
> **vendor**—Vendor identifier for the vendor that is to receive royalty payments when copies of this video are rented.
>
> **rentalFee**—The fee charged less tax to rent this video for the number of days specified in rentalDays.
>
> **lateFee**—The amount charged for each day the video is kept beyond the number of days specified in rentalDays.
>
> **rentalDays**—The number of calendar days the video can be kept for the rentalFee.
>
> **listOfCopies**—The copy numbers for the cartridges stocked in the branches.

Copy—Information about a particular copy of a video.

> **title**—Indicates the title that this copy is associated with.
>
> **number**—A unique copy number for the title above. Copy numbers are unique across branches as well.
>
> **branch**—The branch number of the branch that owns this copy of the video.

Member—Information about individuals who are authorized to rent videos from any company branch.

> **memberId**—A unique identifier for the video store member.
>
> **phone**—Member's daytime phone number.
>
> **creditCard**—The credit card number supplied by the member when he or she joined the video store.

15.2.3 Analysis class diagram

Figure 15-1 shows the class diagram based on the use cases in this increment. Try to limit the model to the elements that are part of this increment. If all objects and attributes are included now, it will be more difficult later to see which ones are not required.

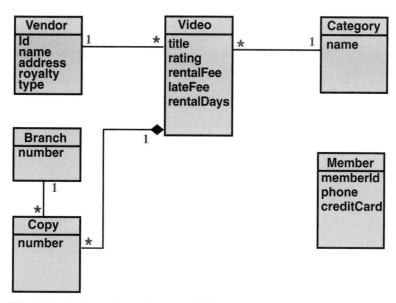

Fig. 15-1 Analysis class diagram with increment one objects and attributes.

15.3 INCREMENT ONE—DESIGN

15.3.1 Use case design

addVideo (title, category, rating, vendorId, rentalFee, lateFee, rentalDays)
The use case design for addVideo, shown in Figure 15-2, creates a new video object with no copies. The vendorId and category must already exist.

addCopy (title, copyNumber, branchNumber)   The use case for addCopy, shown in Figure 15-3, creates a new copy for an existing title. The design allows the control object to retrieve the copylist from the video and work directly with it.

15.4 INCREMENT ONE—CLASS DESIGN

15.4.1 Class specification

The class specification includes the class name, hierarchy, and definition. It shows all attributes. Public attributes are those with a getter (and if necessary a setter) method. Private attributes have neither. Each attribute has a type and if appropriate an initial value. Methods are divided by public and private. Public methods exclude getters. If an attribute has a private setter, it is shown. Event definitions and registration methods are defined here as well.

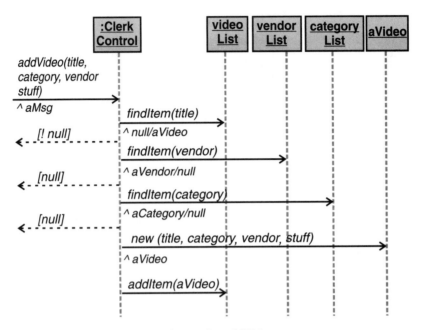

Fig. 15-2 Sequence diagram design for addVideo use case.

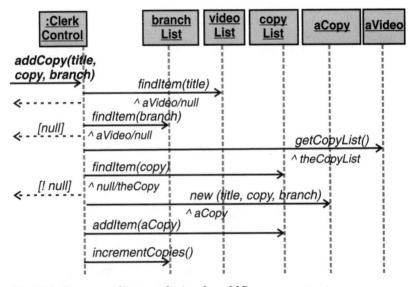

Fig. 15-3 Sequence diagram design for addCopy use case.

Only those attributes and methods defined in the current increment are shown.

Video

Class **Video** subclass of Object, ListItem

Defines a title carried by the store

Attributes (public)

title	String[1..30]
copylist	Vector
category	String[1..15]
rating	{G,PG13,PG,R,NR}
vendor	String[4]
rentalFee	Decimal(5,2)
lateFee	Decimal(5,2)
rentalDays	Integer > 0

Methods—public (excluding getters)

NONE

Methods—private

NONE

Events

NONE

Copy

Class **Copy** subclass of Object, ListItem

Defines a copy carried by a branch

Attributes (public)

title	String[1..30]
copyNumber	String[3]
status	{available}
branch	Integer > 0
$AVAILABLE	0

Methods—public (excluding getters)

NONE

Methods—private

NONE

Events

NONE

Vendor

Class **Vendor** subclass of Object, ListItem

Defines vendor receiving royalty payments

Attributes (public)

id	String[4]
name	String[1..20]
royalty	Decimal(8,2)
type	{fee, percent}
$nextId	Integer > 0(static)(initial = 1000)
$FEE	"fee"
$PERCENT	"percent"

Methods—public (excluding getters)

getNextId() returns **String** {Returns "V" + nextId.}

testResetNextId() return **void** {Sets nextId to 1000.}

Methods—private

AssignNextId() returns **void** {Assigned vendor id to "V"+ nextId. Increments nextId after assignment.}

Events

NONE

Category

Class **Category** subclass of Object, ListItem

Defines a valid category name

Attributes (public)

name	String[1..15]

Methods—public (excluding getters)

NONE

Methods—private

NONE

Events

NONE

Branch

Class **Branch** subclass of Object, ListItem

Defines an active branch

Attributes (public)

number   String[3]

Methods—public (excluding getters)

NONE

Methods—private

NONE

Events

NONE

ListItem

Class **ListItem** pure abstract

Abstract class used by Video, Copy, Branch, Category, Vendor, and Customer to allow them to be the common subtype. This subtype is required to be used as an argument in the methods associated with the ListOfItem class.

Attributes (public)

NONE

Methods—public (abstract)

GetKey () returns **String** {Returns a string that represents the id field. This is used for comparison to the search argument in the findItem method of ListOfItem.}

Methods—private

NONE

Events

NONE

ListOfItem

Class **ListOfItem** subclass of Object

This is a generic list implementation that is reused by several collections in the application.

Attributes (public)

items   Vector

Methods—public (excluding getters)

findItem (String) returns **ListItem** {Returns the first object in the Vector, whose getId() method returns a value equal to the String argument. If no object in the list matches the argument, the method returns void.}

addItem (ListItem) returns **void** {Adds the argument to the vector.}

Methods—private

NONE

Events

NONE

ClerkControl

Class **ClerkControl** subclass of Object

Application class defining all use cases for actor clerk

Attributes (public)

videos	ListOfItem
branches	ListOfItem
categories	ListOfItem
vendors	ListOfVendors
members	ListOfItem

Methods—public (excluding getters and use case methods)

NONE

Methods—private

NONE

Events

NONE

ListOfVendors

Class **ListOfVendors** subclass of Object

Collection for keeping the business's list of authorized vendors

Attributes (public)

items	Vector

Methods—public (excluding use case methods)

FindId (String id) returns **Vendor** {Returns vendor object with a vendorId matching id. Returns null if no vendors in collection have that id.}

FindName (String name) returns **Vendor** {Returns vendor object with a vendor name matching name. Returns null if no vendors in collection have that name.}

addItem(Vendor v) returns **void** {Adds the vendor to the collection.}

elements () returns **Enumeration** {Returns an Enumeration Interface to the items.}

size () returns **int** {Returns the number of items currently in the collection.}

Methods—private

NONE

Events

NONE

ReturnCode

Class **ReturnCode** subclass of Object

Defines the return code and default message for every use case

Attributes (public)

rc	int
msg	String

Methods—public (excluding getters)

NONE

Methods—private

NONE

Events

NONE

ReturnCode_ADD_VENDOR

Class **ReturnCode_ADD_VENDOR** subclass of ReturnCode

Allows specific return information for addVendor use case

Attributes (public)

vendorId	String

Methods—public (excluding getters)

NONE

Methods—private

NONE

Events

NONE

15.4.2 Design class diagram

The design level class diagram (Figure 15-4) adds all the decisions made during use case and class design to the analysis version of the model. These decisions include object identifiers, foreign keys, and redundant data.

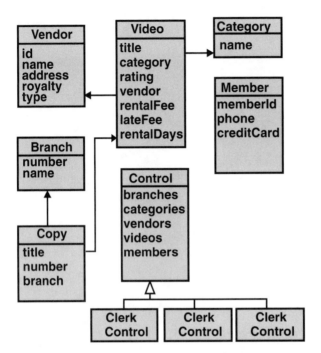

Fig. 15-4 Design class diagram for increment one.

15.5 INCREMENT ONE—TEST PLAN

addCategory

Use case	**addCategory (categoryName)**	
Scenario	OK	
	Pre-condition	Add a new category.
	Validation	Make sure a new category object exists with this category name.
Scenario	Category exists	
	Pre-condition	Add a new category, and then add the same one again.
	Validation	Total number of category objects in category list should be 1.

defineBranch

Use case	**defineBranch (branchNumber)**	
Scenario	OK	
	Pre-condition	Add a new branch number.

	Validation	Make sure that a branch object was created with this number and name.
Scenario	Branch number exists	
	Pre-condition	Add a new branch id; then add the same one again.
	Validation	Total number of branch objects should be 1.

addVideo

Use case	**addVideo (title, category, rating, vendorId, rentalFee, lateFee, rentalDays)**
Scenario	OK
	Pre-condition	Add a new branch, category, and vendor. Add a new video title using the same category and vendor.
	Validation	A new video object should exist with the supplied information.
Scenario	Title exists
	Pre-condition	Add a new branch, category, and two vendors. Add a new video title using the same branch customer and first vendor. Add the exact same video title again, but use the second vendor.
	Validation	The number of video objects should be 1, and it should contain the vendor id of the first vendor added.
Scenario	Invalid category
	Pre-condition	Add a new branch, customer, and vendor. Add a new video using the same branch customer and vendor, and "xxxx" for category.
	Validation	List of videos should be zero.
Scenario	Invalid vendor
	Pre-condition	Add a new branch, customer, and category. Add a new video using the same branch customer and category, and "yyyy" for vendor.
	Validation	List of videos should be zero.

addMember

Use case	**addMember (MemberId, phone, creditCardNumber)**
Scenario	OK

	Pre-condition	Add a new member with memberId, phone, and creditCardNumber.
	Validation	A new member object should exist with the added information.
Scenario	MemberId Exists	
	Pre-condition	Add a new member with an id, phone, and creditCardNumber. Add a second member with the same memberID, but a different credit card number.
	Validation	The number of member objects should be 1, and the credit card number in that object should be the first one added.

addVendor

Use case	**addVendor (vendorName, address, royalty, type)**	
Scenario	OK (vendorId)	
	Pre-condition	Add a vendor with a name, address, royalty, and type; then add a second vendor with a different name.
	Validation	Size of vendor list should be two. The two vendorIds returned should be different. The second vendor object should contain the correct name, id, address, royalty, and type values in their respective attributes.
Scenario	VendorName Exists	
	Pre-condition	Add a vendor with a name, address, royalty, and type; then add a second vendor with the same name.
	Validation	Size of vendor list should be one.

addCopy

Use case	**addCopy (title, copy number, branch number)**	
Scenario	OK	
	Pre-condition	Add a vendor, category, and video. Then add a branch and add a copy with the same number as the branch and the same title as the video.
	Validation	Copy should exist with correct title branch and copy number. Branch number of copies should be 1.

Scenario   Copy number already in use

Pre-condition   Add a vendor, category, and video. Then add a branch and add a copy with the same number as the branch and the same title as the video. Now add a copy with the same title and same copy number.

Validation   Copy list in video should only have one copy.

CHAPTER **16**

First Increment Code Samples

This chapter shows examples of code. It is included for completeness of the example of deliverables for increment one. Subsequent increments will not include any code. For this chapter, the only code provided is

☞ The class definitions
☞ Eight test cases
☞ Three use case methods in the control object

16.1 INCREMENT ONE—TEST CASES

16.1.1 Test init method

The test init method is invoked at the start of every test to ensure that the system is in the well-defined empty state. It will normally empty all the global collection classes and reinitialize class variables and any other state values that could affect the outcome of use cases.

16.1.2 Test main method

The test main method contains all the statements necessary to invoke every test case in the test object. It should count the successful and unsuccessful tests and report the results.

```
public static void main (String[] args) {
           int i = 0;
           System.out.println ("Test run started " + new Date ());
           addCategory_OK (); i++;
           addCategory_OK (); i++;
           addCategory_EXISTS (); i++;
           addVendor_OK (); i++;
           addVendor_EXISTS () ; i++;
           addVideo_OK () ; i++;
           addVideo_EXISTS () ; i++;
           addVideo_INVALID_VENDOR (); i++;
           addVideo_INVALID_CATEGORY (); i++;
           System.out.println ("Total tests run = " + i);
           System.out.println ("Failures = " + failures);
}
```

16.1.3 Test setup methods

Test setup methods are sequences of use case invocations that are used in multiple test cases. This increment has no need for setup methods, but some of the pre-condition use cases may later be combined to make setup methods for future increment test cases.

16.1.4 Scenario test methods

Scenario test methods are shown only for increment one, and only a subset of all the required tests are included. It is assumed that having seen a few test methods, the details of other tests will be obvious.

addCategory

```
private static void addCatagory_OK() {
    //Pre-condition setup
    init();
    //Test and return code validation
    rc = control.addCategory("category name");
    if (rc.getRc() != 10200)
        logError("Test - addCategory (OK) failed - RC");
    //Post-condition validation
    Category v = (Category)control.getCategories().findItem("Category name");
    if (v == null)
        logError("Test - addCategory (OK) failed - Category not added");
}

private static void addCategory_EXISTS() {
    //Pre-condition setup
    init();
    control.addCategory("Category name");
    //Test and return code validation
```

```
            rc = control.addCategory("Category name");
            if (rc.getRc() != 10214)
                logError("Test - addCategory (EXISTS) failed - RC");
            //Post-condition validation
            int i = control.getCategories().size();
            if (i != 1)
                logError("Test - addCategory (EXISTS) failed - Category list size not
                        1 = " + i);
        }
```

addVendor

```
        private static void addVendor_OK() {
            //Pre-condition setup
            init();
            //Test and return code validation
            rc = control.addVendor("vendor1", "the address", 2.00, "rental");
            if (rc.getRc() != 10500)
                logError("Test - addVendor (OK) failed - RC " + rc.getRc());
            //Post-condition validation
            String id = ((ReturnCode_ADD_VENDOR)rc).getVendorId();
            Vendor v = (Vendor)control.getVendors().findId(id);
            if (v == null){
                logError("Test - addVendor (OK) failed - Vendor not added ");
                return
            }
            if (!v.getName().equals("vendor1"))
                logError ("Test - addVendor (OK) failed - Vendor name not stored");
            if (!v.getAddress().equals("the address"))
                logError ("Test - addVendor (OK) failed - Vendor address not stored"
            if (v.getRoyalty() != 2.00)
                logError ("Test - addVendor (OK) failed - Vendor royalty fee not
              stored");
            if (!v.getType().equals("rental"))
                logError ("Test - addVendor (OK) failed - Vendor royalty type not
                        stored");
        }

        private static void addVendor_EXISTS() {
            //Pre-condition setup
            init();
            control.addVendor("vendor1", "the address", 2.00, "rental");
            //Test and return code validation
            rc = control.addVendor ("vendor1", "the address", 2.00, "rental");
            if (rc.getRc() != 10514)
                logError("Test - addVendor (EXISTS) failed - RC");
            //Post-condition validation
            int i = control.getVendors().size();
            if (i != 1)
                logError("Test - addVendor (EXISTS) failed - Vendor list size not
                        1");
        }
```

addVideo

```
private static void addVideo_OK() {
    //Pre-condition setup
    init();
    //Test and return code validation
    rc = control.addVendor("vendor1", "address", 5.00, "fee");
    String vendorId = ((ReturnCode_ADD_VENDOR)rc).getVendorId();
    control.addCategory("category name");
    rc = control.addVideo("title1", "category name", "PG13", vendorId, 2.50,
      1.00, 3);
    if (rc.getRc() != 10400)
        logError("Test - addVideo (OK) failed - RC = " + rc.getRc());
    Video v = (Video)control.getVideos().findItem("title1");
    //Post-condition validation
    if (v == null) {
        logError("Test - addVideo (OK) failed - Video not added");
        return;
    }
    if (!v.getCategory().equals("category name"))
        logError("Test - addVideo (OK) failed - Category not stored");
    if (!v.getRating().equals("PG13"))
        logError("Test - addVideo (OK) failed - Rating not stored");
    if (!v.getVendor().equals(vendorId))
        logError("Test - addVideo (OK) failed - VendorId not stored");
    if (v.getRentalFee() != 2.50)
        logError("Test - addVideo (OK) failed - RentalFee not stored");
    if (v.getLateFee() != 1.00)
        logError("Test - addVideo (OK) failed - LateFee not stored");
    if (v.getRentalDays() != 3)
        logError("Test - addVideo (OK) failed - RentalDays not stored");
}

private static void addVideo_EXISTS() {
    //Pre-condition setup
    init();
    rc = control.addVendor("vendor1", "address", 5.00, "fee");
    String vendorId = ((ReturnCode_ADD_VENDOR)rc).getVendorId();
    control.addCategory("category name");
    control.addVideo("title1", "category name", "PG13", vendorId, 3.00, 1.00,
      3);
    //Test and return code validation
    rc = control.addVideo("title1", "category name", "PG13", vendorId, 4.00,
      2.00, 5);
    if (rc.getRc() != 10414)
        logError("Test - addVideo (EXISTS) failed - RC " + rc.getRc());
    //Post-condition validation
}

private static void addVideo_INVALID_VENDOR() {
    //Pre-condition setup
    init();
    control.addCategory("category name");
    //Test and return code validation
    rc = control.addVideo("title1", "category name", "PG13", "vendorX", 3.00,
      1.00, 3);
```

```
        if (rc.getRc() != 10416)
            logError("Test - addVideo (INVALID_VENDOR) failed - RC");
        //Post-condition validation
    }

    private static void addVideo_INVALID_CATEGORY() {
        //Pre-condition setup
        init();
        rc = control.addVendor("vendor1", "address", 5.00, "fee");
        String vendorId = ((ReturnCode_ADD_VENDOR)rc).getVendorId();
        //Test and return code validation
        rc = control.addVideo("title1", "category X", "PG13", vendorId, 3.00,
            1.00, 3);
        if (rc.getRc() != 10415)
            logError("Test - addVideo (INVALID_CATEGORY) failed - RC " +
                        rc.getRc());
        //Post-condition validation
    }
```

16.2 INCREMENT ONE—IMPLEMENTATION

The implementation involves creating the business classes and its methods, the control classes, and the methods that implement the use cases. The business object method specifications were created as part of design. The specification for the use case methods in the control object are a combination of the use case sequence diagram from design and the use case description (usually a decision table) from analysis. It is possible, however, that neither of these will be available, in which case the implementation will need to be validated to the requirements use case definition.

For increment one, the example includes only the Category, Vendor, and Video business object classes. These were chosen as the minimum business objects to support the addVideo use case, which also requires the addCategory and addVendor use cases. These methods in the control class are shown as well. No other implementation code is shown here.

16.2.1 Category class

```
    public class Category implements ListItem {
        private String name = "";

        public Category (String theCategory) {
            name = theCategory;
        }
        public String getCategory() {
            return name;
        }
        public String getKey() {
            return getCategory();
        }
    }
```

16.2.2 Vendor class

```
public class Vendor {
    private String id = "";
    private String name = "";
    private String address = "";
    private double royalty = 0;
    private String type = "";
    private static int nextId = 1001;

    public Vendor (String theName, String theAddress, double amount, String
                   theType) {
        id = getNewId();
        name = theName;
        address = theAddress;
        type = theType;
        royalty = amount;
    }
    public String getId() {
        return id;
    }
    public String getName() {
        return name;
    }
    public String getNextId() {
        return "V"+nextId;
    }
    public String getNewId() {
        return "V"+nextId++;
    }
    public String getAddress() {
        return address;
    }
    public String getType() {
        return type;
    }
    public double getRoyalty() {
        return royalty;
    }
}
```

16.2.3 Video class

```
public class Video implements ListItem{
    private String title = "";
    private String Category;
    private String rating;
    private String vendor;
    private double rentalFee;
    private double lateFee;
    private int rentalDays;
    private ListOfItem copies;
    public Video
```

```
                    (String theTitle, String theCategory, String theRating, String
                            theVendor, double fee, double late, int days) {
                title = theTitle;
                vendor = theVendor;
                Category = theCategory;
                rating = theRating;
                rentalFee = fee;
                lateFee = late;
                rentalDays = days;
                copies = new ListOfItem();
            }
            public String getTitle() {
                return title;
            }
            public String getKey() {
                return getTitle();
            }
            public String toString() {
                return title;
            }
            public String getVendor() {
                return vendor;
            }
            public String getRating() {
                return rating;
            }
            public String getCategory() {
                return Category;
            }
            public double getRentalFee() {
                return rentalFee;
            }
            public double getLateFee() {
                return lateFee;
            }
            public int getRentalDays() {
                return rentalDays;
            }
        }
```

16.2.4 ListOfItem class

```
    public class ListOfItem
    {
        private Vector items = new Vector();
        public String toString() {
            return items.toString();
        }
        public void addItem(ListItem theItem) {
            items.addElement(theItem);
        }
        public void deleteItem(ListItem theItem) {
            items.removeElement(theItem);
```

```
        }
        public ListItem findItem(String key) {
            Enumeration list = items.elements();
            while (list.hasMoreElements()) {
                ListItem element = (ListItem)list.nextElement();
                if (element.getKey().equals(key))
                    return element;
            }
            return null;
        }
        public int size() {
            return items.size();
        }
        public Enumeration elements() {
            return items.elements();
        }
    }
}
```

16.2.5 ClerkControl class

```
public class ClerkControl {
    private static ListOfItem videos = new ListOfItem();
    private static ListOfItem members = new ListOfItem();
    private static ListOfVendors vendors = new ListOfVendors();
    private static ListOfItem categories = new ListOfItem();
    private static ListOfItem branches = new ListOfItem();
```

Use case addVideo

```
public ReturnCode addVideo
    (String title, String Category, String rating, String vendor, double
      rentFee, double lateFee, int rentDays) {
    Video v = (Video)videos.findItem(title);
    if (v!=null)
        return new ReturnCode(10414,"Title and copy already exist");
    if (vendors.findId(vendor)==null)
        return new ReturnCode(10416,"Vendor not found");
    if (categories.findItem(Category)==null)
        return new ReturnCode(10415,"Category not found");
    v = new Video(title, Category, rating, vendor, rentFee, lateFee,
                    rentDays);
    videos.addItem(v);
    return new ReturnCode(10400,"10,Video added");
}
```

UseCase addVendor

```
public ReturnCode addVendor (String name, String address, double
      royaltyAmount, String royaltyType) {
    if (vendors.findName(name)!=null)
        return new ReturnCode(10514,"10,Vendor exists");
    Vendor v = new Vendor (name, address, royaltyAmount, royaltyType);
    String id = v.getId();
```

```
        vendors.addItem(v);
        return new ReturnCode_ADD_VENDOR(10500,"10,Vendor" + id + "added",id);
    }
```

Use case addCategory

```java
public ReturnCode addCategory(String name) {
    if (categories.findItem(name)!=null)
        return new ReturnCode(10214,"Category already exists");
    Category c = new Category(name);
    categories.addItem(c);
    return new ReturnCode(10200,"10,Category added");
}
```

Supporting methods

```java
public ListOfItem getMembers() { //primarily to support test
    return members;
}

public ListOfItem getCategories() { //primarily to support test
    return categories;
}

public ListOfVendors getVendors() { //primarily to support test
    return vendors;
}

public ListOfItem getBranches() { //primarily to support test
    return branches;
}

public ListOfItem getVideos() { //primarily to support test
    return videos;
}

public void testInit() {
    videos = new ListOfItem();
    members = new ListOfItem();
    categories = new ListOfItem();
    vendors = new ListOfVendors();
    branches = new ListOfItem();
}
```

NOTE: The complete set of Java classes for the implementation and test of the video application can be downloaded as a zip file from **http://www.obps.com/ downloads.html**.

Increment Two

*I*ncrement two continues with the implementation of the video store, but focuses on some of the core use cases of the application. For the data dictionary and class specification, the entire deliverable has been recreated with changes noted.

17.1 INCREMENT TWO—ANALYSIS

Increment Two (Strategy—Deliver sufficient function to train users and evaluate system capability)

Use case	newRentalAgreement
Inputs	None
Outcomes	20100, OK
	20114, Rental agreement active

Use case	rentVideo
Inputs	title, copy number, customer id
Outcomes	20200, OK
	20214, Title reserved
	20215, Customer ineligible

20216, Copy not available
20217, Title not found
20218, Copy not found
20219, Customer not found
20220, No rental agreement
20221, Copy belongs to another branch

Use case	collectRentalFee
Inputs	amount paid
Outcomes	20300, OK (Change due)
	20314, Insufficient amount
	20315, No active rental agreement
	20316, No videos rented

Use case	returnVideo
Inputs	title, copy number
Outcomes	20400, OK
	20401, Overdue (days)
	20402, Next reserved (customer)
	20403, Overdue (days) and next reserved (customer)
	20414, Title not found
	20415, Copy not found
	20416, Copy not rented
	20417, Wrong branch
	20418, Member not found

Use case	reserveVideo
Inputs	title, member id
Outcomes	20500, OK
	20501, Title available
	20514, Title not found
	20515, Member not found
	20516, Member ineligible

Use case	runOverdueReport
Inputs	None
Outcomes	20600, OK

17.1.1 Use case descriptions

Table 17-1 through Table 17-6 show all the decision tables for increment two.

Table 17-1 Decision table for runOverdueReport use case.

Use case: **runOverdueReport ()**								
Conditions								
Overdue videos	F	T						
Actions								
No overdue videos message	X							
List overdue video, date due, member that rented		X						
Set member overdue count		X						

Table 17-2 Decision table for rentVideo use case.

Use Case: **rentVideo(title, copy number, member id)**										
Conditions										
Rental agreement active	F	T	T	T	T	T	T	T	T	T
Video exists		F	T	T	T	T	T	T	T	T
Copy exists			F	T	T	T	T	T	T	T
Member exists				F	T	T	T	T	T	T
Copy available					F	T	T	T	T	T
Copy belongs to this branch						F	T	T	T	T
Member eligible							F	T	T	T
Title has a wait list								F	T	T
Member is on the wait list									F	T
Actions										
Reject	X	X	X	X	X	X	X		X	
Mark copy as rented									X	X
Increment member rented count									X	X
Create new rental									X	X
Store rental in rental agreement and in rentals									X	X
Remove member from the wait list										X

Table 17-3 Decision table for collectRentalFee use case.

Use case: **collectRentalFee (amount)**								
Conditions								
Rental Agreement Active	F	T	T	T				
Videos rented > 0		F	T	T				
Amount > total rental fees			T	F				

Table 17-3 Decision table for collectRentalFee use case. (Continued)

Use case: collectRentalFee (amount)

Actions							
Reject	X	X					
Mark rental complete			X	X			
Return change			X				

Table 17-4 Decision table for returnVideo use case.

Use case: returnVideo (title, copy number)

Conditions							
Title exists	F	T	T	T	T	T	T
Copy exists		F	T	T	T	T	T
Copy rented			F	T	T	T	T
Video is overdue				F	T	T	F
Video is reserved				F	F	T	T
Actions							
Reject	X	X	X				
Mark copy available				X	X	X	X
Decrement rent count of member that rented video				X	X	X	X
Add overdue fine to member					X	X	
Notify clerk of first waiting member						X	X

Table 17-5 Decision table for newRentalAgreement use case.

Use case: newRentalAgreement()

Conditions								
Rental Agreement Exists	T	F						
Actions								
Reject	X							
Create new rental agreement		X						

17.1.2 Data dictionary

The data dictionary is collective. The new entries for increment two are italicized.

Table 17-6 Decision table for reserveVideo use case.

Use case: reserveVideo (title, member Id)								
Conditions								
Title exists	F	T	T	T	T	T	T	T
Member exists		F	T	T	T	T	T	T
Copy available in this branch			T	F	F	F	F	F
Member has fines due				T	F	F	F	F
Member has overdue videos					T	F	F	F
Video has a wait list						F	T	T
Member is on the wait list							T	F
Actions								
Reject	X	X	X	X	X			
Create a wait list for this video						X		
Add member to the wait list						X	X	
Inform clerk video is on shelf		X						

Category—Details of categories that the video store uses to distribute videos, for easy location by customers

> **name**—Company assigned name (e.g., Action, Comedy, Mystery, Drama, Science fiction, etc.). Store must use categories created by business for all videos.

Vendor—Information about the companies that wholesale videos to the company.

> **id**—Unique application assigned vendor number.

> **name**—Video wholesaler name.

> **address**—Wholesaler's street, city, state, and zip. Used for ordering new videos.

> **royalty**—Amount of royalty paid to vendor per rental. Amount represents either a dollar amount or a percentage of rental fee, depending on type attribute.

> **type**—{amount, percent} Indicates the interpretation of the royalty attribute just defined.

Branch—One branch object exists for every store that rents videos.

> **number**—The unique branch identifier. The company assigns this number at the time the branch is created.

name—Branch name, usually based on the city where the store is located, for example, Atlanta North, Deerborn, Upper Darby. The branch name is used in day-to-day communications. This information is not stored in the business object.

Video—Information about each title carried in the branches.

title—Commercial title of the movie. (Sometimes shortened version is used, but every attempt is made to make these unique.)

category—Category where video will be shelved in the video store.

rating—Letter rating assigned by producers of the movie {G, PG, PG13, R, NR}.

vendor—Vendor identifier for the vendor that is to receive royalty payments when copies of this video are rented.

rentalFee—The fee charged less tax to rent this video for the number of days specified in rentalDays.

lateFee—The amount charged for each day the video is kept beyond the number of days specified in rentalDays.

rentalDays—The number of calendar days the video can be kept for the rentalFee.

waitlist—*List of member names that have requested to be notified when an out of stock video becomes available.*

$maxVideos—*The maximum number of videos that a member can have rented at one time.*

Copy—Information about a particular copy of a video.

title—Indicates the title that this copy is associated with.

number—A unique copy number for the title just defined. Copy numbers are unique across branches as well.

branch—The branch number of the branch that owns this copy of the video.

status—*The indication of whether a copy is rented, available, or lost.*

Member—Information about individuals who are authorized to rent videos from any company branch.

memberId—A unique identifier for the video store member.

phone—Member's daytime phone number.

creditCard—The credit card number supplied by the member when they joined the video store.

fines—*The total amount of fines that this member currently owes.*

overdue—*The number of overdue copies for this member at this time.*

Rental—*Information about a copy that is currently rented, or was rented and returned.*

> **title**—*Name of the rented video.*
>
> **copy**—*Copy number associated with the rented title.*
>
> **memberId**—*The Id of the member that rented the video.*
>
> **due**—*The date that the video was to be returned.*
>
> **fee**—*Fee charged to rent the video for the basic number of days.*

RentalAgreement—*Information about a series of rentals joined as a single transaction.*

> **total**—*Total cost of renting all videos currently part of this rental agreement.*
>
> **rentals**—*List of up to 10 rentals that are part of this rental transaction.*
>
> **rentCount**—*The number of videos part of this rental agreement, the number of entries in rentals.*

BetterDate—*Information required for storing and manipulating date information in the application.*

> **gc**—*A complex representation of any date based on the Gregorian Calendar.*

OverDueItem—*Summary information about the number of overdue videos associated with a particular member.*

> **member**—*Identifier for the video store member that has overdue videos.*
>
> **odCount**—*Number of videos currently overdue for this member.*

17.1.3 Class diagram

Figure 17-1 is the composite class diagram for increments one and two. There is no separate analysis version, but design decisions may cause the diagram to change. It will be revisited after increment two is designed. The changes since increment one are in italic boldface.

17.2 INCREMENT TWO—USE CASE DESIGN

17.2.1 Use case design

reserveVideo(memberId, title)

The use case design for reserveVideo is shown in Figure 17-2; it searches all copies of a title for an available copy at that branch. If none are found, it adds the member to the titles waitlist.

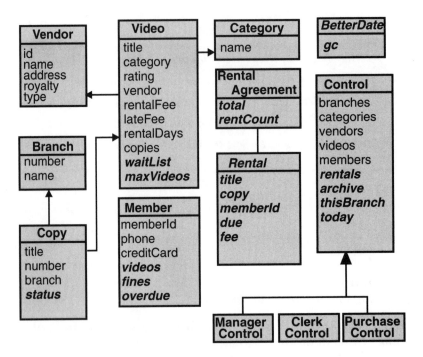

Fig. 17-1 Class diagram for increment two.

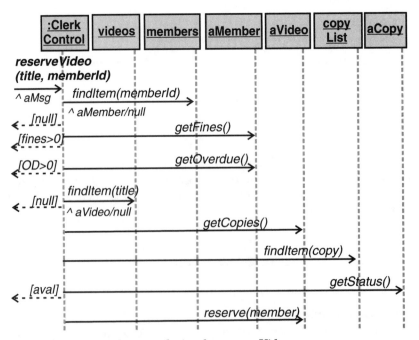

Fig. 17-2 Sequence diagram design for reserveVideo use case.

rentVideo(title, copy, memberId)

The rentVideo use case design is shown in Figures 17-3 and 17-4. The sequence diagram records a rented video by first creating a new rental object containing the title, copy, memberId, and due date (which is calculated by adding the title's rental *days* attribute value to today). It stores the due date in the copy and finally increments the borrower's rent count.

runOverdueReport()

The first half of the runOverdueReport use case design shown in Figure 17-5 searches the rentals for any overdue copy. It reports those copies as overdue and stores the associated memberId in a table; if the member is already in the table, it increments its overdue count.

The second half of the runOverdueReport use case design shown in Figure 17-6 retrieves each stored memberId and reports the id plus the number of overdue copies. It also sets the overdue count in the associated member object.

returnVideo(title, copy)

The returnVideo use case design shown in Figures 17-7 and 17-8 reduces the rent count in the member associated with the rental for this title and copy. It moves the rental object from the rentals list to the archive.

If the video is overdue, it increments the member's fines owed by the overdue amount and decrements their overdue count.

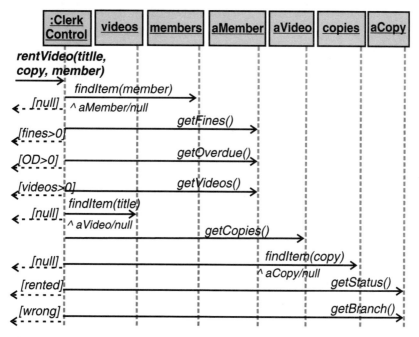

Fig. 17-3 Sequence diagram design for rentVideo use case (part 1).

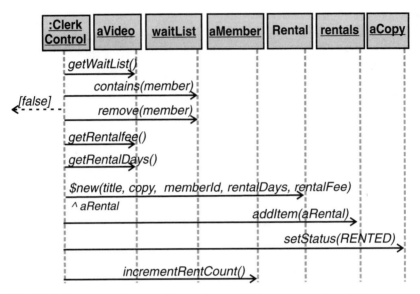

Fig. 17-4 Sequence diagram design for rentVideo use case (part 2).

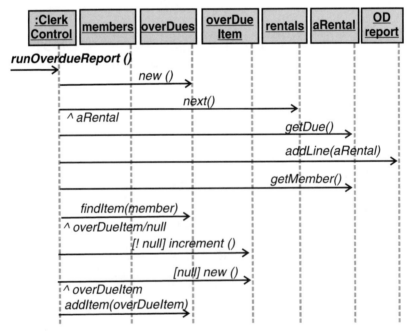

Fig. 17-5 Sequence diagram for the runOverdueReport use case.

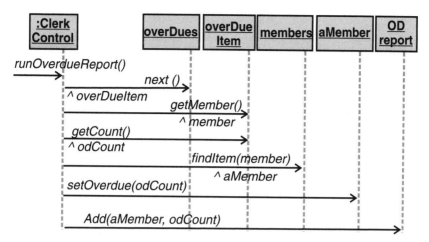

Fig. 17-6 Sequence diagram design for the runOverdueReport use case.

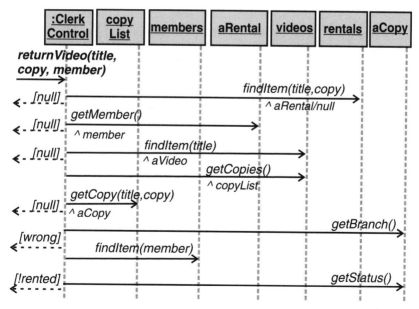

Fig. 17-7 Sequence diagram design for the returnVideo use case (part 1).

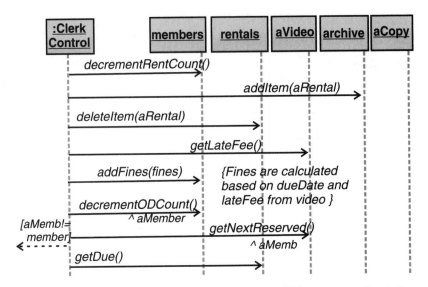

Fig. 17-8 Sequence diagram design for the returnVideo use case (part 2).

17.3 INCREMENT TWO—CLASS DESIGN

17.3.1 Class specification

The class specifications shown contain the details from increment one plus the additions and changes for increment two. New classes and changes to existing classes are shown in *italics*. Static (class) variables are preceded with a $. The $ is not part of the name. Constants are variables written all in capital letters.

Video

Class **Video** subclass of Object, ListItem

Defines a title carried by the store

Attributes (public)

title	String[1..30]
copylist	Vector
category	String[15]
rating	{G,PG13,PG,R,NR}
vendor	String[4]
rentalFee	Decimal(5,2)
lateFee	Decimal(5,2)
rentalDays	Integer > 0

waitlist	*Vector*
$maxVideos	*3*
$G	*"C"*
$PG13	*"PG13"*
$PG	*"PG"*
$R	*"R"*
$NR	*"NR"*

<u>Methods</u>—public (excluding getters)

getNextReserved returns **String** *{returns, but does not remove, the next memberId on the waitlist}*

reserve(String memberId) returns **void** *{adds the memberId to the waitlist}*

remove(String memberId) returns **void** *{removes the memberId from the waitlist}*

<u>Methods</u>—private

NONE

<u>Events</u>

NONE

Copy

<u>Class</u> **Copy** subclass of Object, ListItem

Details of the copies of title currently in inventory

<u>Attributes</u> (public)

title	String[1..30]
copy	String [3]
status	*{AVAILABLE, RENTED}*
branch	Integer > 0
$AVAILABLE	0
$RENTED	*1*

<u>Methods</u>—public (excluding getters)

NONE

<u>Methods</u>—private

NONE

<u>Events</u>

NONE

Vendor

Class **Vendor** subclass of Object, ListItem

Class for keeping details on vendors to which the business is currently paying royalties

Attributes (public)

id	Integer > 0
name	String[1..20]
royalty	Decimal(5,3)
type	{fee, percent}
nextId	Integer > 0(static)(initial = 1000)
$FEE	"fee"
$PERCENT	"percent"

Methods—public (excluding getters)

GetNextId() returns **String** {returns "V" + nextId}

TestResetNextId() returns **void** {sets nextId to 1000}

Methods—private

AssignNextId() returns **void** {assigned vendor id to "V"+ nextId; increments nextId after assignment}

Events

NONE

Category

Class **Category** subclass of Object, ListItem

Class for keeping track of video categories

Attributes (public)

name	String[1..30]

Methods—public (excluding getters)

NONE

Methods—private

NONE

Events

NONE

Branch

Class **Branch** subclass of Object, ListItem

Class for keeping track of branches carrying videos

<u>Attributes</u> (public)

number String[3]

<u>Methods</u>—public (excluding getters)

NONE

<u>Methods</u>—private

NONE

<u>Events</u>

NONE

ListItem

<u>Class</u> **ListItem** pure abstract

Abstract class used by Video, Copy, Branch, Category, Vendor, and Customer to allow them to be the common subtype. This subtype is required to be used as an argument in the methods associated with the ListOfItem class.

<u>Attributes</u> (public)

NONE

<u>Methods</u>—public (abstract)

GetKey() returns **String** {Returns a string that represents the id field. This is used for comparison to search argument in find method of ListOfItem.}

<u>Methods</u>—private

NONE

<u>Events</u>

NONE

ListOfItem

<u>Class</u> **ListOfItem** subclass of Object

This is a generic list implementation that is reused by several collections in the application.

<u>Attributes</u> (public)

items Vector

<u>Methods</u>—public (excluding getters)

findItem (String) returns **ListItem** {Returns the first object in the Vector, whose getId() method returns a value equal to the String argument. If no object in the list matches the argument, the method returns void.}

addItem(ListItem) returns **void** {Adds the argument to the vector)

*elements() returns **Enumeration** {returns an Enumeration Interface to the items}*

*size() returns **int** {returns the number of items currently in the collection}*

*toString() returns the **toString** for the embedded Vector*

Methods—private

NONE

Events

NONE

ClerkControl

Class **ClerkControl** subclass of Object

Application class defining all use cases for actor clerk

Attributes (public)

videos	ListOfItem
branches	ListOfItem
categories	ListOfItem
vendors	ListOfVendors
members	ListOfItem
rentals	*ListOfItem*
archive	*ListOfItem*
thisBranch	*String [3]*
today	*BetterDate*
ra	*RentalAgreement*

Methods—public (excluding use case methods)

*getDate () returns **BetterDate** {returns the value of today}*

*bumpDate (int n) returns **void** {increments today by n days – test method}*

Methods – private

NONE

Events

NONE

ListOfVendors

Class **ListOfVendors** subclass of Object

Collection for keeping the business's list of authorized vendors

<u>Attributes</u> (public)

items Vector

<u>Methods</u>—public (excluding use case methods)

findId(String id) returns **Vendor** {returns vendor object with a vendorId matching id; returns null if no vendors in collection have that id}

findName (String name) returns **void** {returns vendor object with a vendor name matching name; returns null if no vendors in collection have that name}

addItem(Vendor v) returns **void** {adds the vendor to the collection)

***elements** () returns **Enumeration** {returns an Enumeration Interface to the items}*

***size** () returns **int** {returns the number of items currently in the collection}*

<u>Methods</u>—private

NONE

<u>Events</u>

NONE

ReturnCode

<u>Class</u> **ReturnCode** subclass of Object

Defines the return code and default message for every use case

<u>Attributes</u> (public)

rc int
msg String

<u>Methods</u>—public (excluding getters)

NONE

<u>Methods</u>—private

NONE

<u>Events</u>

NONE

ReturnCode_ADD_VENDOR

<u>Class</u> **ReturnCode_ADD_VENDOR** subclass of ReturnCode

Adds specific return information for addVendor use case

Attributes (public)

    vendorId   String

Methods—public (excluding getters)

    NONE

Methods—private

    NONE

Events

    NONE

Return

Class ***ReturnCode_RETURN*** *subclass of ReturnCode*

Adds specific return information for returnVideo use case

Attributes (public)

    odDays   *int*
    nextMember   *String*

Methods—public (excluding getters)

    NONE

Methods—private

    NONE

Events

    NONE

ReturnCode_COLLECT_RENTAL_FEE

Class ***ReturnCode_COLLECT_RENTAL_FEE*** *subclass of ReturnCode*

Adds specific return information for collectRentalFee use case

Attributes (public)

    change   *double*

Methods—public (excluding getters)

    NONE

Methods—private

    NONE

Events

    NONE

BetterDate

Class **BetterDate** *subclass of Object*

A wrapper for an instance of calendar that provides some simple math capabilities on dates

Attributes (public)

gc	*GregorianCalendar*

Methods—public (excluding getters)

bumpDate(int n) *returns* **void** *{adds n days to gc}*

toString() *returns* **String** *{returns a formatted SHORT gc}*

daysTo(BetterDate d) *returns* **int** *{number of days from gc to d}*

daysFrom(BetterDate d) *returns* **int** *{number of days from d to gc}*

isLaterThan(BetterDate d) *returns* **boolean** *{returns true if gc > d, otherwise returns false}*

isSoonerThan(BetterDate d) *returns* **boolean** *{returns true if gc < d, otherwise returns false }*

Methods—private

NONE

Events

NONE

OverDueItem

Class **OverDueItem** *subclass of Object*

Temporary class used only within reports to accumulate information about overdue copies

Attributes (public)

member	*String*
odCount	*int*

Methods—public (excluding getters)

Incr() *returns* **void** *{increments the count in the object by 1}*

Methods—private

NONE

Events

NONE

RentalAgreement

Class **RentalAgreement** *subclass of Object*

Private class used only with the control object to keep track of all copies rented as part of a single transaction.

<u>*Attributes*</u> *(public)*

totals	*double*
rentals	*Rental[10]*
rentCount	*int*

<u>*Methods*</u>—*public (excluding getters)*

> **NONE**

<u>*Methods*</u>—*private*

> **NONE**

<u>*Events*</u>

> **NONE**

Rental

<u>Class</u> **Rental** subclass of Object, ListItem

A detail on a video rental while it is on loan, and for history.

<u>Attributes</u> (public)

title	String
copy	String[3]
memberId	String
due	BetterDate
fee	double

<u>Methods</u>—public (excluding getters)

> **getOverDueString** () returns **String** {returns a string for use in the overdue report}

<u>Methods</u>—private

> **NONE**

<u>Events</u>

> **NONE**

17.3.2 Class diagram

The class diagram for increment two is a revision of the design level class diagram from increment one with new classes and new attributes added. This model will be updated to reflect design decisions made during increment two use case design.

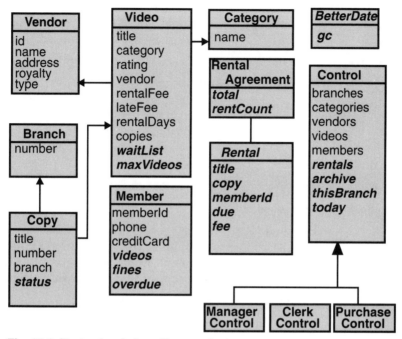

Fig. 17-9 Design level class diagram for increment two.

17.4 INCREMENT TWO—TEST PLAN

newRentalAgreement

Scenario	OK	
	Pre-condition	Create new rental agreement.
	Validation	New rental agreement exists.
Scenario	Rental agreement exists	
	Pre-condition	Create new rental agreement, attempt to create another rental agreement.
	Validation	Original rental agreement should still exist.

rentVideo (title, copy, memberId)

Scenario	OK	
	Pre-condition	Add vendor, category, branch, video, and two copies of the video. Create a new rental agreement, add new member, and then have that member rent one copy of the video.

| Validation | Exactly one rental is created with member, video, and copy. Member rent count is 1, and video copy is marked as rented. |

Scenario	Title not found
Pre-condition	Add vendor, category, branch, video, and two copies of the video. Add a new member, create a rental agreement, and then attempt to rent a different video title than the one added along with any copy to that member.
Validation	Member rent count should be 0.

Scenario	Copy does not exist
Pre-condition	Add category, vendor, member, a video, and two copies of the video. Create a new rental agreement, and then attempt to rent a different copy of that video title to the member.
Validation	Member rent count equals 0.

Scenario	MemberId not found
Pre-condition	Add branch, category, vendor, video, and two copies. Create a new rental agreement, and then attempt to rent one copy of that video title to any member.
Validation	There should be no rental records, and the video copy should be available.

Scenario	Copy already rented
Pre-condition	Add category, vendor, member, a video, and two copies of the video. Create a rental agreement, and rent the first copy of the video to the member. Then rent the same copy to the same member.
Validation	The first copy status should still be rented.

Scenario	Copy belongs to another branch
Pre-condition	Add category, vendor, member, a video, and two copies of the video. Change the current branch number. Create a rental agreement, and rent the first copy of the video to the member.
Validation	The first copy status should still be rented.

Scenario   Member has overdue videos

Pre-condition   Add category, vendor, member, a video, and two copies of the video. Create a new rental agreement, rent the first copy of the video to the member, and collect the correct rental fee. Then make the date 4 days later, and run the overdue report. Finally create a new rental agreement and have the member attempt to rent the other copy of the video.

Validation   The second video copy should be available, and the member rent count should be 1.

Scenario   Member owes fines

Pre-condition   Add category, vendor, member, a video, and two copies of the video. Create a new rental agreement, rent the first copy of the video to the member, and collect the correct rental fee. Then make the date 4 days later, and return the rented video. Then attempt to rent the second copy of the video to the member.

Validation   Make sure number of rentals equals 0, and rental agreement total and count both equal zero.

Scenario   No rental agreement exists

Pre-condition   Add category, member, video, and two copies of the video. Add a member and attempt to have that member rent the first copy of the video.

Validation   Rental list size should equal zero.

Scenario   Member has max rentals

Pre-condition   Add a category, vendor, two members, three videos, and a total of five copies. Rent any three copies to the member, and collect the rental fee. Create second rental agreement and try to rent a different copy of the video to the same member.

Validation   Fourth copy should still be available, and number of rentals should be 3.

reserveVideo (title, memberId)

Scenario   OK

Pre-condition   Add a category, vendor, video, two members, and two copies of the video. Create a rental agreement and have the first member rent both copies of the video. Then have the second member reserve the same title.

Validation   Video's waitlist should have one memberID, and it should be the second member's id.

Scenario   Title is available

Pre-condition   Add a category, vendor, video, two members, and two copies of the video. Create a rental agreement and have the first member rent the video. Then have the second member reserve the same title.

Validation   Video waitlist should be empty.

Scenario   Title does not exist

Pre-condition   Add a member, and have them reserve any title.

Validation   Return code value.

Scenario   MemberId not found

Pre-condition   Add a category, vendor, a member, a video, and two copies of the video. Create a rental agreement, have the member rent both copies of the video, collect the correct rental fee, and then have a nonexistent member attempt to reserve the video.

Validation   Video's waitlist should be empty.

Scenario   Member has overdue videos

Pre-condition   Add category, vendor, member, a video, and two copies of the video. Create a rental agreement, rent the copy of the video to the member, and collect the correct rental fee. Then make the date 4 days later, and run the overdue report. Then have the member attempt to reserve the video.

Validation   Video's waitlist should be empty.

Scenario   Member owes fines

Pre-condition   Add category, vendor, member, a video, and two copies of the video. Create a rental agreement, rent the copy of the video to the member, and collect the correct rental fee. Then make the date 4 days later, and have the member return the rented video. Finally have the member attempt to reserve the video.

Validation   Video's waitlist should be empty.

collectRentalFee (amount)

Scenario   OK

Pre-condition   Add category, vendor, member, a video, and two copies of the video. Create a rental agreement, and then rent the copy of the video to the member. Collect a rental fee with the exact amount required.

Validation   No rental agreement should exist, and the rentals list should contain one record. The change amount returned in the return code object should be zero.

Scenario   No videos rented

Pre-condition   Add category, vendor, member, a video, and two copies of the video. Create a rental agreement, and then immediately collect a rental fee for zero dollars.

Validation   Rental agreement should still exist.

Scenario   Amount is too little

Pre-condition   Add category, vendor, member, a video, and two copies of the video. Create a rental agreement, and then rent the copy of the video to the member. Collect a rental fee with an amount less than the actual amount owed according to the rental agreement.

Validation   Rental agreement should still exist, and change due in the return code should be a negative number equal to the difference between the amount collected and the total in the rental agreement.

Scenario   Change due

Pre-condition   Add category, vendor, member, a video, and two copies of the video. Create a rental agreement, and then rent the copy of the video to the member. Collect a rental fee with an amount greater than the rental fee.

Validation   Rental agreement should be null, and return code should contain the change due.

Scenario   No rental agreement open

Pre-condition   Collect a rental fee with any amount.

Validation   Return code validation only.

return (title, copy)

Scenario   OK

Pre-condition   Add category, vendor, member, a video, and two copies of the video. Create a rental agreement, and then rent both copies of the video to the member. Collect a rental fee with the exact amount specified. Return the first copy.

Validation   Copy should be available, member rent count should be 1, rental list should be 1, and the archive should contain the returned rental. Member fines should be zero as well.

Scenario   Video is overdue

Pre-condition   Add category, vendor, member, a video, and two copies of the video. Create a rental agreement, and then rent both copies of the video to the member. Collect a rental fee with the exact amount specified. Make the date 5 days later, and run the overdue report. Now return the first rented copy.

Validation   Copy should be available, member rent count should be 1, rental list size should be 1, and archive size should be 1 as well. Member fines should be equal to the overdue charge for 2 days. Overdue days in the return code object should be equal to 2.

Scenario   Title is reserved

Pre-condition   Add category, vendor, member, a video, and
                two copies of the video. Create a rental
                agreement, and then rent both copies of the
                video to the member. Collect a rental fee
                with the exact amount specified. Add a sec-
                ond member, and have them reserve the
                video. Now have the first member return
                one of the two copies that they rented.

Validation   Copy should be available, member rent
                count should be 1, rental list size should be
                0, and archive size should be 1. Return code
                should contain the name of the reserving
                member.

Scenario   Video is overdue and title is reserved

Pre-condition   Add category, vendor, member, a video, and
                two copies of the video. Create a rental
                agreement, and then rent both copies of the
                video to the member. Collect a rental fee
                with the exact amount specified. Add a sec-
                ond member and have them reserve the
                video. Make the date 5 days later, and then
                return one of the videos.

Validation   Copy should be available, member rent
                count should be 1, rental list and archive
                sizes should both be 1. Member fines should
                be equal to the overdue charge for 2 days.
                Overdue days and reserving member should
                be in the return code object.

Scenario   Copy not rented

Pre-condition   Add category, vendor, member, a video, and
                two copies of the video. Create a rental
                agreement, and then rent 1 copy of the video
                to the member. Collect a rental fee with the
                exact amount specified. Return the copy,
                and then return the same copy again.

Validation   Returned copy should be available, member
                rent count should be 1, and the size of the
                archive should be 1.

NOTE: IT WILL NOT BE POSSIBLE TO TEST THE LAST THREE SCENARIOS SINCE THEIR PRE-CONDITIONS CANNOT BE ESTABLISHED.

Scenario	Title not found	
	Pre-condition	IMPOSSIBLE: Can't delete a video with copies, and can't delete a rented copy.
	Validation	N/A
Scenario	Copy not found	
	Pre-condition	IMPOSSIBLE: Can't delete a rented copy.
	Validation	N/A
Scenario	Member no longer exists	
	Pre-condition	IMPOSSIBLE: Can't delete a member with unreturned copies.
	Validation	N/A

runOverdueReport ()

Scenario	OK—No overdue videos	
	Pre-condition	Add a category, vendor, and title. Add two copies of the title. Add a member, and have the member rent the video. Run the overdue report.
	Validation	Report should be empty (visual check). Member overdue count should be zero.
Scenario	OK—There are overdue videos	
	Pre-condition	Add category, vendor, member, a video, and two copies of the video. Create a rental agreement, and rent both copies of the video to the member. Collect a rental fee with the exact amount specified. Make the date 4 days later. Run the overdue report.
	Validation	Member should have an overdue count of 2. Both videos and the member should show up on overdue report (check visually).

CHAPTER 18

Increment Three

*T*his increment adds the remainder of the necessary functions to run most day-to-day transactions. It adds some new attributes to Rental, Copy, and Control to support getAvailability and the usage reports.

18.1 INCREMENT THREE—ANALYSIS

Increment Three (Strategy—Continue with increment two strategy—now include all use cases except those that do simple cleanup)

Use case	rentOverride
Inputs	title, copy number, member id
Outcomes	30200, OK
	30214, Title not found
	30215, No rental agreement active
	30216, Copy not found
	30217, Member not found
Use case	payFine
Inputs	member id, amount

Outcomes   30100, OK
             30101, Change due (amount)
             30102, Still owes(amount)
             30114, Member not found
             30115, Member has no fines outstanding

Use case   getAvailability
Inputs   title, branch
Outcomes   30300, On shelf (category)
             30301, Due back (date)
             30302, Available at (list of branches)
             30314, Title not found

Use case   runRoyaltyReport
Inputs   from date, to date
Outcomes   30400, OK

Use case   runUsageReport
Inputs   from date, to date
Outcomes   30500, OK

18.1.1 Use case descriptions

Table 18-1 through Table 18-5 are the complete set of decision tables for increment three.

Table 18-1 Decision table for runUsageReport use case.

Use case: **runUsageReport (fromDate, toDate)**								
Conditions								
Rentals exist inclusive within specified range	T	F						
Actions								
Return empty report		X						
Return count of rentals by title for the range given	X							

Table 18-2 Decision table for getAvailability use case.

Use case: getAvailability (title, branchId)									
Conditions									
Title exists	F	T	T	T	T	T			
Copies exist in branchId				T	F	F			
Copies available in branchId			T	F	F	F			
Copies available in another branch					T	F			
Branch exists		F	T	T	T	T			
Actions									
Reject	X	X							
Return Category			X						
Return availability date				X					
Return list of branches that have a copy					X				
Return title not carried						X			

Table 18-3 Decision table for payFine use case.

Use case: payFine (memberId, amount)									
Conditions									
Member exists	F	T	T	T	T				
Member owes fines		F	T	T	T				
Fines > amount			T		F				
Fines < amount				T	F				
Actions									
Reject	X	X							
Reduce fines by amount			X						
Set fines to zero				X	X				
Indicate change owed				X					

Table 18-4 Decision table for runRoyaltyReport use case.

Use case: runRoyaltyReport (fromDate, toDate, vendorId)

Conditions								
Vendor specified (not null)	T		T	F				
Vendor exists	F		T					
Rentals exist inclusive within specified range		F	T	T				
Actions								
Reject	X							
Return empty report		X						
Return royalty total for specified vendor			X					
Return royalty totals for all vendors				X				

Table 18-5 Decision table for rentOverride use case.

Use case: rentOverride (title, copy number, member id)

Conditions								
Video exists	F	T	T	T				
Member exists		F	T	T				
Copy exists			F	T				
Actions								
Reject	X	X	X					
Mark video rented				X				
Increment member rented count				X				
Create rental record and add to rental list				X				
Add rental fee to rental agreement total				X				

18.1.2 Data dictionary

The data dictionary is cumulative. The entries that are new for increment three are italicized.

> **Category**—Details of categories that the video store uses to distribute videos, for easy location by customers.
>
> > **name**—Company assigned name; e.g., Action, Comedy, Mystery, Drama, Science fiction, etc. Store must use categories created by business for all videos.

Vendor—Information about the companies that wholesale videos to the company.

> **id**—Unique application assigned vendor number.

> **name**—Video wholesaler name.

> **address**—Wholesaler's street, city, state, and zip. Used for ordering new videos.

> **royalty**—Amount of royalty paid to vendor per rental. Amount represents either a dollar amount or a percentage of rental fee, depending on type attribute.

> **type**—{amount, percent} Indicates the interpretation of the royalty attribute.

Branch—One branch object exists for every store that rents videos.

> **number**—The unique branch identifier. The company assigns this number at the time the branch is created.

> **name**—Branch name, usually based on the city where the store is located; e.g., Atlanta North, Deerborn, Upper Darby. The branch name is used in day-to-day communications but recorded in the business object.

Video—Information about each title carried in the branches.

> **title**—Commercial title of the movie. (Sometimes shortened version is used, but every attempt is made to make these unique.)

> **category**—Category where video will be shelved in the video store.

> **rating**—Letter rating assigned by producers of the movie {G, PG, PG13, R, NR}.

> **vendor**—Vendor identifier for the vendor that is to receive royalty payments when copies of this video are rented.

> **rentalFee**—The fee charged less tax to rent this video for the number of days specified in rentalDays.

> **lateFee**—The amount charged for each day the video is kept beyond the number of days specified in rentalDays.

> **rentalDays**—The number of calendar days the video can be kept for the rentalFee.

> **waitlist**—List of member names that have requested to be notified when an out-of-stock video becomes available.

> **$maxVideos**—The maximum number of videos that a member can have rented at one time.

Copy—Information about a particular copy of a video.

> **title**—Indicates the title that this copy is associated with.
>
> **number**—A unique copy number for the title. Copy numbers are unique across branches as well.
>
> **branch**—The branch number of the branch that owns this copy of the video.
>
> **status**—The indication of whether a copy is rented, available, or lost.
>
> *dueDate*—*The date that this copy, if rented, is due to be returned.*

Member—Information about individuals who are authorized to rent videos from any company branch.

> **memberId**—A unique identifier for the video store member.
>
> **phone**—Member's daytime phone number.
>
> **creditCard**—The credit card number supplied by the member when they joined the video store.
>
> **videos**—The number of videos currently rented by this member.
>
> **fines**—The amount of fines that have not yet been paid by this member.
>
> **overdue**—The number of overdue videos for this member.

Rental—Information about a copy that is currently rented, or was rented and returned.

> **title**—Name of the rented video.
>
> **copy**—Copy number associated with the rented title.
>
> **memberId**—The id of the member that rented the video.
>
> **due**—The date that the video was to be returned.
>
> **fee**—Fee charged to rent the video for the basic number of days.
>
> *rentDate*—*The date that this rental was created.*

RentalAgreement—Information about a series of rentals joined as a single transaction.

> **total**—Total cost of renting all videos currently part of this rental agreement.
>
> **rentals**—List of up to ten rentals, that are part of this rental transaction.
>
> **rentCount**—The number of videos part of this rental agreement, the number of entries in rentals.

BetterDate—Information required for storing and manipulating date information in the application.

gc—A complex representation of any date based on the Gregorian Calendar.

OverDueItem—Summary information about the number of overdue videos associated with a particular member.

member—identifier for the video store member that has overdue videos.

odCount—number of videos currently overdue for this member.

UsageItem—*Summary information about the video usage, and vendor royalty data.*

title—*Identifier for the Usage and Royalty reports.*

count—*Number rentals for this title.*

amount—*Amount or revenue generated by this title.*

18.1.3 Class diagram

Figure 18-1 shows the class diagram with all the new classes and attributes for increment three. Information for the current increments is in bold italics.

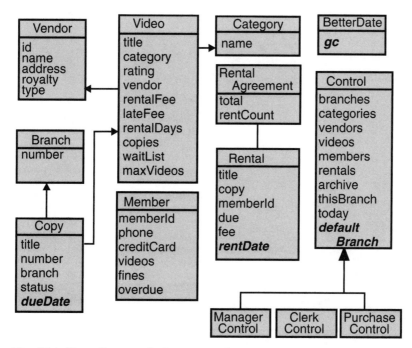

Fig. 18-1 Class diagram for increment three.

18.2 INCREMENT THREE—USE CASE DESIGN

18.2.1 Use case design

getAvailability(title, branch) The use case design for getAvailability shown in Figure 18-2 looks at every copy of the title looking for an available copy at the specified branch. As it is searching, it remembers the earliest due date for rented copies from the branch and keeps track of all branches that stock the title. If an available copy is found, that fact is reported; if not, it reports the earliest due date for that title. If there are no copies in the specified branch, it reports all the branches where it is carried.

18.3 INCREMENT THREE—CLASS DESIGN

18.3.1 Class specification

Video

Class **Video** subclass of Object, ListItem

Defines a title carried by the store.

Attributes (public)

title	String[1..30]
copylist	Vector

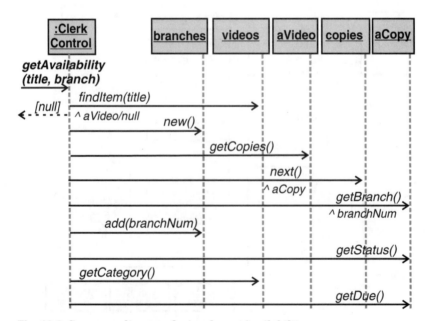

Fig. 18-2 Sequence diagram design for getAvailability use case.

category	String[15]
rating	{G,PG13,PG,R,NR}
vendor	String[4]
rentalFee	Decimal(5,2)
lateFee	Decimal(5,2)
rentalDays	Integer > 0
waitlist	Vector
$maxVideos	3
$G	"C"
$PG13	"PG13"
$PG	"PG"
$R	"R"
$NR	"NR"

<u>Methods</u>—public (excluding getters)

getNextReserved returns **String** {Returns, but does not remove, the next memberId on the waitlist.}

reserve(String memberId) returns **void** {Adds the memberId to the waitlist.}

<u>Methods</u>—private

NONE

<u>Events</u>

NONE

<u>Class</u> **Copy** subclass of Object, ListItem

Details of the copies of title currently in inventory.

<u>Attributes</u> (public)

title	String[1..30]
copy	Integer > 0
status	{AVAILABLE}
branch	Integer > 0
$AVAILABLE	0
$RENTED	1

due	*BetterDate*

<u>Methods</u>—public (excluding getters)

setDue(BetterDate) returns void {creates an instance for due}

<u>Methods</u>—private

NONE

<u>Events</u>

NONE

Vendor

Class **Vendor** subclass of Object, ListItem

Class for keeping details on vendors to which the business is currently paying royalties.

Attributes (public)

id	Integer > 0
name	String[1..20]
royalty	Decimal(5,3)
type	{fee, percent}
nextId	Integer > 0(static)(initial =1000)
$FEE	"fee"
$PERCENT	"percent"

Methods—public (excluding getters)

GetNextId() returns **String** {Returns "V" + nextId.}

TestResetNextId() returns **void** {Sets nextId to 1000.}

Methods—private

AssignNextId() returns **void** {Assigned vendor id to "V"+ nextId. Increments nextId after assignment.}

Events

NONE

Category

Class **Category** subclass of Object, ListItem

Class for keeping track of video categories.

Attributes (public)

name	String[1..30]

Methods—public (excluding getters)

NONE

Methods—private

NONE

Events

NONE

Branch

Class **Branch** subclass of Object, ListItem

Class for keeping track of branches carrying videos.

Attributes (public)

number   String[3]

Methods—public (excluding getters)

NONE

Methods—private

NONE

Events

NONE

ListItem

Class **ListItem** pure abstract

Abstract class used by Video, Copy, Branch, Category, Vendor, and Customer to allow them to be the common subtype. This subtype is required to be used as an argument in the methods associated with the ListOfItem class.

Attributes (public)

NONE

Methods—public (abstract)

GetKey() returns **String** {Returns a string that represents the id field. This is used for comparison to search argument in find method of ListOfItem.}

Methods—private

NONE

Events

NONE

ListOfItem

Class **ListOfItem** subclass of Object

This is a generic list implementation that is reused by several collections in the application.

Attributes (public)

items   Vector

Methods—public (excluding getters)

findItem (String) returns **ListItem** {Returns the first object in the Vector, whose getId() method returns a value equal to the String argument. If no object in the list matches the argument, the method returns void.}

addItem(ListItem) returns **void** {Adds the argument to the vector.)

elements() returns **Enumeration** {Returns an Enumeration Interface to the items.}

size() returns **int** {Returns the number of items currently in the collection.}

Methods—private

NONE

Events

NONE

ClerkControl

Class **ClerkControl** subclass of Object

Application class defining all use cases for actor clerk

Attributes (public)

videos	ListOfItem
branches	ListOfItem
categories	ListOfItem
vendors	ListOfVendors
members	ListOfItem
rentals	ListOfItem
archive	ListOfItem
thisBranch	String [3]
today	BetterDate
ra	RentalAgreement

defaultBranch	*String[3]*

Methods—public (excluding use case methods)

NONE

getDate () returns **BetterDate** {Returns the value of today.}

bumpDate (int n) returns **void** {Increments attribute today by n days – test method.}

Methods—private

NONE

Events

NONE

Class **ListOfVendors** subclass of Object

Collection for keeping the business's list of authorized vendors.

Attributes (public)

items   Vector

Methods—public (excluding use case methods)

findId(String id) returns **Vendor** {Returns vendor object with a vendorId matching id. Returns null if no vendors in collection have that id.}

findName (String name) returns **void** {Returns vendor object with a vendor name matching name. Returns null if no vendors in collection have that name.}

addItem(Vendor v) returns **void** {Adds the vendor to the collection.}

elements () returns **Enumeration** {Returns an Enumeration Interface to the items.}

size () returns **int** {Returns the number of items currently in the collection.}

Methods—private

NONE

Events

NONE

ReturnCode

Class **ReturnCode** subclass of Object

Define the return code and default message for every use case.

Attributes (public)

rc   int
msg   String

Methods—public (excluding getters)

NONE

Methods—private

NONE

Events

NONE

ReturnCode_ADD_VENDOR

Class **ReturnCode_ADD_VENDOR** subclass of ReturnCode

Add specific return information for addVendor use case.

Attributes (public)

> **vendorId**   String

Methods—public (excluding getters)

> **NONE**

Methods—private

> **NONE**

Events

> **NONE**

ReturnCode_RETURN

Class **ReturnCode_RETURN** subclass of ReturnCode

Adds specific return information for returnVideo use case.

Attributes (public)

> **odDays**   int
> **nextMember**   String

Methods—public (excluding getters)

> **NONE**

Methods—private

> **NONE**

Events

> **NONE**

ReturnCode_COLLECT_RENTAL_FEE

Class **ReturnCode_COLLECT_RENTAL_FEE** subclass of ReturnCode

Adds specific return information for collectRentalFee use case.

Attributes (public)

> **change**   double

Methods—public (excluding getters)

> **NONE**

Methods—private

> **NONE**

Events

> **NONE**

ReturnCode_PAY_FINE

*Class **ReturnCode_PAY_FINE** subclass of ReturnCode*

Adds specific return information for payFine use case.

Attributes (public)

category	*double*
dueBack	*BetterDate*
branches	*String[]*

Methods—public (excluding getters)

    NONE

Methods—private

    NONE

Events

    NONE

ReturnCode_GET_AVAILABILITY

*Class **ReturnCode_GET_AVAILABILITY** subclass of ReturnCode*

Adds specific return information for getAvailability use case.

Attributes (public)

    difference   *double*

Methods—public (excluding getters)

    NONE

Methods—private

    NONE

Events

    NONE

BetterDate

Class **BetterDate** subclass of Object

A wrapper for an instance of calendar that provides some simple math capabilities on dates.

Attributes (public)

    gc   GregorianCalendar

Methods—public (excluding getters)

    bumpDate(int n) returns **void** {Adds n days to gc.}

    toString() returns **String** {Returns a formatted SHORT gc.}

daysTo(BetterDate d) returns **int** {Number of days from gc to d.}

daysFrom(BetterDate d) returns **int** {Number of days from d to gc.}

isLaterThan(BetterDate d) returns **boolean** {Returns true if gc > d; otherwise, returns false.}

isSoonerThan(BetterDate d) returns **boolean** {Returns true if gc < d; otherwise, returns false.}

Methods—private

NONE

Events

NONE

OverDueItem

Class **OverDueItem** subclass of Object

Temporary class used only within runOverdueReport to accumulate information about overdue copies.

Attributes (public)

member	String
odCount	int

Methods—public (excluding getters)

Incr() returns **void** {Increments the count in the object by 1.}

Methods—private

NONE

Events

NONE

UsageItem

*Class **UsageItem** subclass of Object*

Temporary class used within runRoyaltyReport and runUsageReport to accumulate information about vendor's fees and rental history.

Attributes (public)

title	*String*
count	*int*
amount	*double*

Methods—public (excluding getters)

***Incr()** returns **void** {Increments the count in the object by 1.}*

Methods—private

NONE

Events

NONE

RentalAgreement

Class **RentalAgreement** subclass of Object

Private class used only with the control object to keep track of all copies rented as part of a single transaction.

Attributes (public)

totals	double
rentals	Rental[10]
rentCount	int

Methods—public (excluding getters)

NONE

Methods—private

NONE

Events

NONE

Rental

Class **Rental** subclass of Object, ListItem

A detail on a video rental while it is on loan, and for history.

Attributes (public)

title	String
copy	String[3]
memberId	String
due	BetterDate
fee	double
rentDate	*BetterDate*

Methods—public (excluding getters)

getOverDueString () returns **String** {Returns a string for use in the overdue report.}

Methods—private

NONE

Events

NONE

18.3.2 Class diagram

The design version of the class diagram shown in Figure 18-3 is the same as the analysis view.

18.4 INCREMENT THREE—TEST PLAN

Use case rentOverrride

Scenario	OK	
	Pre-condition	Add a vendor, category, title, and two copies of a video. Add a member, create a rental agreement, and have them rent one copy of the video using rent override.
	Validation	Rentals size should be 1; have the title and copy number of the rented video and a due date of today plus video rental days. Copy should be marked as rented and member's rent count should be 1.

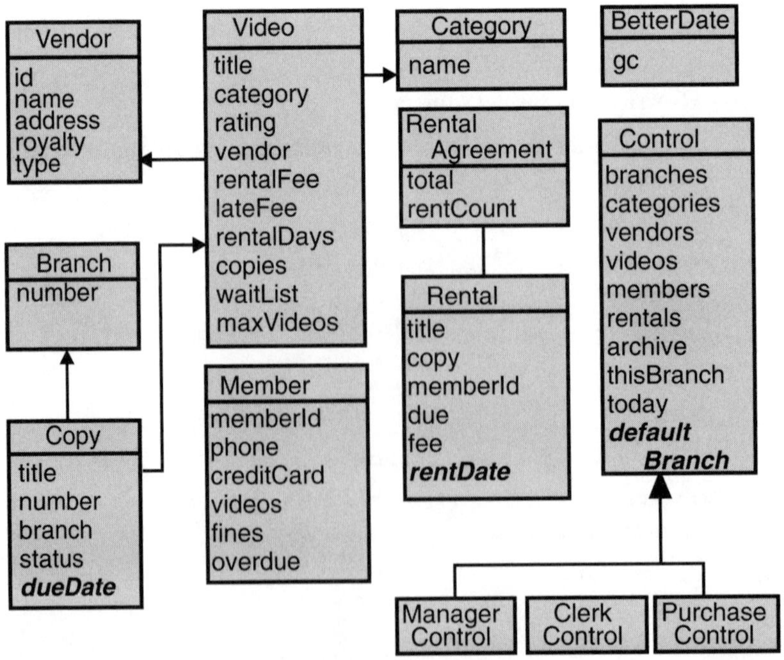

Fig. 18-3 Design class diagram for increment three.

Scenario	OK—Member has max rentals	
	Pre-condition	Add a vendor, category, three titles, and a total of five copies of the videos. Add two members, create a rental agreement, and have one member rent three titles. Then using rent override, have them attempt to rent a fourth video.
	Validation	Member rent count should be 4. The fourth rented copy should have a status of rented. A rental should exist with the title and copy of the fourth rented video and the correct due date, and the total number of rentals should be 4.
Scenario	OK—Member has overdue videos	
	Pre-condition	Add a vendor, category, title, and two copies of a video. Add a member, create a rental agreement, and have them rent one copy of the video. Make the date 6 days later, and run the overdue report. Then using rent override, have the member rent the other copy of the video.
	Validation	Member rent count should be 2. The second rented copy should have a status of rented. A rental should exist with the title and copy of the second rented video and the correct due date, and the total number of rentals should be 2.
Scenario	OK—Member has fines due	
	Pre-condition	Add a vendor, category, title, and two copies of a video. Add a member, create a rental agreement, and have them rent one copy of the video. Make the date 6 days later, run the overdue report, and have the member return the overdue video. Then using rent override, have the member rent the other copy of the video.
	Validation	Member rent count should be 1. The second rented copy should have a status of rented. A rental should exist with the title and copy of the second rented video and the correct due date, and the total number of rentals should be 1.

Scenario   Title not found

Pre-condition   Add a vendor, category, title, and two copies of a video. Add a member, create a rental agreement, and have them rent one copy of the video. Then using rent override, have member attempt to rent a copy of a nonexistent video.

Validation   Validate return code. Member rent count should be 0.

Scenario   Copy not found

Pre-condition   Add a vendor, category, title, and two copies of a video. Add a member, create a rental agreement, and attempt to rent a nonexistent copy of the video using rent override.

Validation   Member rent count should be 0.

Scenario   MemberId not found

Pre-condition   Add a vendor, category, title, and two copies of a video. Add a member, create a rental agreement, and attempt to rent one copy of the video to a nonexistent member using rent override.

Validation   Copy status should still be available, and number of rentals should be zero.

Scenario   No rental agreement

Pre-condition   Add a vendor, category, title, and two copies of a video. Add a member, and have that member attempt to rent one copy of the video using rent override.

Validation   Number of rentals should still be 0.

Use case payFine

Scenario   OK

Pre-condition   Add a vendor, category, title, and two copies of a video. Add a member, create a rental agreement, and have the member rent one copy. Make the date 6 days later, and have the member return the video. (Fine should be $6.00.) Have the member pay the exact amount owed.

Validation   Member fines should be zero. Return code change due should be zero as well.

Scenario   MemberId not found

Pre-condition   Add a vendor, category, title, and two copies of a video. Add a member, create a rental agreement, and have the member rent one copy. Have a nonexistent member try to pay a fine amount.

Validation   Validate return code.

Scenario   Member has no outstanding fines

Pre-condition   Add a vendor, category, title, and two copies of a video. Add a member, create a rental agreement, and have the member rent one copy. Have one member attempt to pay a fine.

Validation   Return code fines due should be zero, and the member should still have a value of zero for fines due.

Scenario   Change due

Pre-condition   Add a vendor, category, title, and two copies of a video. Add a member, create a rental agreement, and have the member rent one copy. Make the date 6 days later, and have the member return the video. (Fine should be $6.00.) Have the member pay $10.00.

Validation   Member fines due should be 0. Return code change due should be $4.00.

Scenario   Member still owes fines

Pre-condition   Add a vendor, category, title, and two copies of a video. Add a member, create a rental agreement, and have the member rent one copy. Make the date 6 days later, and have the member return the video. (Fine should be $6.00.) Have the member pay only $3.50 toward the amount owed.

Validation   Member fines owed should now be $2.50. Return code fines still owed should be $2.50 as well.

Use case getAvailability

Scenario   Available at other branches

Pre-condition   Add three branches and four video titles, and a total of nine copies of the videos spread over the three branches. Add three members, and have them rent a total of five videos. Get availability for a title at a branch that does not carry that title.

Validation
Return code should contain a list of the branches that do carry the title, whether the title is currently available at those branches or not.

Scenario   Due back by

Pre-condition   Add three branches and four video titles, and a total of nine copies of the videos spread over the three branches. Add three members, and have them rent a total of five videos. Get availability for a title at a branch that does not currently have any available copies, but that has two or more copies due back.

Validation
The return code should contain the date of the copy that is due back the earliest at the specified branch.

Scenario   OK—An available copy is on the shelf

Pre-condition   Add three branches and four video titles, and a total of nine copies of the videos spread over the three branches. Add three members, and have them rent a total of five videos. Get availability for a title at a branch where there is at least one copy of that title not currently rented.

Validation
Return code should contain the category name of the available title.

Scenario   Not carried

Pre-condition   Add three branches and four video titles, and a total of nine copies of the videos spread over the three branches. Add three members, and have them rent a total of five videos. Get availability for a title not currently carried by any branch.

Validation   Validate return code value.

Use case runRoyaltyReport

Scenario   OK—All vendors

Pre-condition   Add three branches, three vendors, four video titles, and a total of nine copies of the videos spread over the vendors and branches. Add three members, and have them rent a total of five videos. Return all five videos on time. Run the royalty report to include all five videos.

Validation   Validate return code. Visually check that each vendor has the correct royalty fee computed.

Scenario   OK—A single vendor

Pre-condition   Add three branches, three vendors, four video titles, and a total of nine copies of the videos spread over the vendors and branches. Add three members, and have them rent a total of five videos. Return all five videos on time. Run the royalty report to include all five videos, but only a single vendor.

Validation   Report should be a subset of the preceding one, showing only the selected vendor.

Use case runUsageReport

Scenario   OK—Records found in date range

Pre-condition   Add three branches, three vendors, four video titles, and a total of nine copies of the videos spread over the vendors and branches. Add three members, and have them rent a total of five videos. Return all five videos on time. Run the usage report to include all five videos.

Validation   Visually check the report to see that each title has the correct number of rentals.

Increment Four

This chapter presents the deliverables for the fourth and final increment. It is mostly the delete use cases. All the decision tables but only two sequence diagrams are included.

19.1 INCREMENT FOUR—ANALYSIS

Increment four (Strategy—rest of system)

Use case	cancelRentalAgreement
Inputs	None
Outcomes	40100, OK
	40114, No rental agreement active

Use case	unreserveVideo
Inputs	title, member id
Outcomes	40200, OK
	40214, Video not found
	40215, Member not on list

Use case	setCopyStatus
Inputs	title, copy number, status

Outcomes	40300, OK
	40314, Title not found
	40315, Copy not found
Use case	removeBranch
Inputs	branch number
Outcomes	40400, OK
	40414, Branch does not exist
	40415, Branch has copies
Use case	removeCopy
Inputs	title, copy number
Outcomes	40500, OK
	40501, Last copy
	40514, Title not found
	40515, Copy not found
	40516, Copy rented
Use case	removeVideo
Inputs	title
Outcomes	40600, OK
	40614, Copies exist
	40615, Title not found
Use case	removeMember
Inputs	member id
Outcomes	40700, OK
	40714, Member id not found
	40715, Member has videos rented
	40716, Member owes fines
Use case	removeVendor
Inputs	vendor id
Outcomes	40800, OK
	40814, Vendor not found
	40815, Vendor has associated titles
Use case	transferCopies
Inputs	old branch number, new branch number
Outcomes	40900, OK
	40914, New branch not found
	40915, Old branch has no copies
Use case	reassignVendor
Inputs	old vendor id, new vendor id
Outcomes	41000, OK
	41014, vendor not found
	41015, Old vendor has no videos

19.1.1 Use case descriptions

Table 19-1 through Table 19-10 are the decision tables showing detailed business rules for the use cases in this increment. Even though every use case has a formal decision table, some of them could be discarded once the analysis review is complete.

Table 19-1 Decision table for removeCopy use case.

Use case: removeCopy (title, copy)

Conditions									
Title exists	F	T	T	T	T				
Copy exists		F	T	T	T				
Copy is rented			T	F	F				
Copy is the only copy of the title				F	T				
Actions									
Reject	X	X	X						
Remove copy				X	X				
Inform clerk that that was the last copy					X				

Table 19-2 Decision table for removeVideo use case.

Use case: removeVideo (title)

Conditions								
Title exists	F	T	T					
Title has copies		T	F					
Actions								
Reject	X	X						
Delete title			X					

Table 19-3 Decision table for removeMember use case.

Use case: removeMember (memberId)								
Conditions								
Member exists	F	T	T	T				
Member has videos rented		T	F	F				
Member has fines due			T	F				
Actions								
Reject	X	X	X					
Remove member				X				

Table 19-4 Decision table for removeVendor use case.

Use case: removeVendor (vendorId)								
Conditions								
Vendor exists	F	T	T					
Vendor owns video titles		T	F					
Actions								
Reject	X	X						
Remove vendor			X					

Table 19-5 Decision table for setCopyStatus use case.

Use case: setCopyStatus (title, copy, status)								
Conditions								
Title exists	F	T	T					
Copy exists		F	T					
Actions								
Reject	X	X						
Change copy status to supplied value			X					

Table 19-6 Decision table for cancelRentalAgreement use case.

Use case: cancelRentalAgreement ()

Conditions								
Rental agreement exists	F	T	T					
Rental agreement has rented copies		F	T					
Actions								
Reject	X							
Cancel (remove) rental agreement		X	X					
Mark already rented copies as available			X					
Reduce member rent count by number of rented copies			X					
Remove rentals for the agreement from rental file			X					

Table 19-7 Decision table for removeBranch use case.

Use case: removeBranch (branchNumber)

Conditions								
Branch with branchNumber exists	F	T	T					
Branch owns copies		T	F					
Actions								
Reject	X	X						
Remove branch			X					

Table 19-8 Decision table for unreserveVideo use case.

Use case: unreserveVideo (title, memberId)

Conditions								
Title exists	F	T	T					
MemberId is on wait list		F	T					
Actions								
Reject	X	X						
Remove memberId from wait list			X					

Table 19-9 Decision table for transferCopies use case.

Use case: transferCopies (fromBranchNumber, toBranchNumber)

Conditions								
FromBranchNumber exists	F	T	T	T				
ToBranchNumber exists		F	T	T				
Copies associated with fromBranchNumber			F	T				
Actions								
Reject	X	X						
Change owning branch for all copies currently owned by fromBranchNumber to toBranchNumber				X				
Report that fromBranchNumber currently has no copies			X					

Table 19-10 Decision table for reassignVendor use case.

Use case: reassignVendor (vendorId1, vendorId2)

Conditions								
VendorId1 exists	F	T	T	T				
VendorId2 exists		F	T	T				
Videos are currently assigned to vendorId1			F	T				
Actions								
Reject	X	X						
Change associated vendorId for all videos associated with vendorId1 to vendorId2				X				
Report no videos are currently associated with vendorId1			X					

19.1.2 Data dictionary

The data dictionary is cumulative. The entries that are new for increment four are *italicized*.

Category—Details of categories that the video store uses to distribute videos, for easy location by customers.

name—Company assigned name; e.g., Action, Comedy, Mystery, Drama, Science fiction, etc. Store must use categories created by business for all videos.

Vendor—Information about the companies that wholesale videos to the company.

   id—Unique application assigned vendor number.

   name—Video wholesaler name.

   address—Wholesaler's street, city, state, and zip. Used for ordering new videos.

   royalty—Amount of royalty paid to vendor per rental. Amount represents either a dollar amount or a percentage of rental fee, depending on type attribute.

   type—{amount, percent} Indicates the interpretation of the royalty attribute.

   number of titles—*The total number of titles for which this vendor receives a royalty payment.*

Branch—One branch object exists for every store that rents videos.

   number—The unique branch identifier. The company assigns this number at the time the branch is created.

   numberOfCopies—*The total number of copies currently assigned to this branch.*

   name—Branch name, usually based on the city where the store is located; e.g., Atlanta North, Deerborn, Upper Darby. The branch name is used in day-to-day communications but not recorded in the business object.

Video—Information about each title carried in the branches.

   title—Commercial title of the movie. (Sometimes shortened version is used, but every attempt is made to make these unique.)

   category—Category where video will be shelved in the video store.

   rating—Letter rating assigned by producers of the movie {G, PG, PG13, R, NR}.

   vendor—Vendor identifier for the vendor that is to receive royalty payments when copies of this video are rented.

   rentalFee—The fee charged less tax to rent this video for the number of days specified in rentalDays.

   lateFee—The amount charged for each day the video is kept beyond the number of days specified in rentalDays.

   rentalDays—The number of calendar days the video can be kept for the rentalFee.

waitlist—List of member names that have requested to be notified when an out of stock video becomes available.

$maxVideos—The maximum number of videos that a member can have rented at one time.

Copy—Information about a particular copy of a video.

title—Indicates the title that this copy is associated with.

number—A unique copy number for the title. Copy numbers are unique across branches as well.

branch—The branch number of the branch that owns this copy of the video.

status—The indication of whether a copy is rented, available, or lost.

dueDate—The date that this copy, if rented, is due to be returned.

Member—Information about individuals who are authorized to rent videos from any company branch.

memberId—A unique identifier for the video store member.

phone—Member's daytime phone number.

creditCard—The credit card number supplied by the member when they joined the video store.

videos—The number of videos currently rented by this member.

fines—The amount of fines that have not yet been paid by this member.

overdue—The number of overdue videos for this member.

Rental—Information about a copy that is currently rented, or was rented and returned.

title—Name of the rented video.

copy—Copy number associated with the rented title.

memberId—The id of the member that rented the video.

due—The date that the video was to be returned.

fee—Fee charged to rent the video for the basic number of days.

rentDate—The date that this rental was created.

RentalAgreement—Information about a series of rentals joined as a single transaction.

total—Total cost of renting all videos currently part of this rental agreement.

rentals—List of up to ten rentals that are part of this rental transaction.

rentCount—The number of videos part of this rental agreement, the number of entries in rentals.

BetterDate—Information required for storing and manipulating date information in the application.

gc—A complex representation of any date based on the Gregorian Calendar.

OverDueItem—Summary information about the number of overdue videos associated with a particular member.

member—Identifier for the video store member that has overdue videos.

odCount—Number of videos currently overdue for this member.

19.1.3 Class diagram

Figure 19-1 shows the class diagram with all the new classes and attributes for increment four. Information for the current increments is in bold italics. No new classes were added for this increment.

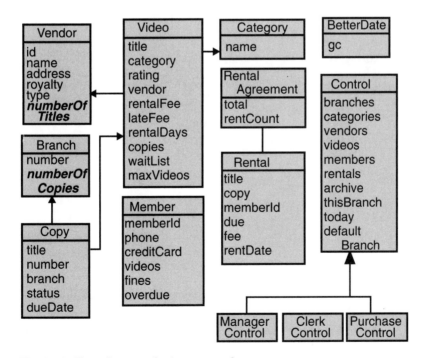

Fig. 19-1 Class diagram for increment four.

19.2 INCREMENT FOUR—USE CASE DESIGN

19.2.1 Use case design

CancelRentalAgreement() The cancelRentalAgreement use case in Figure 19-2 checks to see if any videos have been rented and, if so, deletes the associated rental object and decrements the member's rent count. The *ra* attribute in the control object is set to null.

RemoveCopy(title, copy) The removeCopy use case in Figure 19-3 gets the copy and ensures that it is not rented. It decrements the branch's copy count and, after deleting the copy from the title's copy list, informs the clerk if it was the last copy for that title.

19.3 INCREMENT FOUR—CLASS DESIGN

19.3.1 Class specification

Video

Class **Video** subclass of Object, ListItem

Defines a title carried by the store.

Attributes (public)

title	String[1..30]
copylist	Vector
category	String[15]
rating	{G,PG13,PG,R,NR}
vendor	String[4]
rentalFee	Decimal(5,2)
lateFee	Decimal(5,2)
rentalDays	Integer > 0
waitlist	Vector
$maxVideos	3
$G	"C"
$PG13	"PG13"
$PG	"PG"
$R	"R"
$NR	"NR"

Methods—public (excluding getters)

getNextReserved returns **String** {returns, but does not remove, the next memberId on the waitlist}

reserve(String memberId) returns **void** {Adds the memberId to the waitlist}

setVendorId(String) returns void {}

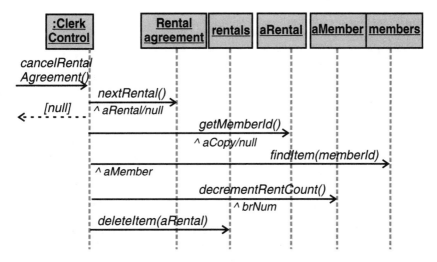

Fig. 19-2 Sequence diagram for cancelRentalAgreement use case.

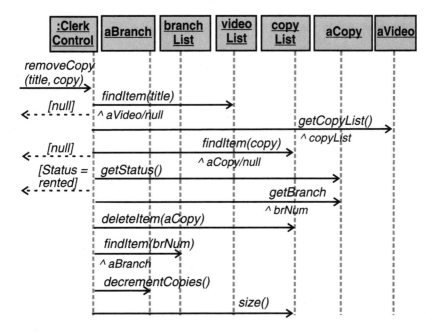

Fig. 19-3 Sequence diagram for removeCopy use case.

Methods—private

NONE

Events

NONE

Copy

Class **Copy** subclass of Object, ListItem

Details of the copies of title currently in inventory.

Attributes (public)

title	String[1..30]
copy	Integer > 0
status	{AVAILABLE}
branch	Integer > 0
$AVAILABLE	0
$RENTED	1
due	BetterDate

Methods—public (excluding getters)

setDue(BetterDate) returns void {creates an instance for due}

setBranch(String) returns void {}

setStatus(status) returns void {}

Methods—private

NONE

Events

NONE

Vendor

Class **Vendor** subclass of Object, ListItem

Class for keeping details on vendors to which the business is currently paying royalties.

Attributes (public)

id	Integer > 0
name	String[1..20]
royalty	Decimal(5,3)
type	{fee, percent}
nextId	Integer > 0(static)(initial =1000)
$FEE	"fee"
$PERCENT	"percent"
numberofTitles	Integer ≥ 0

Methods—public (excluding getters)

GetNextId() returns **String** {Returns "V" + nextId.}

TestResetNextId() returns **void** {Sets nextId to 1000.}

IncrementVideoCount() *returns **void** {adds 1 to number of titles for this vendor}*

Methods—private

AssignNextId() returns **void** {Assigned vendor id to "V"+ nextId. Increments nextId after assignment.}

Events

NONE

Category

Class **Category** subclass of Object, ListItem

Class for keeping track of video categories.

Attributes (public)

    name   String[1..30]

Methods—public (excluding getters)

NONE

Methods—private

NONE

Events

NONE

Branch

Class **Branch** subclass of Object, ListItem

Class for keeping track of branches carrying videos.

Attributes (public)

    number   String[3]
    numberOfCopies   *Integer > 0*

Methods—public (excluding getters)

IncrementCopyCount() *returns **void** {adds 1 to copies for this branch}*

Methods—private

NONE

Events

NONE

ListItem

<u>Class</u> **ListItem** pure abstract

Abstract class used by Video, Copy, Branch, Category, Vendor, and Customer to allow them to be the common subtype. This subtype is required to be used as an argument in the methods associated with the ListOfItem class.

<u>Attributes</u> (public)

NONE

<u>Methods</u>—public (abstract)

GetKey() returns **String** {Returns a string that represents the id field. This is used for comparison to search argument in find method of ListOfItem.}

<u>Methods</u>—private

NONE

<u>Events</u>

NONE

ListOfItem

<u>Class</u> **ListOfItem** subclass of Object

This is a generic list implementation that is reused by several collections in the application.

<u>Attributes</u> (public)

items   Vector

<u>Methods</u>—public (excluding getters)

findItem (String) returns **ListItem** {Returns the first object in the Vector, whose getId() method returns a value equal to the String argument. If no object in the list matches the argument, the method returns void.}

addItem(ListItem) returns **void** {Adds the argument to the vector.}

elements() returns **Enumeration** {Returns an Enumeration Interface to the items.}

size() returns **int** {Returns the number of items currently in the collection.}

<u>Methods</u>—private

NONE

<u>Events</u>

NONE

ClerkControl

Class **ClerkControl** subclass of Object

Application class defining all use cases for actor clerk.

Attributes (public)

videos	ListOfItem
branches	ListOfItem
categories	ListOfItem
vendors	ListOfVendors
members	ListOfItem
rentals	ListOfItem
archive	ListOfItem
thisBranch	String [3]
today	BetterDate
ra	RentalAgreement
defaultBranch	String[3]

Methods—public (excluding use case methods)

getDate () returns **BetterDate** {Returns the value of today.}

bumpDate (int n) returns **void** {Increments today by n days – test method.}

Methods—private

NONE

Events

NONE

ListOfVendors

Class **ListOfVendors** subclass of Object

Collection for keeping the business's list of authorized vendors.

Attributes (public)

items	Vector

Methods—public (excluding use case methods)

findId(String id) returns **Vendor** {Returns vendor object with a vendorId matching id. Returns null if no vendors in collection have that id.}

findName (String name) returns **void** {Returns vendor object with a vendor name matching name. Returns null if no vendors in collection have that name.}

addItem(Vendor v) returns **void** {Adds the vendor to the collection.}

elements () returns **Enumeration** {Returns an Enumeration Interface to the items.}

size () returns **int** {Returns the number of items currently in the collection.}

Methods—private

NONE

Events

NONE

ReturnCode

Class **ReturnCode** subclass of Object

Define the return code and default message for every use case.

Attributes (public)

rc	int
msg	String

Methods—public (excluding getters)

NONE

Methods—private

NONE

Events

NONE

ReturnCode_ADD_VENDOR

Class **ReturnCode_ADD_VENDOR** subclass of ReturnCode

Add specific return information for addVendor use case.

Attributes (public)

vendorId	String

Methods—public (excluding getters)

NONE

Methods—private

NONE

Events

NONE

ReturnCode_RETURN

<u>Class</u> **ReturnCode_RETURN** subclass of ReturnCode

Add specific return information for returnVideo use case.

<u>Attributes</u> (public)

odDays	int
nextMember	String

<u>Methods</u>—public (excluding getters)

NONE

<u>Methods</u>—private

NONE

<u>Events</u>

NONE

ReturnCode_COLLECT_RENTAL_FEE

<u>Class</u> **ReturnCode_COLLECT_RENTAL_FEE** subclass of ReturnCode

Adds specific return information for collectRentalFee use case.

<u>Attributes</u> (public)

change	double

<u>Methods</u>—public (excluding getters)

NONE

<u>Methods</u>—private

NONE

<u>Events</u>

NONE

ReturnCode_PAY_FINE

<u>Class</u> **ReturnCode_PAY_FINE** subclass of ReturnCode

Adds specific return information for payFine use case.

<u>Attributes</u> (public)

category	double
dueBack	BetterDate
branches	String[]

Methods—public (excluding getters)

NONE

Methods—private

NONE

Events

NONE

ReturnCode_GET_AVAILABILITY

Class **ReturnCode_GET_AVAILABILITY** subclass of ReturnCode

Adds specific return information for getAvailability use case.

Attributes (public)

difference   double

Methods—public (excluding getters)

NONE

Methods—private

NONE

Events

NONE

BetterDate

Class **BetterDate** subclass of Object

A wrapper for an instance of calendar that provides some simple math capabilities on dates.

Attributes (public)

gc   GregorianCalendar

Methods—public (excluding getters)

bumpDate(int n) returns **void** {Adds n days to gc.}

toString() returns **String** {Returns a formatted SHORT gc.}

daysTo(BetterDate d) returns **int** {Number of days from gc to d.}

daysFrom(BetterDate d) returns **int** {Number of days from d to gc.}

isLaterThan(BetterDate d) returns **boolean** {Returns true if gc > d; otherwise, returns false.}

isSoonerThan(BetterDate d) returns **boolean** {Returns true if gc < d; otherwise, returns false.}

Methods—private

NONE

Events

NONE

OverDueItem

Class **OverDueItem** subclass of Object

Temporary class used only within runOverdueReport to accumulate information about overdue copies.

Attributes (public)

member	String
odCount	int

Methods—public (excluding getters)

Incr() returns **void** {Increments the count in the object by 1.}

Methods—private

NONE

Events

NONE

UsageItem

Class **UsageItem** subclass of Object

Temporary class used within runRoyaltyReport and runUsageReport to accumulate information about vendor's fees and rental history.

Attributes (public)

title	String
count	int
amount	double

Methods—public (excluding getters)

Incr() returns **void** {Increments the count in the object by 1.}

Methods—private

NONE

Events

NONE

RentalAgreement

Class **RentalAgreement** subclass of Object

Private class used only with the control object to keep track of all copies rented as part of a single transaction. Once the collectRentalFee use case completes the rental object is deleted.

Attributes (public)

totals	double
rentals	Rental[10]
rentCount	int

Methods—public (excluding getters)

NONE

Methods—private

NONE

Events

NONE

Rental

Class **Rental** subclass of Object, ListItem

A detail on a video rental while it is on loan, and for history.

Attributes (public)

title	String
copy	String[3]
memberId	String
due	BetterDate
fee	double
rentDate	BetterDate

Methods—public (excluding getters)

getOverDueString () returns **String** {Returns a string for use in the overdue report.}

Methods—private

NONE

Events

NONE

19.3.2 Class diagram

Figure 19-4 shows the class diagram with all of the new classes and attributes for increment four. Information for the current increments is in ***bold italics***.

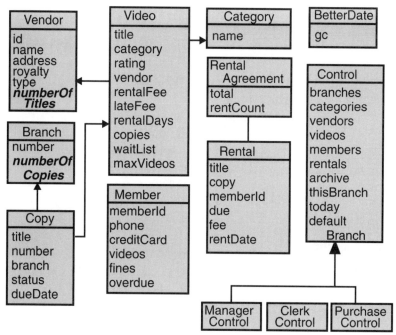

Fig. 19-4 Design level class diagram for increment four.

19.4 INCREMENT FOUR—TEST PLAN

removeCopy(title, copy)

Scenario	OK	
	Pre-condition	Add a category, vendor, title, branch, and two copies of the title. Then remove the first copy.
	Validation	Number of copies should be 1, and the first copy should not be found.
Scenario	OK—Last copy	
	Pre-condition	Add a category, vendor, title, branch, and two copies of the title. Then remove both copies.
	Validation	Number of copies should be zero.
Scenario	Title does not exist	
	Pre-condition	Add a category, vendor, title, branch, and two copies of the title. Then remove a copy for a nonexistent title.
	Validation	Copy size should be 2.

Scenario   Copy does not exist

Pre-condition Add a category, vendor, title, branch, and
               two copies of the title. Then remove a third
               copy of the title.

Validation   Copy size should be 2.

Scenario   Copy is rented

Pre-condition Add a category, vendor, title, member,
               branch, and two copies of the title. Create a
               rental agreement and rent the second copy.
               Collect the rental fee and try to delete the
               second copy.

Validation   Copy size should be 2, and the second copy
               should still be there.

removeVideo(title)

Scenario   OK

Pre-condition Add a category, vendor, title, branch, and
               two copies of the title. Remove both copies;
               then remove the video.

Validation   Number of videos should be 0.

Scenario   Title not found

Pre-condition Remove any title name.

Validation   Return code.

Scenario   Title has copies

Pre-condition Add a category, vendor, title, branch, and
               two copies of the title. Then remove the title.

Validation   Video title should be found.

removeMember (memberId)

Scenario   OK

Pre-condition Add a member, and remove it immediately.

Validation   Number of members should be 0.

Scenario   Member not found

Pre-condition Remove any member id.

Validation   Return code.

Scenario   Member has videos rented

Pre-condition Add a category, vendor, title, member,
               branch, and two copies of the title. Create a
               rental agreement and rent both copies. Col-
               lect the rental fee and try to delete the
               member.

	Validation	Member rent count should be 1, and member should still exist.
Scenario		Member owes fines
	Pre-condition	Add a category, vendor, title, member, branch, and two copies of the title. Create a rental agreement, rent the second copy, and collect the rental fee. Make the date 5 days later, run the overdue report, and return the video. Try to rent the other copy to the same member.
	Validation	Member should still exist.

removeVendor (vendorId)

	Scenario	OK
	Pre-condition	Add a vendor and remove it.
	Validation	Number of vendors should be 0.
Scenario		Vendor not found
	Pre-condition	Add a vendor and remove it using the vendor name instead of the vendor id.
	Validation	Number of vendors should be 1.
Scenario		Vendor has titles
	Pre-condition	Add a category, vendor, title, branch, and two copies of the title. Remove the vendor
	Validation	Vendor should still exist.

setCopyStatus(title, copy, status)

	Scenario	OK
	Pre-condition	Add a category, vendor, title, branch, and two copies of the title. Set the second copy's status to missing.
	Validation	Retrieve the copy and check that the status was set correctly.
Scenario		Title not found
	Pre-condition	Add a category, vendor, title, branch, and two copies of the title. Set the status of one copy to rented, but misspell the title.
	Validation	The status of both copies should be available.

Scenario   Copy not found

Pre-condition   Add a category, vendor, title, branch, and
                two copies of the title. Set the status of a
                third copy to missing.

Validation   The status of both copies should be avail-
                able.

cancelRentalAgreement()

Scenario   OK

Pre-condition   Add a category, vendor, title, branch, and
                two copies of the title. Create a rental agree-
                ment and cancel it.

Validation   Rental agreement should be null.

Scenario   OK, has rentals

Pre-condition   Add a category, vendor, title, branch, mem-
                ber, and two copies of the title. Create a
                rental agreement, rent both copies, and can-
                cel the rental agreement.

Validation   Number of rentals should be 0. Members
                rent count should be 0, rental size should
                be 0, and status of both copies should be
                available.

Scenario   No rental agreement active

Pre-condition   Add a category, vendor, title, branch, and
                two copies of the title. Cancel the rental
                agreement.

Validation   Number of rentals should be 0. Members
                rent count should be 0. Status of both copies
                should be available.

removeBranch (branchNumber)

Scenario   OK

Pre-condition   Add a branch and remove it immediately.

Validation   Number of branches should be 0.

Scenario   Branch not found

Pre-condition   Add a branch and remove a different one.

Validation   Number of branches should be 1.

Scenario   Branch has copies

Pre-condition   Add a category, vendor, title, branch, and two copies of the title. Attempt to remove the branch.

Validation   Number of branches should be 1, and branch should still exist.

unreserveVideo(title, memberId)

Scenario   OK

Pre-condition   Add a category, vendor, title, branch, and two copies of the title. Add a member, create a rental agreement, rent both copies, and collect rental fee. Add a second member and have it reserve and unreserve the title.

Validation   Title waitlist should be empty.

Scenario   Video title not found

Pre-condition   Add a member and remove them from the waitlist of a nonexistent title.

Validation   Return code.

Scenario   Member not on waitlist

Pre-condition   Add a category, vendor, title, branch, and two copies of the title. Add a member, create a rental agreement, rent both copies, and collect rental fee. Have the member reserve the title. Add a second member and have him or her unreserve the title.

Validation   Waitlist should contain only the first member.

reassignVendor(vendorId1, vendorId2)

Scenario   OK

Pre-condition   Add a category, vendorId1, title, branch, and two copies of the title. Create a vendorId2 and reassign the vendorId1 with it.

Validation   Title should now have vendorId equal to vendorId2.

Scenario   VendorId2 not found

Pre-condition   Add a category, vendor, title, branch, and two copies of the title. Replace the vendor with vendor id of xxxx.

Validation   Title should still contain vendorId1.

Scenario   VendorId1 has no titles

Pre-condition   Add a category, vendorId1, and branch. Replace the vendorId1 with the vendorId2.

Validation   Return code

transferCopies(branchNumber1, branchNumber2)

Scenario   OK

Pre-condition   Add a category, vendor, title, branch, and two copies of the title. Add a second branch and reassign the first branch's copies to it.

Validation   Branch number of both copies should be the new branch number.

Scenario   Branch number 2 does not exist

Pre-condition   Add a category, vendor, title, branch, and two copies of the title. Reassign the existing branch's copies to a nonexistent one.

Validation   Branch number of both copies should be the original branch number.

Scenario   Branch number 1 does not exist

Pre-condition   Add a category, vendor, title, branch, and two copies of the title. Reassign a nonexistent branch to the one added.

Validation   Branch number of both copies should be the original branch number.

Other Deliverables

This chapter describes some of the other deliverables that are developed as part of the OODP. Specifically, it shows examples of

- ☞ State diagrams
- ☞ User interface designs
- ☞ User interface objects
- ☞ User interface test control objects

20.1 STATE DIAGRAMS

State diagrams are most useful during analysis to help identify missing use cases. But they have value as well in design to better understand the relationship of objects, methods, and associated states. For this small video store problem, they have been included outside of all increments and not within a particular phase. The diagrams shown here would most likely have evolved throughout the incremental development process.

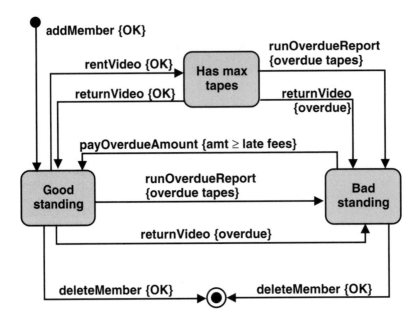

Fig. 20-1 Member object state diagram.

20.1.1 Member

Figure 20-1 shows the state transitions for the member object. The member good standing state is defined by attribute values in its object and by the due-Date attribute in all rentals that refer to the member object. The bad standing state is defined as the logical not of the good standing state, since it can occur in either of two different ways—the member owes fines or the member has overdue videos. The logical not of multiple conditions that must all be true is a series of conditions, of which only one needs to be false.

The state diagram in Figure 20-2 explodes the bad standing state so that the transition between its substates can be examined.

State definitions Good standing

☞ Member.finesOwed = 0.0
☞ Rentals.(member).dueDate <= today
    (Rentals.(member).dueDate should be interpreted as the **dueDate** *in the* **rental** *object referred to from the* **member** *object)*

Has max tapes
    Member.videos = 3

Bad standing
    ~ Good standing

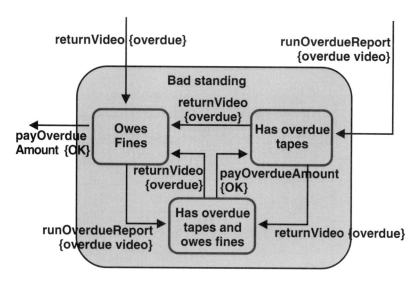

Fig. 20-2 Substates of member object bad standing state.

20.1.2 Video

The state diagram for the Video object is shown in Figure 20-3. The **known** state is defined as a video with no copies. If there is at least one copy that is not rented, the video is in the **available** state. A video is in the **unavailable** state when all its copies are either rented or missing. Notice that a video can go to the **waitlisted** state only from the **unavailable** state. Once, the video is in the **waitlisted** state; it remains there until the waitlist is empty. The rule is that only members on the waitlist can rent a waitlisted video; therefore, it is possible to have tapes available and still be in the **waitlisted** state.

The last possibility makes the diagram as drawn incorrect. Consider the case where a video has three copies, all of which are rented. Assume that a member calls and asks to be added to the waitlist. Later, if all three copies are returned and the waitlisted member rents one of the returned copies, the video is now in the available state. This means that there must be a legal transition from **waitlisted** directly to **available**. The scenario on that line would be rentVideo {OK}, but this is the same OK scenario as the one that transformed the video from **waitlisted** to **unavailable**. Since there cannot be identical scenarios that transform objects from one state to different states, it must be the case that waitlisted has at least two substates. The corrected state model is shown in Figure 20-4. The **returnVideo {OK2}** scenario is the case when *"the video is rented by the last member on the waitlist."* Logically this is not a separate path through the code, but it can be identified with a different pre-condition *(exactly one member on the list)*, and a unique post-condition *(zero members on the waitlist)*. This points out the importance of capturing business

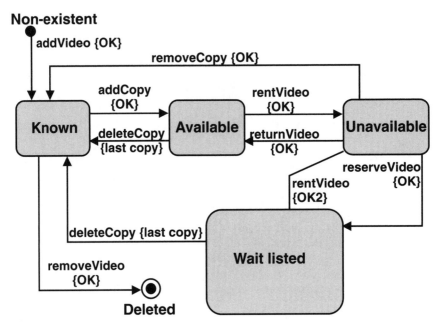

Fig. 20-3 State diagram for video object.

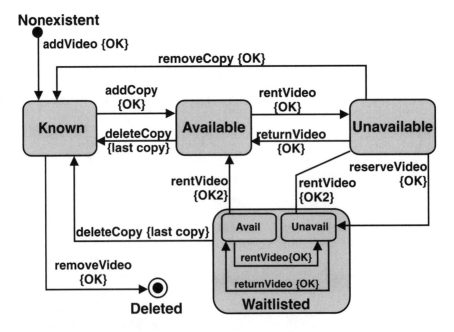

Fig. 20-4 Revised state diagram for the video object.

rules in the use case description rather than on these supplemental analysis models.

State definition

Known

> Video.copyList.size = 0
>
> Video.waitlist.size = 0

Available

> Video.copyList.size > 0
>
> At least one Copy.(Video).status = available
>
> Video.waitlist.size = 0

Unavailable

> Video.copyList.size > 0
>
> No copies of video have a status of available
>
> Video.waitlist.size = 0

Waitlisted(unavailable)

> Video.copyList.size > 0
>
> No copies of video have a status of available
>
> Video.waitlist.size > 0

Waitlisted(available)

> Video.copyList.size > 0
>
> At least two copies of video have a status of available
>
> Video.waitlist.size > 0

20.1.3 Copy

The state diagram for the copy object is shown in Figure 20-5, and the attribute values that define each of those states are listed below.

State definition

Available

> Copy.status = available

Rented

> Copy.status = rented

Missing

> Copy.status = missing

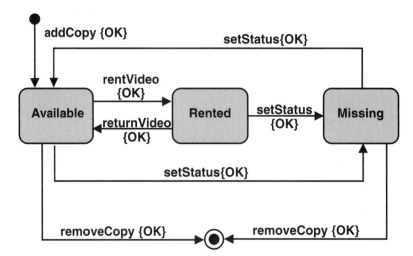

Fig. 20-5 State diagram for a copy object.

20.1.4 Rental

The state diagram for the rental object is shown in Figure 20-6, and the attribute values that define each of those states are listed next.

State definition
Rented

> The rental object belongs to rental list

Archived

> The rental object belongs to archive list

20.2 USER INTERFACE DESIGN

Figure 20-7 is an example of a user interface design for the actor "supervisor."

20.2.1 User interface implementation

Only that portion of the user interface implementation that adds vendors is shown. The addVendor() method executes when the user clicks the Execute button and the Add Vendor radio button is selected. The addVendor method retrieves the vendor id, the vendor address, the royalty type, and the royalty (amount) from the interface and sends this information to the control object method for addVendor(...). A response message and a generated vendor id are retrieved from the ReturnCode object; the message is placed in the message area label on the interface and the vendor id is placed in the vendor id input text field. There is an example of the corresponding test control object for testing that the addVendor() user interface method sends the correct message for to the control object.

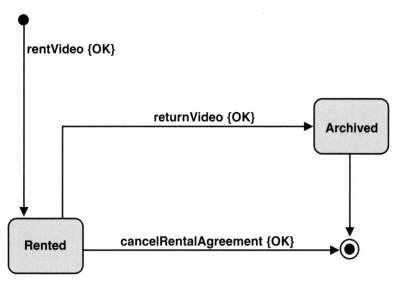

Fig. 20-6 State diagram for a rental object.

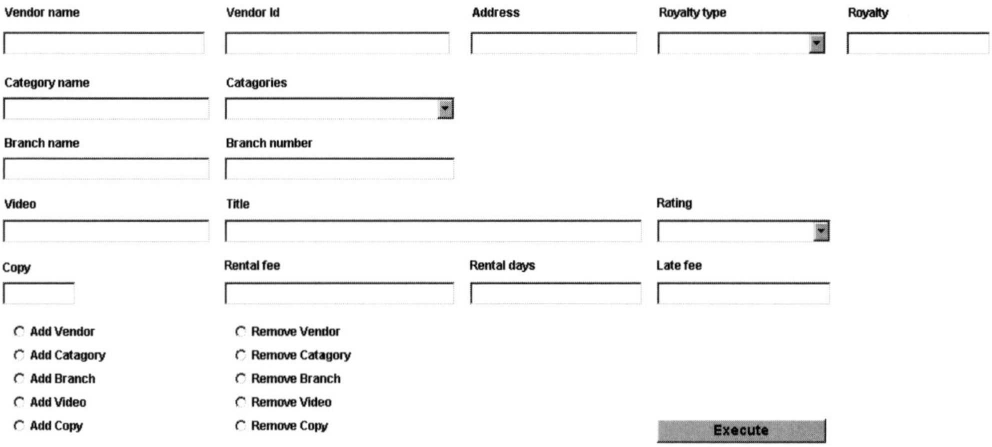

Fig. 20-7 User interface for video store maintenance operations.

20.2.2 User interface object

Partial user interface Figure 20-8 shows the partial user interface that accompanies the code examples that follow. The names of the interface fields containing the input data are written diagonally on each interface object.

User interface methods

```
public void addVendor() {
        vendorName = getVendorNameText().getText();
        if (vendorName == null || vendorName.equals("")) {
            showMessage("900,Vendor name missing");
            return;
        }
        vendorAddress = getVendorAddressText().getText();
        if (vendorAddress == null || vendorAddress.equals("")) {
            showMessage("900,Vendor address missing");
            return;
        }
        vendorRoyalty = getVendorRoyaltyAmount().getText();
        if (vendorRoyalty == null || vendorRoyalty.equals("")) {
            showMessage("900,Vendor royalty amount missing");
            return;
        }
        vendorType = getVendorType().getSelectedItem();
        if (vendorType == null || vendorType.equals("")) {
            showMessage("900,Please select a valid vendor type");
            return;
        }
```

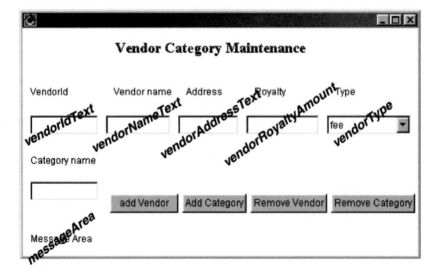

Fig. 20-8 Partial user interface with support methods.

```
                    try {
                        vendorRoyaltyAmount=Double.valueOf(vendorRoyalty).doubleValue();
                    }
                    catch (NumberFormatException e) {
                        showMessage("900,Please enter a valid royalty amount");
                        return;
                    }
                    ReturnCode_ADD_VENDOR rc = (ReturnCode_ADD_VENDOR)
                    control.addVendor(vendorName, vendorAddress, vendorRoyaltyAmount,
                            vendorType);
                    showMessage(rc.getMsg() + " Vendor Id = " + rc.getVendorId());
                    getVendorIDText().setText(rc.getVendorId());
                    return;
        }
```

20.2.3 Test user interface control class

```
    public ReturnCode_ADD_VENDOR addVendor(String name, String address, double
        royaltyAmount, String royaltyType) {
        switch (addVendorSwitch) {
            case (0): {
                    addVendorSwitch = 1;
                    return new ReturnCode_ADD_VENDOR(10500,
                    "VendorId "+ name +" added", null);
            }
            case (1):{
                    addVendorSwitch = 0;
                    return new ReturnCode_ADD_VENDOR(10514, "Vendor"+name+
                                                    "exists", null);
            }
        }
        return new ReturnCode_ADD_VENDOR(99,
            "VendorId "+ "id" +
            " name = " + name +
            " address = " + address +
            " royalty  = " + royaltyAmount +
            " type " + royaltyType +
            " added","generated id");
    }
```

Reference

This section includes the glossary, the bibliography, and three other appendices.

The glossary contains the terminology of OODP. It does not cover terms from object technology. The first appendix (bibliography) is a set of references that can be of value to the reader of this book in finding additional details or views on topics related to object-oriented software development. When a topic in this book had a direct reference to another source, that source was cited within that topic.

There are three additional appendixes. Appendix B is a detail of the process architecture for OODP, with all steps and dependencies. Appendix C contains instructions on how to build your own OT metric-based estimating model using a spreadsheet. Appendix D summarizes by activity the correctness questions and the rules and guidelines presented in the first 13 chapters of the book.

Glossary

analyst Development team member responsible for gathering and recording the business rules of the use cases.

application The union of all the use cases in the requirements; excludes the user interface. Also refers to the implementation of the use cases in the control class.

attribute Name by which the information within the object's state is referred to in the use case descriptions, definitions, and design.

business object An object with no application logic; this is the surrogate of the persistent business data.

class design That phase of OODP where the details of the class specification are recorded, based on the requirements from use case design.

class diagram Graphical view of the objects, their attributes, and associations. Created during analysis and usually refined during design. This is the object-oriented version of the data model.

client The person for whom the software system is being developed. The individual or group of individuals that define the requirements and sign off on the business rules.

constraint UML term for a rule or relationship that cannot be recorded as part of the basic class diagram. OODP term for an invariant, or method precondition.

customer The individual for whom the application runs. The user of the system may or may not be the same person as the client. Often the customer is the same person that the client considers a customer.

data model Collection of entities and their attributes used to represent a relational data base. The non-object-oriented equivalent of the class diagram.

designers Development team members that refine the analysis use case descriptions into design, often using a sequence diagram to represent the messaging visually.

development The activities of requirements, analysis, design, and implementation. Excludes test and user interface development.

implementers The programming language coders that do some very low level design and develop the classes and their methods.

invariant A constraint that must always be true. It is the responsibility of the methods that change attributes participating in the constraint to guarantee that it remains true.

method parameter The name and type of an input to the method, and the identifier by which the value passed to the method will be known within the body of the method.

method pre-condition A constraint associated with a method. It defines something that must be true before the method is invoked. It is the responsibility of the one who invokes the method with a pre-condition to make sure that the method pre-condition is true before sending the message that will run that method.

object attribute See *attribute*.

requirements The informal statement of need presented by the client. These are not the use case definitions developed during the requirements activity as a formal response to the requirements.

scenario pre-condition A set of conditions, defined in terms of the values of the use case inputs and the business object attributes, that define when the scenario is in effect.

scenario post-condition The final values of the business object attributes for a scenario, expressed in terms of the scenario pre-condition and, when necessary, use case inputs and additional business object attributes.

system (product) The combination of the application, the user interface, and, when appropriate, any hardware.

test Those activities within the process that deliver test plans and test cases and that test the completed use cases.

testers Those members of the development team responsible for writing the test plan, developing the test cases, and testing the use cases.

use case definition The use case, as defined during requirements, that identifies its inputs, outcomes, and outputs.

use case description The use case, as developed during analysis, complete with all the business rules for each scenario.

use case design The use case, as refined in design, showing all of the messages between objects that are required to correctly implement the use case description. This is the structure that will be the basis for the use case implementation.

use case outcome One of several logical results of a use case, as defined by the client during requirements. A use case outcome may be refined into one or more use case scenarios during analysis.

use case parameter The information required to run the use case, as defined by the client, including its name and type. The name is the identifier by which the input value will be known within the body of the use case definition, description, and design.

use case scenario The logical result of a use case as defined by the client during analysis. Each scenario has a unique pre-condition and post-condition.

user See *customer.*

user interface design Activity within OODP where the physical layout (look and feel) of the user interface, in graphical form, is assembled to allow the client and/or user to see the visual access to the application.

user interface development Activity within OODP where the user interface design is implemented and brought to realization in the target programming language.

variable Name by which objects are referred to in an object-oriented program. Variables can be objects or atomic values, like primitives. Every attribute is also a program variable.

Sources and References

1. [Baker72]   F. T. Baker, "Chief programmer team management of production programming," *IBM Systems Journal*, vol. 11, no. 1, 1972.

2. [Beck89]   Kent Beck and Ward Cunningham, "A laboratory for teaching object-oriented thinking," *Proceeding of OOPSLA '89*, vol. 24, no. 10, pp.1–6, 1989.

3. [Beizer83]   Boris Beizer, *Software Testing Techniques*, New York, Van Nostrand Reinhold, 1983.

4. [BenAri82]   M. Ben-Ari, *Principles of Concurrent Programming*, Englewood Cliffs, NJ: Prentice Hall, 1982.

5. [Boehm81]   Barry Boehm, *Software Engineering Economics*, Englewood Cliffs, NJ: Prentice Hall, 1981.

6. [Boehm88]   Barry Boehm, "A spiral model of software development and enhancement," *Computer*, vol. 21, no. 5, pp. 61–72, May 1988.

7. [Booch96]   Rational Software Corporation, "The Unified Modeling Language for Object-Oriented Software Development," July 1996.

8. [Brooks75]   Frederick Brooks, *The Mythical Man-Month*, Reading, MA: Addison-Wesley Publishing Co., 1975.

9. [Brooks87]   Frederick Brooks, "No silver bullet: Essence and accidents of software engineering," *IEEE Computer*, vol. 20, no. 4, pp. 10–19, April 1987.

10. [Collins95]   Dave Collins, *Designing Object-Oriented User Interfaces*, Reading, MA: Benjamin/Cummings Publishing Company, 1995.

11. [Demarco79]   Tom Demarco, *Structured Analysis and Software Specification*, Englewood Cliffs, NJ: Yourdon Press, 1979.

12. [Demarco82]   Tom Demarco, *Controlling Software Projects*, Englewood Cliffs, NJ: Prentice Hall, 1978.

13. [Demarco87]   Tom Demarco and Tim Lister, *Peopleware*, New York: Dorset House, 1987.

14. [Dyer92]   Michael Dyer, *The Cleanroom Approach to Quality Software Development*, New York: John Wiley & Sons, 1992.

15. [Fagan86]   Michael Fagan, "Advances in software inspections," *IEEE Transactions on Software Engineering*, vol. 12, no. 7, pp. 744–751, 1987.

16. [Fenton91]   Norm Fenton, *Software Metrics: A Rigorous Approach*, London: Chapman & Hall, 1991.

17. [Firesmith95]   Donald G. Firesmith and Edward M Eykholt, *Dictionary of Object Technology—The Definitive Desk Reference*, New York: SIGS Books Inc., 1995.

18. [Flanagan96]   David Flanagan, *Java in a Nutshell*, Sebastopol, CA: O'Reilly & Associates, 1996.

19. [Fowler97]   Martin Fowler and Kendall Scott, *UML Distilled, Applying the Standard Object Modeling Language*, Reading, MA: Addison-Wesley, 1997.

20. [Gamma95]   Erich Gamma, Richard Helm, Ralph Johnson, and John Vlissides, *Design Patterns: Elements of Reuseable Object-Oriented Software,* Reading, MA: Addison-Wesley Publishing Co., 1995.

21. [Gibson90]   E. Gibson, "Objects—Born and Bred," *BYTE*, vol. 14, no. 10, pp. 245–254, October 1990.

22. [Gilb76]   Tom Gilb, *Software Metrics*, Bromley, England: Chartwell-Bratt, 1976.

23. [Gilb88]   Tom Gilb, *Principles of Software Engineering Management*, Reading, MA: Addison-Wesley, 1988.

24. [Goldberg95]   Adele Goldberg and Kenneth S. Rubin, *Succeeding with Object Technology: Decision Frameworks for Project Management*, Reading, MA: Addison-Wesley Publishing Co., 1995.

25. [Harel87]   David Harel, "Statecharts: A visual formalism for complex systems," *Science of Computer Programming*, vol. 8, pp. 231–274, 1987.

26. [Humphrey89]   Watts Humphrey, *Managing the Software Process*, Reading, MA: Addison-Wesley Publishing Co., 1989.

27. [Jackson83]   Michael Jackson, *Systems Development*, Englewood Cliffs, NJ: Prentice Hall, 1983.

28. [Jacobson92]   Ivar Jacobson, Magnus Christerson, Patrik Jonsson, and Gunnar Overgaard, *Object-Oriented Software Engineering: A Use Case Driven Approach*, Reading, MA: Addison-Wesley Publishing Company, 1992.

29. [Johnson88]   Ralph E. Johnson and Brian Foote, "Designing reusable classes," *Journal of Object-Oriented Programming*, vol. 1, no. 2, pp. 22–35, 1988.

30. [Jones86]   T. Capers Jones, "Programming Productivity," New York: McGraw-Hill, 1986.

31. [Knuth81]   Donald E. Knuth, *The Art of Computer Programming*, Volumes 1–3, Reading, MA: Addison-Wesley Publishing Co., 1973, 1981.

32. [Kowal88]   James A. Kowal, *Analyzing Systems*, Englewood Cliffs, NJ: Prentice Hall, 1988.

33. [LaLonde94]   Wilf LaLonde and John Pugh, *Smalltalk V*, Englewood Cliffs, NJ: Prentice Hall, 1994.

34. [Lieberherr88]   K. Lieberherr, I. Holland, G. Lee, and A. Riel, "An objective sense of style," *IEEE Computer*, vol. 21, no. 6, 1988.

35. [Lieberherr89]   K. Lieberherr and I. Holland, "Formulation and benefits of the law of Demeter," *SIGPLAN Notices*, vol. 24, no. 3, March 1989.

36. [Linger79]   Richard C. Linger, Harland Mills, and R. Witt, *Structured Programming: Theory and Practice*, Reading, MA: Addison-Wesley, 1979.

37. [Lorenz94]   Mark Lorenz and Jeff Kidd, *Object-Oriented Software Metrics*, Englewood Cliffs, NJ: Prentice Hall, 1994.

38. [McCabe76]   Tom McCabe, "A complexity measure," *IEEE Transactions on Software Engineering.* vol. 2, no. 4, pp. 308–320, December 1976.

39. [McMenamin]   Stephen M. McMenamin and John F. Palmer, *Essential Systems Analysis*, Englewood Cliffs, NJ: Prentice Hall, 1984.

40. [Meyer88]   Bertrand Meyer, *Object-Oriented Software Construction*, Englewood Cliffs, NJ: Prentice Hall, 1988.

41. [Mills80]   Harland Mills, "Software of Certifiable Reliability," Unpublished correspondence, 1980.

42. [Mills83]   Harland D. Mills, *Software Productivity*, New York: Little, Brown & Co., 1983.

43. [Mills87]   Harland D. Mills, Michael Dyer, and Richard C. Linger, "Cleanroom software engineering," *IEEE Software*, vol. 4, no. 5, pp. 68–88, September, 1987.

44. [Musa87]   J. Musa, A. Iannino, and K. Okumoto, *Software Reliability: Measurement, Prediction, Application*, New York: McGraw-Hill, 1987.

45. [Parnas72]   David Parnas, "On the criteria to be used in decomposing systems into modules," *Communications of the ACM*, vol. 15, no. 2, pp. 1053–1058.

46. [Poore83]   J. H. Poore, H. D. Mills, and D. Mutchler, "Planning and Certifying Software System Reliability," *IEEE Software*, pp. 88–99, January 1993.

47. [Pressman92]   Roger S. Pressman, *Software Engineering: A Practitioner's Approach*, New York: McGraw-Hill International Editions, 1992.

48. [Putnam78]   Larry Putnam, "A general empirical solution to the macro software sizing and estimating problem," *IEEE Transactions on Software Engineering*, vol. 4, no. 4, pp. 345–361, 1978.

49. [Radice88]   R. A. Radice and R. W. Phillips, *Software Engineering: An Industrial Approach*, Englewood Cliffs, NJ: Prentice Hall, 1988.

50. [Rowlett93a]   Tom Rowlett, "Productivity and Quality Metrics for Software Development," IBM Technical Report TR54.743, April 1993.

51. [Rowlett93b]   Tom Rowlett, "Managing the Risk of Aggressive Software Schedules," IBM Technical Report TR54.738, March 1993.

52. [Rowlett98]   Tom Rowlett, "Building an object oriented process around use cases," *Journal of Object-Oriented Programming*, vol. 11, no. 1, pp. 53–58, March-April 1998.

53. [Rubin92]   Kenneth S. Rubin and Adele Goldberg, "Object Behavior Analysis," *Communications of the ACM*, vol. 35, no. 9, pp. 48–62, September 1992.

54. [Rubin94]   Kenneth S. Rubin, "Object Behavior Analysis (OBA)," in Andrew Hutt, editor, *Object Analysis and Design: Description of Methods*, New York: John Wiley & Sons, 1994.

55. [Rumbaugh91]   James Rumbaugh, Michael Blaha, William Premerlani, Frederick Eddy, and William Lorensen, *Object-Oriented Modeling and Design*, Englewood Cliffs, NJ: Prentice Hall, 1991.

56. [Taylor90]   David A. Taylor, *Object-Oriented Technology: A Manager's Guide*, Reading, MA: Addison-Wesley Publishing Company, 1990.

57. [Wegner87]   Peter Wegner, "Dimensions of object-based language design," *Proceeding of OOPSLA '87*, Orlando Special Issue of *SIGPLAN* Notices, vol. 22, no. 12, pp. 168–182, 1987.

58. [WirfsBrock90]   Rebecca Wirfs-Brock, Brian Wilkerson, and Lauren Wiener, *Designing Object-Oriented Software*, Englewood Cliffs, NJ: Prentice Hall, 1990.

59. [Yourdon79]   Edward Yourdon and Larry Constantine, *Structured Design: Fundamentals of a Discipline of Computer Programming and System Design*, Englewood Cliffs, NJ: Prentice Hall, 1979.

60. [Yuan95]   George Yuan, "A Depth-First Process Model for Object-Oriented Development with Improved OOA/OOD Notations," *Report on Object Analysis and Design*, vol. 2, no. 1, May-June 1995.

The Complete Use Case Process Details

This section provides the details of the use case based process. Each activity includes all the essential process elements as described in Figure B-1. This process is based on the flow and methods described in this book. It may be necessary to modify the specifics of this process for any given project. Following the process details is a graphical representation of the flow and dependencies between the activities. The details of the correctness questions are described in the individual chapters and in Appendix D.

B.1 REQUIREMENTS GATHERING

Requirement	Textual statement of need.
Deliverables	Use case definitions; initial list of objects/attributes, and actors; incremental plan.
Activity	
Method	For each noun, categorize as object/attribute, actor, or other. For each actor, list the probable use cases. For each use case, identify and record their typed inputs, logical outcomes, and any returned information. Partition the use cases into increments so that no use case is dependent on another use case that is defined in a subsequent increment.

Definition of process terms	
Requirement	Define the input to the activity. This is the "what," which will be refined using the **Activity-Method**, to create the **Deliverable.**
Deliverable	The outputs, the forms that they will take. List all deliverables.
Activity Details	
Method	Describe the steps to create the **Deliverables** from the **Requirement**. List the details of each **Deliverable**, and any alternatives if appropriate.
Assumptions	What must be true about the **Requirement** if the **Method** is to be applied correctly? It is considered a pre-condition of the input.
Correctness	Describe how each **Deliverable's** correctness and completeness are to be determined. What must be true about the **Deliverable**, in terms of the **Requirement**? List all checks to be made.
Risk	Can a subsequent process activity begin before all **Deliverables** in this activity have been determined to be **Correct**? If so, what are the guidelines?

Fig. B-1 A process architecture.

Assumptions	Textual requirements are a reasonably complete description of needs.
Correctness	Customer agrees that all use cases and their outcomes have been identified.
	Verify that no use case in the first increment is dependent on one that is not part of the first increment.
Risk	Proceed to analysis when customer/team agrees that all major use cases have been identified, and development estimates that less than 10 percent of the total use case have been undiscovered. A use case with only a subset of its outcomes included in an increment, may require that the complete use case be retested when the remaining scenarios are added.

B.2 TEST PLANNING

Requirement	Use case definitions.
Deliverables	Narrative details on how each scenario will be tested; list of attributes required to have read access in this increment.

Activity

| Method | For every outcome of each use case (for the current increment), describe the test cases; this includes the number of tests, how the pre-condition state will be achieved, and how the post-condition state will be validated. |

Assumptions   Use cases that meet the correctness criteria from requirement gathering.

Correctness   All scenarios have at least one test case, and all use cases considered critical (customer and team decide) have at least two different test cases for each of their nonerror scenarios.

Risk   Details of post-condition validation will need to be reviewed after use case business rules are added during analysis. This may necessitate redesign of some test cases.

B.3 ANALYSIS (AND APPLICATION SPECIFICATION)

Requirement   Use case definitions (for current increment); initial list of objects and attributes.

Deliverables   Use case descriptions (decision tables); data dictionary; class diagram.

Activity

Method   For every scenario of the use cases, describe the pre-condition in terms of system attributes and use case inputs; describe the final value of any attributes changed in this scenario. For every object and attribute used in a use case, create a data dictionary entry, and add the attribute to the class diagram.

Assumptions   Use cases must meet correction criteria for requirements gathering.

Correctness   No term from the domain is defined twice in the data dictionary. All attributes and objects in a use case appear on the class diagram and as a data dictionary entry. Every class diagram entry and every data dictionary entry appear in some use case.

Customer agrees that all scenarios have a complete description of pre-condition and state changes. All nouns used in the description are either defined in the input or are references to attributes in the state.

Risk   Since all use cases will not be detailed, in some cases correctness questions might be addressed only verbally and informally with the customer. Customer may not understand requirements well enough to guarantee that all use cases and scenarios have been identified.

B.4 USER INTERFACE IMPLEMENTATION AND TEST

Requirement   Use case definitions; scenario semantics; use case signature (screen designs).

Deliverables   A set of user interfaces that sends the correct messages to the control object for every use case associated event.

Activity

Method   For each use case, gather the required information, validate its type, and send a message to the control object passing that information. Interpret the control method's response, and communicate it to the user.

Assumptions   Use case definitions meet correctness criteria from requirements gathering, and scenario semantics are understood. Screen designs are complete and approved by the client.

Correctness   User interface can demonstrate that it can send a correct message (valid inputs and in the correct order) to the correct method in the control object for every use case. Customer agrees that the UI reacts correctly for every scenario.

Risk   All scenario semantics may not be well defined at the beginning of interface design.

B.5 TEST CASE DESIGN AND DEVELOPMENT

Requirement   Use case descriptions; test plan.

Deliverables   A method in the test object for every test case in the test plan.

Activity

Method   For each test case in the test plan, place the system in the empty state, record the use cases and the specific values for inputs, which will be sent to the control object to establish the pre-condition for this scenario test. Write the test with input values based on the use case parameters in the pre-condition setup. Evaluate the returnCode for completeness and correctness, and log any discrepancies. Write messages to interrogate the business objects attributes and validate that the correct post-condition state was achieved. Log all discrepancies. All tests should be developed based on the system's initialized state; that is, there are no existing objects, other than the control object and empty collections.

Assumptions   Test plan is described using only use cases included in this increment and prior increments.

Correctness   Has a test case been created for every test in the test plan? Are test case attribute validations thorough (is at least every changed attribute checked)? Class owners agree to provide read access to all checked attributes. All errors in the returnCode or post-condition are logged.

Risk   Attributes required not to change would be an error condition if they were altered, but it is not reasonable to check every unchanged attribute. It may be unreasonable to require that every test use the empty state as its initial state.

B.6 USE CASE DESIGN

Requirement   Use case descriptions, test attribute references.

Deliverables   Design of use cases recorded using a sequence diagram; new method specifications; design level class diagram.

Activity

Method   For each use case, create a sequence diagram that shows the messages required to: first, determine the correct scenario, and second, perform the required attribute modifications. All scenarios for the use case can be included on the same diagram. For each message, document its class, input parameters and their type, any returned value and its type, and changes to all the receiving object's attributes, as well as those of its collaborators.

For each class, describe any required references to objects of other classes. Include the type of reference (pointer, key, etc.). For all attributes and methods, record their logical visibility. Ensure that a getter is provided for all attribute references required by the test group.

Assumptions   Either a use case description for each complex use case exits, or the use case's pre- and post-conditions are known, and there is a use case definition that meets the correctness criteria of requirements gathering.

Correctness   Any data that are not part of the state of an object must be either passed in by a message sent to the object or returned from a message sent to another object. All information required across method invocations is part of the object's state, and these attributes must be reflected in the design model. Are all collections created as a result of many-to-many associations shown on the design model. All newly created, nonlocal objects have been saved in a collection or are referred to by another persistent object.

Risk   Design team agrees that a use case with no sequence diagram can be implemented directly from the existing use case documentation.

B.7 CLASS DESIGN

Requirement   Use case descriptions; method specifications; use case designs.

Deliverables   Class specification.

Activity

Method   Based on the method specifications and use case design, document each attribute's visibility, type, and initial value and for each method in the class document its signature, visibility, and type.

Assumptions   Method specifications as described with correctness criteria from use case design.

Correctness   Is every constraint recorded on the class diagram or in the class specification captured in the business rule of some analysis use case description? Does every setter method have a use case that requires it? Do method specifications support the use case design of every use case in which they participate? Do all subclasses preserve the valid values of attributes in the superclass? When overriding methods, do the new methods return the identical values of their superclass counterpart?

Risk   Class specification may exceed the requirements of use case design at the discretion of the class owner.

B.8 IMPLEMENTATION

Requirement   Use case descriptions; class specifications; use case designs.

Deliverables   Classes.

Activity

Method   Design and write each method for each class as specified.

Assumptions   Method and class specifications as described with correctness criteria from use case design and class design.

Correctness   A public getter method exists for all logically public (read only) methods. Both getter and setter methods exist for all logically public (read/write) methods. No public getter or setter methods exist for logically private state variables. The method's design is correct with respect to its specification. The control method's implementation agrees with the sequence diagram and the use case decision table, if they exist.

Risk   Test of a use case can begin when all methods required for that use case and all pre-req use cases are complete.

B.9 USE CASE TEST

Requirement   Test cases; compiled classes.

Deliverables   Test results.

Activity

Method   Create a main method in the test object that invokes every test case. It should keep track of the total test run and the number that failed. When all tests have run, it should create the log report showing the details of all failures.

Assumptions   All methods required for a test case are available and have been correctly compiled.

Correctness   Every test case runs correctly on a set of classes that are unchanged from the first test to the last.

Risk   In some cases, it may not be necessary to rerun all test cases after a small fix, if it can be determined which tests are unaffected by the fix.

B.10 INTERFACE AND APPLICATION INTEGRATION

Requirement   Tested use cases; classes; user interface; test plan.

Deliverables   Integrated tested product.

Activity

Method   Combine the application and user interface classes. Retest the scenarios using the UI as a driver instead of the test cases. Use the test plan as a guide to walk through the user transactions that establish the test pre-condition, then test the scenario. It is not necessary to validate system state after the test.

Assumptions   All the requirements meet their correctness criteria from their corresponding activity.

Correctness   All scenarios have been run and the user interface response (next window, disabled buttons, displayed information, etc.) have been agreed to as correct by the customer.

Risk   It may not be necessary to test explicitly every scenario by itself, if they are tested as part of establishing the state of other scenarios.

Figure B-2 shows the complete OODP flow graphically.

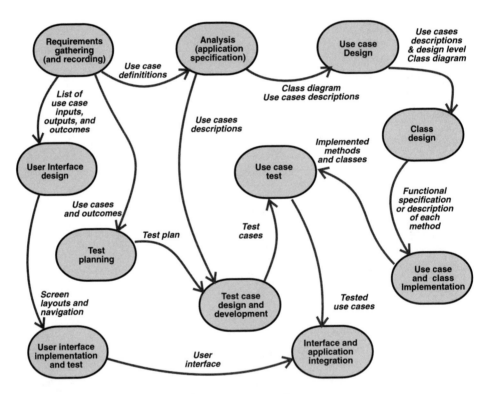

Fig. B-2 The object-oriented development process flow.

Building an Estimating Model Using a Spreadsheet

*T*his appendix provides detailed instructions on how to build an estimating model using a spreadsheet. It explains how to identify the best metric from several candidate metrics. The data shown are fictitious and are provided for demonstration only. As with any estimating model, it is best to use real data from several projects that are representative of the type of software that the local organization builds.

The spreadsheet formulas in these exercises were developed on Quatro Pro version 8.0. They have been run using EXCEL 97 and Lotus 123 97. When the exact formula is given, it is enclosed in brackets [ ]. Do not enter the brackets. Figure C-1 shows how to adapt the cell formulas for EXCEL and Lotus 123 spreadsheets.

C.1 LINEAR REGRESSION

This section builds a model to estimate project effort and duration based on requirement's deliverables. It starts with use cases, scenarios, objects, nouns as candidate metrics. It uses statistical correlation to determine the best predictor of project effort and then uses those metrics to build the estimating model.

For Lotus 123

Changes are noted in the individual exercises.

For EXCEL

Change all "@" in the functions to "="

Range definition should be represented with a ":" rather than ".."

When testing for a non-empty cell in an IF statement, use E5<>" " instead of just E5

Fig. C-1 Changes to cell formulae for Lotus 123 and EXCEL.

■ Create a new spreadsheet with the rows and columns shown in Figure C-2. This will represent the historical data from seven previous projects. This spreadsheet will work with as few as three projects' worth of data. And often there will be only two or three columns of potential metrics.

Try to include as much data as possible. The only criterion should be: "Can these items be *counted* during requirements," since only information available at that point in the process will be useful to develop an estimate during that phase.

■ In column **A**, rows **11** through **13**, place the three literals ("Correlation," "Slope," and "Intercept"). Beginning in column **C**, we will calculate these values using the data in that column and the effort in column **B**.

■ In **C11**, place the formula: **[@CORREL($B3..$B9,C3..C9)]**. This computes the correlation between Scenarios and Effort. Recall that correlation

	A	B	C	D	E	F
1	Project	Actual		Use		
2	number	effort	Scenarios	cases	Nouns	Actors
3	1	4	1	1	25	2
4	2	30	5	5	30	1
5	3	45	12	3	19	2
6	4	60	20	8	20	2
7	5	95	40	10	30	2
8	6	120	65	18	27	3
9	7	119	102	22	50	2

Fig. C-2 Basic effort and deliverable data.

is a measure of how closely related these pairs of values are. (This formula will work for 123 since correlation a:b is the same as correlation b:a.)

■ Do the same for Slope **(C12)** and Intercept **(C13)** using the formulae **[@SLOPE($B3..$B9,C3..C9)]** and **[@INTERCEPT($B3..$B9,C3..C9)]**, respectively.

LOTUS 123 users should enter:
[@REGRESSION(C3..C9,$B3..$B9,101))] for slope and
[@REGRESSION(C3..C9,$B3..$B9,1)] for intercept.

■ These three cells can now be copied to cells **D11..F13**. *(Select cells C11, C12, and C13. Select copy from the edit menu. Select cells D11 through F11. Select paste from the edit menu.)*

The first row (correlation) shows us that based on the data, nouns and actors apparently have no relation to project effort, but use cases and scenarios do. The next two rows provide the values to create the formula for calculating effort, given either scenarios or use cases. The formula is Effort $= I + (S * X)$, where X is either the number of use cases or the number of scenarios, and I and S are the corresponding values for intercept and slope. To see the formula's effect, we will recalculate effort for scenarios and use cases, using these formulae.

■ Add the labels shown in Figure C-3, in columns **H** and **I** of rows **1** and **2**. The formulae will be built below these columns.

■ In cell **H3** calculate effort as the intercept value from cell **C13** plus the product of the slope from cell **C12** and the number of scenarios in **C3**. Use the following formula: **[+C$13+(C3*C$12)]**. Adding the dollar signs will allow propagation of the equation to the rest of this column and all of the next.

■ Copy cell **H3** to rows **4** thru nine in the same column and rows **3** through **9** in the next column **(I)**. *(Select cell H3. Select copy from the edit menu. Select cells H4 to H9. Select paste from the edit menu. Select cells I3 to I9. Select paste from the edit menu.)*

In some cases, the formula gets pretty close to actual effort, and in others it is not so accurate. That is because the regression formula creates a straight line that passes as close to, but not necessarily through, as many of the actual values as possible.

	H	I
1	Best fit	Best fit
2	scen/ef	UC/eff

Fig. C-3 Titles for columns H and I.

C.2 EXPONENTIAL REGRESSION

Sometimes the best fit formula for predicting effort is not a straight line, but a curve. In this case, it is referred to as exponential, meaning the slope is not fixed. In those cases, the formula for Effort looks like: $E = a * b^c$, where b is the known metric such as scenarios or use cases. In this case, we want to solve for the values of a and c.

Using logarithms on the formula it can be refined as follows:

$$\log(E) = \log(a * b^c)$$

$$\log(E) = \log(a) + \log(b^c)$$

$$\log(E) = \log(a) + \log(b) * c$$

This gives a formula that approximates the model used for linear regression. So using the log of effort and the log of the metric, linear regression analysis will provide **c** as the slope and $\log(a)$ as the intercept.

To build the nonlinear model, create five new columns: one that contains the log of effort and the others that contain the log of the independent variables.

- In rows **14** and **15**, starting in column **B**, enter the text shown in Figure C-4.
- In rows **16** through **22** of column **B** calculate the log of effort located in **B3** through **B9**. Then copy these formulae to the next four rows. This will calculate the log of the values for scenarios, use cases, nouns, and actors. *In **B16** place the formula [@log(**B3**)]. Select cell **B16**, then click copy from the edit pull down. Select cells **B17..B22**, and click paste from the edit pull down. Select cells **C16..F22**, and again click paste from the edit pull down.*
- Recompute the correlation slope and intercept as before. In rows **25, 26,** and **27** of column **A**, put the text "Correlation," "Slope," and "Intercept." Also add a fourth text string below in row **28** "10^intercept."

Recall in preceding formula that the intercept that is computed is the **log(a)**, so to compute **a** for the exponential formula take the antilog of the intercept.

- Fill in the formulae as follows:
  In **C25** enter [@CORREL($B16..$B22,C16..C22)]

	B	C	D	E	F
14	---------------------------------- Log of ----------------------------------				
15	Effort	Scenarios	Use cases	Nouns	Actors

Fig. C-4 Titles for columns B through F.

In **C26** enter [**@SLOPE($B16..$B22,C16..C22)**].

In **C27** enter [**@INTERCEPT($B16..$B22,C16..C22)**]

LOTUS 123 users should enter:

In **C25** enter [**@CORREL(C16..C22,$B16..$B22)**]

In **C26** enter [**@REGRESSION(C16..C22,$B16..$B22,101))**] for slope.

In **C27** enter [**@REGRESSION(C16..C22,$B16..$B22,1)**] for intercept.

■ Finally in **C28** enter [**+10^C27**].

By using **$B** instead of plain **B** in the formulae, the cells **C25..C28** can be copied to **D25..F28**.

Examine that the correlation values show that nouns and actors are still not a predictor of effort, and use cases seem to work equally as well either linearly or exponentially. However, scenarios, with a logarithmic correlation of .966, will probably work better using the nonlinear model.

■ Add a third best fit column. In the **J** column in rows **1** and **2** put "Log best fit," and "Scen/eff." Then just below (**J3**) put the exponential formula *Effort = antilog(Intercept) * (scenarios^{slope})* [**+C$28*(C3^C$26)**].

■ Copy this formula to the next six rows.

C.3 USING THE MODEL TO CALCULATE EFFORT

Assume a new project that has 19 scenarios and 6 use cases.

■ Enter these two numbers in the corresponding columns (**C** and **D**) of row **10**. Label the row "new project." Now copy **H9..J9** to **H10..J10**.

These are the estimates for Effort using each of the three models. Since all the values are rather close, use any one as the initial estimate. If they were widely scattered, it may indicate that one or all of the models are flawed. If only one is out of bounds, take the average of the closest two, or go back and build the exponential model for use cases.

Figure C-5 shows the spreadsheet results, and a graphic representation of the regression data.

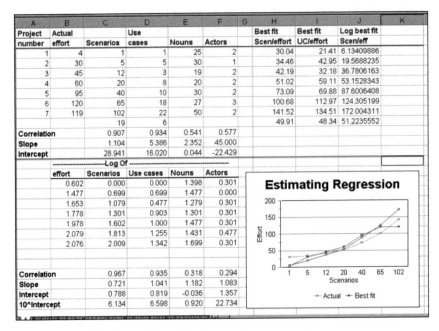

	A	B	C	D	E	F	G	H	I	J	K
	Project number	Actual effort	Scenarios	Use cases	Nouns	Actors		Best fit Scen/effort	Best fit UC/effort	Log best fit Scen/eff	
	1	4	1	1	25	2		30.04	21.41	6.13409886	
	2	30	5	5	30	1		34.46	42.95	19.5688235	
	3	45	12	3	19	2		42.19	32.18	36.7806163	
	4	60	20	8	20	2		51.02	59.11	53.1528343	
	5	95	40	10	30	2		73.09	69.88	87.6006408	
	6	120	65	18	27	3		100.68	112.97	124.305199	
	7	119	102	22	50	2		141.52	134.51	172.004311	
			19	6				49.91	48.34	51.2235552	
Correlation			0.907	0.934	0.541	0.577					
Slope			1.104	5.386	2.352	45.000					
Intercept			28.941	16.020	0.044	-22.429					

--Log Of--

	effort	Scenarios	Use cases	Nouns	Actors
	0.602	0.000	0.000	1.398	0.301
	1.477	0.699	0.699	1.477	0.000
	1.653	1.079	0.477	1.279	0.301
	1.778	1.301	0.903	1.301	0.301
	1.978	1.602	1.000	1.477	0.301
	2.079	1.813	1.255	1.431	0.477
	2.076	2.009	1.342	1.699	0.301
Correlation	0.967	0.935	0.318	0.294	
Slope	0.721	1.041	1.182	1.083	
Intercept	0.788	0.819	-0.036	1.357	
10^Intercept	6.134	6.598	0.920	22.734	

Estimating Regression

Fig. C-5 Completed sample estimating model spreadsheet.

Summary of Correctness Questions and Guidelines

This appendix repeats all the OODP activity correctness questions presented in the first 13 chapters. It also summarizes the guidelines and rules for creating many of the individual deliverables of OODP. Both parts are organized by OODP activity, which allows the reader to locate the chapter of the book where a detailed description and discussion of the elements of the rules can be found.

D.1 CORRECTNESS QUESTIONS

D.1.1 Requirements

Checking requirements correctness and completeness

☞ Have all use cases within the scope of the application been considered?
☞ Are the use case inputs and their types correct?
☞ Have all the outcomes and the outputs for each use case been identified?

D.1.2 Analysis

The correctness questions for scenarios within a use case

☞ The pre-conditions must cover the input space completely; that is, there can be no state of the system that is not covered by some pre-condition.

☞ The pre-conditions must be disjoint. This means that there can be no system state that is satisfied by more than one pre-condition.

☞ The post-conditions must be unique. That means that no two scenarios can have the same post-condition. Violating this rule may merely mean that the two scenarios need to be combined, but often it is an indication that a portion of the post-condition of one of the scenarios was omitted.

☞ The business rules must not be ambiguous. This fourth rule is not as easy to enforce as the others.

D.1.3 Use case design

Correctness questions for a use case design

☞ Does the signature of the control method for this use case match the signature that was defined in the requirements?

☞ Is every recipient of a message and every parameter on the message either:

✗ Part of the state of the object that is sending the message,

✗ Passed in as a parameter to the method sending the message,

✗ Returned from a previous message sent within the current method?

☞ Do the signature and semantics of every message support the design of the methods that use it?

☞ For every scenario in the use case:

✗ Does the control method correctly apply the business rules to check its pre-condition?

✗ Does the control method make the correct updates to establish the post-condition?

✗ Are any state changes made that are not required by the scenario?

☞ Is every attribute assumed to be part of an object's state recorded on the class diagram?

☞ Is every persistent object that is created initialized and saved in a collection?

D.1.4 Class design

☞ Is every constraint recorded on the class diagram or in the class specification captured in the business rule of some analysis use case description?

☞ Does every setter method have a use case that requires it?

☞ Does each method specification support the use case design of every use case in which it participates?

☞ Do all subclasses preserve the valid values of attributes in the superclass?

☞ When overriding methods, do the new methods return the identical values of their superclass counterpart?

D.1.5 Implementation

Implementing from a sequence diagram

☞ Is every message in the sequence diagram implemented as a method in the appropriate class? *(Is there a method for every design message sent?)*

☞ Do the parameters of the messages in the sequence diagram agree with respect to type and order with the implemented message? *(Was the message transcribed into code correctly?)*

☞ Is each method's implementation correct?

    ✗ When a method is implemented from its design specification, is the implemented method correct with respect to that specification?

    ✗ When no method specification was created during design, does the implementation of the method invoked by the message agree with respect to parameter type and order, and return type, with the message recorded on the sequence diagram?

☞ Does the logic of the control method's implementation (loops, conditions, algorithms) agree with the business rules of the use case's analysis specification? *(Does the control method implement the use case business rules?)*

Implementing from a decision table

☞ Does the logic of the control method implementation (loops, conditions, algorithms) agree with the business rules of the use case's analysis specification?

☞ Does the control method implement the use case business rules?

☞ Do the methods used by the control method support the implementation of the use case? When these are simple getter methods, the answer is usually a trivial yes.

Implementing from requirements

☞ Does the number of paths through the code match the number of outcomes in the requirements?

☞ If returned information is required for a scenario, is it included in the return object?

☞ Does the implementation for each scenario logically and reasonably agree with the stated outcome?

D.1.6 Test planning

☞ Do the use cases that establish the pre-condition refer only to use cases in this or a previous increment?

☞ Can every scenario of every use case be tested in this increment; if not, how has the fact that a re-test is required been documented?

☞ Has development agreed to provide the test support methods to give access to the business objects for the purpose of scenario post-condition evaluation?

☞ Do the clients and use case owners agree that test coverage is complete and sufficient?

☞ Is every post-condition check possible, given the pre-condition?

D.1.7 User interface implementation

☞ Does the user interface invoke the correct use case method in the control object?

☞ Are the parameters of the use case method in the correct order and of the correct type?

☞ Does the user interface react correctly to the scenario reported by the returnCode object?

☞ Are the correct message and associated returned information displayed?

D.2 RULES AND GUIDELINES

D.2.1 Requirements

The rules of use case granularity

☞ The use case must be **complete**, i.e., contain enough information that the application can process the request completely without returning to the user for additional information.

☞ The use case should be a **discrete** unit of work. Business processes should be decomposed into individual use cases each with its own inputs and outcomes.

☞ Keep use cases **simple**, by avoiding multiple identical inputs when these inputs logically belong to separate transactions.

Finding use cases from objects, attributes, and other use cases

☞ Every attribute must have a use case that sets its value and another that reads its value. Look at every attribute and ask if there is a use case that

- ✗ Initializes this attribute,
- ✗ Uses its value,
- ✗ Changes its value.

☞ For every object is there a use case that

- ✗ Creates the object,
- ✗ Deletes the object?

☞ Almost every use case will have an inverse. Examine each use case and ask if there is an inverse that should be included.

Finding outcomes

Use the client's knowledge of the domain to find the outcomes based on business policy. Use the guidelines for outcomes based on inputs to discover other potential outcomes.

☞ Look at each use case input and ask if there is an outcome related to it being *logically invalid*. That means that the input represents data that should exist in the system but does not.

☞ *Duplication*. For use cases that add new objects, one scenario may be that the object or its identifier already exists within the system.

☞ *Business rules* are the outcomes defined by the client. Scan the requirements for words like: *if*, *when*, *until*, and *must*. Then have the client elaborate to define the outcome.

Use case dependency for incremental planning

☞ Use case A is dependent on use case B, if B is necessary to create a precondition state for any scenario in use case A.

Partitioning strategies

When defining the use cases for a partition, there are several project-related strategies that will affect which use cases are included. The strategy for each increment may be different.

☞ *Easiest first*. Select simpler use cases that will allow the team time to evaluate the methods and tools.

☞ *Target use cases for operational support*. Select use cases that allow the client and system users to perform some operations tasks, such as loading the database.

☞ *Most functionality as soon as possible*. Select use cases that will demonstrate as much of the system's capability as soon as possible. As part of this strategy, consider delaying use cases that delete objects or perform simple attribute updates.

☞ *Support end user training.* Choose use cases that provide most application operations, but not enough to run in production mode.

Guidelines for incremental planning

☞ *Use case effort does not distribute evenly across increments.* Effort per use case will decrease with each increment. The recommendation is to make the first increment the smallest in terms of functionality, and gradually to build up to larger increments. The exception is the last increment, which should be smaller and easier so any required redesign can be accommodated.

☞ *Plan on surprises in the first increment.* During the first increment, the team is likely to discover overlooked use cases and complexity issues. If increment one takes longer than planned, it does not necessarily follow that every other increment will as well.

☞ *Plan at a detailed level only for the current increment.* Then plan to re-plan at the start of each new increment. The lessons learned in one increment will change the way you approach the next increment.

☞ *Defer changes after analysis to the next increment.* Although it may seem more practical to go ahead and incorporate a change to a use case while it is being developed, the benefit of having all requirements go through analysis is enormous.

☞ *Include all of a use case's scenarios in the same increment.* When only some of the scenarios of a use case are operational, testing the outcome becomes fragmented, and the testing of the omitted scenario may get overlooked when it is completed.

☞ *Finish increments in 4 months or less.* Although increments one and two need to be relatively short, productivity will suffer with too many small increments.

D.2.2 Analysis

Guidelines for recording business rules to eliminate ambiguity

☞ *Use only terms from the data dictionary.* The use case should be written using a combination of business object, attributes, and input parameters defined for the use case.

☞ *Use identical words when the meaning is identical.* Avoid synonyms and use the same words over and over to ensure that the semantics are clear.

☞ *Avoid adjectives just to improve readability.* Remember that the goal is precision; avoid adjectives not integral to the problem domain.

☞ *Use formulae instead of ambiguous verb phrases.* The terms of the formulae should be the inputs, the attributes, and their values.

Rules for creating a correct state diagram

☞ Every state must be reachable from the initial state, using some sequence of transactions. (Reachable means along some path using the transitions.)

☞ The final state must be reachable from every state.

☞ Every state must be definable in terms of values of business object attributes.

☞ Every transition must have at least one scenario of some use case that is its trigger.

☞ The object may not exist in more than one state at any time between use cases.

☞ A use case scenario may not transition from the same old state to different new states.

Rules of consistency for the analysis models

☞ Does every noun that is part of a use case description appear in the data dictionary and on the object model?

☞ Is the use of aliases in use case descriptions appropriate?

☞ Are all ambiguous use case terms replaced with their nonambiguous alternatives?

☞ Does every class diagram object appear in some use case?

☞ For every attribute in the class diagram, is there both a use case that creates the attribute and one that uses it?

☞ For enumerated attributes, does every value appear in a use case where the associated attribute is set to that value, and potentially another use case where that value is used?

D.2.3 Use case design

Most common pitfalls of object-oriented design correctness

☞ Forgetting to acquire addressability to an object before sending it a message

☞ Not saving a newly created object

☞ Forgetting to label objects, attributes, returned objects, and parameters consistently

☞ Making design decisions about object-to-object references and not recording them on the class diagram

OODP variations on sequence diagram notation

☞ Interface objects are omitted.

☞ Returned information is not indicated with a separate event arrow; instead it is written below the line and preceded with a ^.

☞ When the use case exits with an error condition, the return to the interface is shown as a dashed line.

☞ Returned data are included only when it is not obvious, or the variable name is required for use in a subsequent message.

☞ Conditions on messages and loop notation are included only if necessary for understanding the design.

☞ Braces {} are used for comments on functionality not recordable as part of the sequence diagram.

D.2.4 Class design

Single object invariant rules

☞ Each method may assume that the invariant is true at the beginning of the method.

☞ It is okay for the attribute to be in an invalid state while a method is executing, provided that it is not possible for another thread to access that attribute while in the invalid state.

☞ Each method must exit with the invariant true.

Responsibilities of the use case owner

☞ Write and validate the use case with the client.

☞ Review the test plan for their use cases.

☞ Be aware of how other use case designs impact theirs.

☞ Approve the use case design.

☞ Review ALL change requests.

☞ Approve changes impacting their use case.

Responsibilities of class owners

☞ Ensure that complete documentation is provided for each class.

☞ Determine visibility, type, and initial values for attributes.

☞ Determine visibility for methods.

☞ Arbitrate conflicts relating to duplicate or similar method names or behavior.

☞ Review all class design decisions.

D.2.5 Persistence

Method operation categories to consider for persistence

☞ Retrieving an object from a collection

☞ Changing the value of an attribute within an object

☞ Creating a new object

☞ Removing an object from a collection

D.2.6 Implementation

Suggested guidelines for implementing directly from requirements

☞ There are no more than three outcomes.

☞ The number of scenarios equals the number of outcomes.

☞ Each business rule has a single simple condition.

☞ If a scenario exists that changes state, its rule is algorithmically trivial.

☞ If these conditions are not met or the subsequent correctness questions are difficult to answer, consider creating a temporary sequence diagram, decision table, or both.

Rules for implementation of managed type constraints

☞ It is allowable to violate a constraint/type within a method as long as

✗ It is restored before exiting the method,

✗ All other threads are blocked while the attribute is in its invalid state.

☞ The object must be created with the attributes in a valid state. This can be accomplished by providing an initial value for each attribute or using the technique known as lazy initialization. That is where the getter method performs initialization when it is first invoked.

☞ A method may assume that all attributes are in a valid state when the method is invoked. The first two rules essentially guarantee this one.

☞ If a method determines that an invalid state has occurred, it should roll back all state changes. It must do this while ensuring that no other thread has gained access to any altered attribute, and return a status to the invoking method informing it of the error.

Rules for using pre-conditions

☞ It must be possible and reasonable for the calling method to guarantee the pre-condition.

☞ If the pre-condition is not met, then any external effects should not be catastrophic.

Guidelines when considering breaking encapsulation

☞ Do not use public attributes as a convenience. Force the team to justify each attribute separately.

☞ Never anticipate the need to override encapsulated data. Wait until the problem arises. Avoid the temptation to design around encapsulation.

☞ A public attribute is not an excuse to bypass the get/set interface. After a public attribute is created to circumvent a performance problem in one part of the application, do not treat the attribute as public in another part of the application, unless that part of the application can also justify the need to access the attribute directly.

☞ Record the names of methods using direct access to an attribute adjacent to the public attribute in the class specification. This will allow identification of potentially broken code if the design of the data within the object containing the public attributes changes.

Rules for updating skeleton control class

☞ A new use case is added.

☞ The order, number, or type of a parameter of a use case changes.

☞ The returnCode object's content changes.

D.2.7 Test case development

Development setup responsibilities to the test team

☞ A skeleton control object that has the signature (but no body) of every method in the increment

☞ All the ReturnCode subclasses

☞ The business object classes with the getters required by test to do post-condition validation

Rules for running and evaluating test case results

☞ Run all test cases before making changes to the code.

☞ Try to repair all defects before the next test run.

☞ If intermediate code versions are tested before all bugs are repaired, be sure to run the entire test suite when all fixes have been applied.

☞ Do not allow changes due to new requirements, if at all possible, until all tests have run successfully.

☞ The final test run should complete with no failures.

D.2.8 User interface implementation

Recommendations for use case return codes

☞ Reserve a range of numbers for every use case. For example, if the values are five digit numbers, use the first three to identify the use case.

☞ Use the last two digits as a subrange for successful vs. unsuccessful scenarios.

☞ Successful scenarios might use numeric return codes in the range 0 to 14.

☞ Error scenarios would use 15 through 89.

☞ 90 through 99 could be reserved for the default processing exception responses.

D.2.9 Maintenance

Rules for removing decision tables

☞ Error scenarios are rejections of invalid inputs due to missing objects, and are not complex state violations.

☞ The OK scenario's business rules are obvious from the use case name.

The rules for omitting or discarding the sequence diagrams

☞ The team feels that understanding how the use case should be designed is not appreciably improved by reading the sequence diagram?

☞ If a decision table exists, the control method and supporting business object methods can be implemented directly from it.

☞ If the use case description was not created during analysis or subsequently discarded, a correct implementation can be developed directly from the requirements.

Rules for evaluating changes

☞ Determine the true scope of the change by identifying "hidden requirements." There are guidelines that follow that can help in that process.

☞ Present all discovered use cases to the client to ensure that they are required. Some will obviously be needed based on dependencies, but others may be deleted or deferred at the client request. The analyst will need to provide guidance in this area, since there may be functionality that the client considers unnecessary but is absolutely essential for other required functions.

☞ Evaluate changes for cost. Using the list accepted by the client, calculate the extra cost (effort) and schedule slip.

Rules for identifying hidden changes in new requirements

☞ The *inverse rule* states that "Most use cases have another use case that has the effect of reversing the original."

☞ The *parameter attribute rule* states that "Every use case parameter should map to some attribute in a business object." This is not a one-to-one relationship but rather is many to one. More than one input parameter will possibly map to the same attribute.

☞ The *new object–use case rule* states that "When a new class is defined,

   ✗ There must be a use case to create the object,

   ✗ Another use case to destroy existing objects, and

   ✗ It must have a unique identifier attribute."

☞ The *attribute use case rule* says that "Every attribute needs a use case to set its value, another use case to use that value, and optionally a third to change its value."

☞ The *parameter scenario rule* asks, "Is there a scenario that validates each use case input?"

☞ The *scenario state rule* requires that "Every successful scenario of a non-query use case must be remembered as a modification of one or more attributes."

☞ The *scenario state rule* corollary says, "Scenarios and input states should map as well."

D.2.10 Project management

Ideal pilot project characteristics

☞ Small enough to be completed within 4 months or less.

☞ Large enough to exercise most of the aspects of the technology.

☞ Simple enough to not overwhelm the developers to the point where they cannot pay adequate attention to the way they are developing the software.

☞ Complex enough that the organization will have the sense that "it will work" on the rest of their projects.

☞ Focuses on a single technology.

☞ A team with some experience with the technology, or if that is not possible, make sure that they are recently trained, enthusiastic, and augmented with an expert mentor.

☞ A project or subproject well off the critical path.

Steps of process improvement

☞ Examine the final work product for the most serious defects.

☞ Determine where in the process the defect was inserted.

☞ Given the insertion point of the defect, determine if either

    ✗ The methods of that activity could be improved to create fewer defects in the future.

    ✗ The correctness question and the review at the end of the activity could be elaborated to catch the error before the deliverable is turned over to the next activity.

☞ Evaluate the effect of the change by examining the deliverables created from the modified process.

Skill identification based on work definition

☞ Define the activities.

☞ Define the deliverables.

☞ Define the tasks associated with each deliverable.

☞ Describe the skills required based on creating that deliverable.

Skill categories

☞ Cannot create the deliverable or perform the task. (Level 0)

☞ Can perform the task with guidance from others. (Level 1)

☞ Can perform the task without guidance. (Level 2)

☞ Can guide others in performing the task. (Level 3)

☞ Can teach others to perform the task. (Level 4)

Skill identification techniques (least reliable to most reliable)

☞ Experience resumes with references to where and when the individual has performed this task in the past.

☞ Direct interrogation on the ability of the individual to create the required deliverable.

☞ Testing to see if they are capable of creating the deliverable as required by the task.

☞ First-hand knowledge based on observation of the individual on a prior project.

Index

Solutions from experts you know and trust.

| Articles | Free Library | eBooks | Expert Q & A | Training | Career Center | Downloads | MyInformIT |

Login   Register   About InformIT

Topics
Operating Systems
Web Development
Programming
Networking
Certification
and more...

www.informit.com

✔ Free, in-depth articles and supplements

✔ Master the skills you need, when you need them

✔ Choose from industry leading books, ebooks, and training products

✔ Get answers when you need them - from live experts or InformIT's comprehensive library

✔ Achieve industry certification and advance your career

Expert Access

Free Content

Visit *InformIT* today
and get great content
from **PH PTR**

Prentice Hall and InformIT are trademarks of Pearson plc /
Copyright © 2000 Pearson

Prentice Hall: Professional Technical Reference

http://www.phptr.com/

PRENTICE HALL

Professional Technical Reference
Tomorrow's Solutions for Today's Professionals.

www.phptr.com

Keep Up-to-Date with
PH PTR Online!

We strive to stay on the cutting edge of what's happening in professional computer science and engineering. Here's a bit of what you'll find when you stop by **www.phptr.com**:

@ Special interest areas offering our latest books, book series, software, features of the month, related links and other useful information to help you get the job done.

Deals, deals, deals! Come to our promotions section for the latest bargains offered to you exclusively from our retailers.

$ Need to find a bookstore? Chances are, there's a bookseller near you that carries a broad selection of PTR titles. Locate a Magnet bookstore near you at www.phptr.com.

! What's new at PH PTR? We don't just publish books for the professional community, we're a part of it. Check out our convention schedule, join an author chat, get the latest reviews and press releases on topics of interest to you.

✉ Subscribe today! Join PH PTR's monthly email newsletter!

Want to be kept up-to-date on your area of interest? Choose a targeted category on our website, and we'll keep you informed of the latest PH PTR products, author events, reviews and conferences in your interest area.

Visit our mailroom to subscribe today! **http://www.phptr.com/mail_lists**